INSIDE THE ATLANTIC TRIANGLE

DAVID MACKENZIE

Inside the Atlantic Triangle

CANADA AND THE ENTRANCE
OF NEWFOUNDLAND INTO
CONFEDERATION, 1939–1949

UNIVERSITY OF TORONTO PRESS
Toronto Buffalo London

© University of Toronto Press 1986
Toronto Buffalo London
Printed in Canada

ISBN 0-8020-2587-0

Canadian Cataloguing in Publication Data

MacKenzie, David Clark, 1953–
  Inside the Atlantic triangle

  Bibliography: p.
  Includes index.
  ISBN 0-8020-2587-0

  1. Newfoundland – Annexation to Canada.
  2. Newfoundland – History – 1934–1949.* 3. Canada –
  Relations – Newfoundland. 4. Newfoundland – Relations –
  Canada. I. Title.

  FC2174.M24 1986   971.8'03   C85-099867-0
  F1123.M24 1986

49,505

This book is dedicated to my mother and father.

Contents

Preface

This book examines the evolution of Canadian policy towards New-foundland during the decade leading up to Confederation in 1949. The outbreak of war in 1939 produced relatively few changes in Canadian-Newfoundland relations but, in 1940, with the Allied collapse in Europe and the base-destroyer deal which introduced an American presence in Newfoundland, the Canadian government was forced to take a more active interest in that country's welfare. Over the course of the war the Canadians increasingly provided for the defence of Newfoundland, and a vigorous effort was made to preserve and enhance Canada's influence there.

The war period is divided into three general sections. The first begins with the fall of France, when the invasion of North America was con-sidered a distinct possibility and Newfoundland was turned into a bulwark in the defence of this continent. The second examines New-foundland's role in the prosecution of the war effort. As a base for convoy defence, St John's played a major part in the Battle of the Atlantic. The third section looks at Newfoundland's contribution as a stepping-stone for the invasion of Europe. The establishment of the Goose Bay airbase and the Atlantic ferry system transformed New-foundland's role from a defensive to an offensive one.

As the strain of war and the need to defend Newfoundland eased, so too did the interest of the Canadian military planners. But this was not the case for a small group of officials clustered around the Department of External Affairs, men such as Norman Robertson, Lester Pearson, R.A. MacKay, and Hugh Keenleyside, who had been forced to deal with the 'Problem of Newfoundland.' These men recognized that Canada would continue to have a vital stake in Newfoundland's future. Only a handful of politicians sustained an uninterrupted interest in the matter. This group, which included Mackenzie King, Louis St Laurent, C.D. Howe, and Brooke Claxton, gradually came to see that economically, strategically, and politically, Confederation was the only logical solution to the problem of Newfoundland.

On the part of the United Kingdom, there was an underlying current of pro-Confederate feelings, tempered by British self-interest and sentimental ties to Britain's oldest colony. As the war progressed Britain's financial difficulties overcame sentimental attachments and the United Kingdom became more open to considering ways to divest itself of its responsibility for Newfoundland. When the Canadians showed some interest in Newfoundland at the end of the war, the British jumped at the opportunity to make the union of Canada and Newfoundland their goal.

The ultimate decision about Confederation was for the Newfoundlanders to make among themselves. But the Canadian and British governments could limit and define the alternatives from which the Newfoundlanders could choose, and in this way could influence the outcome of the two referendums held to decide the country's future. The Canadian government as greatly aided in its efforts to implement Confederation by an able group of civil servants, a co-operative British government, and an energetic Confederate campaign in Newfoundland, led by J.R. 'Joey' Smallwood. This book traces the growth and development of these factors, in an effort to take the union of Canada and Newfoundland out of the realm of local Newfoundland politics and to set it in its larger context of Canadian-Newfoundland relations in the 1940s and within the North Atlantic Triangle as a whole.

There are a number of people who must be thanked for the aid that they have given me along the way. Professor Robert Bothwell directed this work from its earliest stages as a doctoral thesis at the University of Toronto, and I am sincerely grateful for his support. Professor John English and the Hon. J.W. Pickersgill gave of their time to read the manuscript and make numerous helpful suggestions. I would also like to thank Virgil Duff of the University of Toronto Press for his efforts in helping me turn a manuscript into a book, and Beverley Beetham Endersby for copyediting this book. I was also fortunate to receive generous financial support while conducting the research for this book, and I would like to thank the University of Toronto and the Social Sciences and Humanities Research Council of Canada for doctoral fellowships and the Centre for International Studies and the Associates of the University of Toronto, Inc. for travel grants. Most important, I am deeply grateful to Teresa Lemieux for the commitment, support, and energy that she gave to me from the very start. Without her this book would not have been written.

Transcripts/Translations of Crown-copyright records in the Public Record Office appear by permission of the Controller of H.M. Stationery Office.

This book has been published with the help of a grant from the Social Science Federation of Canada, using funds provided by the Social Sciences and Humanities Research Council of Canada, and from the Publications Fund of University of Toronto Press.

Abbreviations

ATFERO   Atlantic Ferry Organization
CHR   *Canadian Historical Review*
CJEPS   *Canadian Journal of Economics and Political Science*
CPAS   Canadian Pacific Air Services
CRO   Commonwealth Relations Office
CSC   Chiefs of Staff Committee
CWC   Cabinet War Committee
DCER   *Documents on Canadian External Relations*
DEA   Department of External Affairs
DND   Department of National Defence
DO   Dominions Office
DRCN   *Documents on Relations between Canada and Newfoundland*, volume 1
ICCNR   Interdepartmental Committee on Canada-Newfoundland Relations
ICICA   Interdepartmental Committee on International Civil Aviation
JSC   Joint Staff Committee
NAW   National Archives, Washington
NPA   Newfoundland Provincial Archives
PAC   Public Archives of Canada
PCO   Privy Council Office
PJBD   Permanent Joint Board on Defence
PRO   Public Record Office, Kew

INSIDE THE ATLANTIC TRIANGLE

1

Introduction

The island of Newfoundland lies at the eastern limits of the Gulf of St Lawrence, inside the 'North Atlantic Triangle' in a physical as well as an historical sense. Geographically, Newfoundland is very much a part of the North American continent; to the west the Strait of Belle Isle separates the island from the mainland by only a handful of miles, while to the south, the tip of Cape Breton lies across the Cabot Strait, a distance of fifty-five miles at the closest point. But the proximity of the island to the mainland is deceiving in several ways: the Strait of Belle Isle is closed to shipping for much of the year, and, although access to Cabot Strait is much longer, the shipping routes between Newfoundland and Canada are rarely free from the hazards of fog and ice; moreover, the only significant population centre in Newfoundland during the 1930s, St John's, was five day's journey from Montreal by boat.

Newfoundland is the tenth largest island in the world, with an area of roughly 42,000 square miles. The terrain is dotted with low rolling hills and a large number of rivers and lakes. The coastline comprises nearly 6,000 miles of ragged bays and inlets which furnish many natural harbours. Labrador is considerably larger, with a territory of 100,000 square miles. In the 1930s very little was known about Labrador; there had been few surveys undertaken, access to the interior was limited, the population was small, and few possessed the capital necessary for development. However, many Newfoundlanders viewed Labrador as an area of vast potential wealth, which once opened to development would prove to be a panacea for their troubled economy.[1]

In 1935 the population of Newfoundland and Labrador was 289,515. The Avalon Peninsula housed 47 per cent of the total, including the

39,886 people who resided in St John's. Most of the remainder of the population lived in the more than 1,000 settlements scattered around the coast. Immigration to Newfoundland was almost exclusively from the British Isles, in particular from Ireland and the English west country. The population as a whole was fairly evenly divided on religious grounds among three churches: Anglican, Roman Catholic, and United Church of Canada.[2]

The climate of Newfoundland is comparable to that of southern Alaska. The Labrador current has a cooling effect, and Newfoundland experiences long winters and has an average mean temperature of 41° F. The soil and climate, moreover, are not suited to large-scale agriculture. Short summers with cool and cloudy weather severely limit the growing season even in those few areas where the soil conditions are adequate. Consequently, farms tended to be small and geared mainly to filling local needs. The census of 1935 listed the number of farmers in Newfoundland as 4,339.

Traditionally, the centre of the Newfoundland economy has always been the catching and selling of fish. From the sixteenth century onwards the Grand Banks have attracted fishermen from all over the world, and much of the early history of Newfoundland can be seen as a function of the fishing industry. A variety of fish can be found in Newfoundland waters, but the primary focus of the industry is cod, which thrives on the nearly ideal conditions – temperature, food supply, and high degree of salinity in the water – of the Grand Banks. The dried codfish industry was the mainstay of the Newfoundland fishery during the 1930s. It comprised three main sections, the inshore fishery, the Labrador fishery, and the Bank fishery, which as a group accounted for an average of $6,390,684 of a total export value of Newfoundland fish of $7,912,250 from 1931 to 1935. The principal markets for Newfoundland cod were Portugal, Spain, Italy, and Greece, but there was also some export to Brazil and the West Indies.[3]

Not surprisingly, the bait fishery played an important role in the industry as a whole. The catch consisted mainly of herring, capelin, and squid, the last also being exported in small quantities to the United States and the Far East. Other branches of the fishery included salmon fishing, sealing, whaling, and lobster trapping. Salmon, seal skins, and seal oil were valuable exports, as were, to a lesser degree, canned whale meat and lobster. Mention should also be made of the fresh-fish industry which was helped by improved freezing techniques in the 1930s. Although this branch of the industry was not enormously significant in the 1930s, the Commission of Government believed that the future of Newfoundland's fishery lay here and with the fresh-fish market in the United States.

The role of the fishing industry in the local economy in Newfoundland was central: in 1935 the cod fishery alone employed more than 34,000 men.[4] Severe class divisions evolved between the merchants, who bought and exported the catch and imported and distributed needed goods, and the fishermen, who remained dependent on the merchants for their livelihood. The merchant class spread into other areas in the domestic economy, including shipping, banking, insurance, and some manufacturing. Inevitably this class wielded strong influence economically, politically, and socially. The fishermen, in contrast lived from day to day with little control over their environment; perpetually in debt; and at all times dependent on the goodwill of the merchant class for a fair price.[5]

The two other major natural resources of Newfoundland were its forests and mineral wealth. Because of the weak soil and adverse growing conditions, forest land in Newfoundland was not abundant, and the areas that did exist comprised mainly spruce and fir. Less than 25 per cent of the island supported forest cover, and there was practically none in the interior. Traditionally, much of the forest near the coast was used by Newfoundlanders for domestic purposes, and at the turn of the century there were almost nine hundred small sawmills producing board mainly for these needs. In 1909 the Harmsworth interests (owners of London's *Daily Mail*) opened a pulp and paper mill at Grand Falls under the control of their Anglo-Newfoundland Development Company Ltd. Virtually the total output of newsprint produced here up to the Second World War was shipped for use by the *Daily Mail*. A second pulp and paper mill was established in 1923, and after a succession of owners it fell under the control of the Bowater-Lloyd interests of England (the International Power and Paper Company) in 1937. In 1933 the two mills employed approximately 1,400 men, plus 3,000 more in the woods during the cutting season, and paid out approximately $6 million per year in wages.[6]

Throughout Newfoundland there was a considerable variety of minerals but only a few were found in sufficient quantities to be commercially profitable. The two major minerals were the iron-ore deposits in Bell Island and the copper deposits in the vicinity of Buchans. The deposits of iron ore at Wabana on Bell Island were of high quality and mining operations were opened in 1895 by Nova Scotian interests.

The Dominion Steel and Coal Corporation, which ran this operation, also controlled the limestone quarries at Aquathana. Although more than 2,000 men were normally employed by this company, the number dropped to just over 1,000 during the depression. In 1928 the copper-lead-zinc deposits at Buchans were opened up by the Buchans Mining Co. which in turn was controlled by the Anglo-Newfoundland Development Company Ltd and the American Smelting and Refining Co. This operation was of less importance than that at Wabana but gave employment to 350 men. Fluorspar was also mined in small quantities at St Lawrence, and limestone was quarried at Humbermouth and Cobbs Arm as well as at Aquathana.[7]

Between the wars the major customer for Wabana ore was Germany; Canada was a close second, followed by the United Kingdom and the United States. Almost all the limestone went to Canada while the copper was shipped primarily to the United States. Like the forest industry, the mining industry was largely controlled by outside interests.

The importance of these industries is evident in the export statistics. Between 1936 and 1940 the average value of fishing exports was $7,445,383, while the value of mining exports was relatively higher, averaging out at $8,104,826. Most lucrative were the exports of forest products; the average for the five-year period was $14,870,389. The three exports together brought in more than $30 million, out of the total export figure of $30,958,389 – over 95 per cent of Newfoundland's total exports.[8]

In the 1930s Newfoundland's best customers were the United Kingdom and the United States. The United Kingdom bought an average of 37 per cent of Newfoundland's exports between 1936 and 1940, mainly newsprint but also some fresh/frozen salmon, dried cod, seal skins, and seal oil. In the same time period the United States purchased 24.1 per cent of Newfoundland's exports, mainly copper and newsprint, but also some seal skins and seal oil. Canada took less than 10 per cent of Newfoundland's exports, primarily iron ore for the Sydney steel industry. At the turn of the century, export to Brazil, Portugal, Spain, and Italy accounted for over 50 per cent of Newfoundland's total but from 1936 to 1940 this had dropped to 9 per cent, an indication of the decline in relative importance of dried cod.[9]

Domestic manufacturing and secondary industry in Newfoundland at this time were on a relatively minor scale, employing fewer than 6,000 people. As a result Newfoundland was very dependent on the outside world for many basic goods, such as foodstuffs, textiles, furniture, oil products, machinery, and hardware, among other products. Between the two world wars 92 per cent of all of Newfoundland's imports came from Canada, the United Kingdom, and the United States, with Canada the leading supplier at 37 per cent to 40 per cent.[10]

Clearly, foreign trade was an essential element in Newfoundland's economy. On the export side a large segment of the population was directly dependent on world demand and prices, and as a result their standard of living rose and fell in response to the expansion or contraction of trade with the outside world. On the import side, the Newfoundland tariff was used primarily for revenue purposes and consequently was high on items such as clothing and foodstuffs in general despite domestic 'shortages.' However, machinery needed for resource industries was allowed to enter at low rates and often free. Customs and excise duties during the 1920s and 1930s on average accounted for between 65 per cent and 75 per cent of the Newfoundland government's total revenue. Moreover, most duties were rated on an ad valorem basis and therefore tended to fluctuate with the quantity as well as the value of imports.[11]

Income taxes and corporation taxes increased in relative importance during the 1930s, but still accounted for only a small percentage of total revenue. For example, in 1933–4 the income tax collected amounted to $824,000 out of a total government revenue of $8,906,000, of which $6,406,000 was from tariff duties. Because of the nature of the work done, especially by fishermen, income taxes were difficult to assess and collect. Also there was a traditional dislike for direct taxation among Newfoundlanders, and successive governments found it politically easier to increase tariff rates instead.[12] Furthermore, the non-industrial nature of the economy and the absence of large corporations produced few areas for increased government revenue through taxation. Low domestic production led to more reliance on the tariff as a source of revenue. These factors made Newfoundland's economy precarious at the best of times, and in the depression they proved to be disastrous.

Politically, Newfoundland evolved during the nineteenth century from a brawling and sparsely populated fishing colony into a self-governing dominion. The institutions of democracy – representative government and then responsible government – were duly granted and Newfoundland followed its sister colonies in Canada on the road to nationhood. Nevertheless, Newfoundland's political and constitutional evolution did not simply parallel that of the rest of British North America; Newfoundland's unique geographical and political situation sparked an independent course of development. There were, for example, few real political parties. For the most part, allegiances continuously shifted with the times, and the divisions within Newfoundland society tended to be more along religious lines. Moreover, political and economic power was concentrated to a significant degree in a small merchant-dominated group centred in St John's. [13]

Relations between Canada and Newfoundland during this period were marked with a certain amount of apprehension, hesitation, and mutual suspicion. The idea of Confederation had seemed to many to be a 'natural' development geographically and ethnically, and the cause had garnered wide-range support from a variety of sources in both countries. But concomitant with this, strong forces rallied to oppose closer relations and at all times made Confederation difficult, if not impossible.

In Newfoundland the merchant class had traditionally opposed Confederation; union would mean increased competition from mainland business and the introduction of prohibitive mainland taxes, two strong inducements for the maintenance of independence. In addition, the large Roman Catholic population in Newfoundland believed that Confederation would leave them as an unprotected minority in a largely Protestant Canada, despite the large Catholic population in Quebec.[14]

There also existed over a long period of time a pervasive anti-French bias in Newfoundland. Throughout Newfoundland's history France had been the traditional enemy, both in war and in peace. By the late nineteenth century fear of invasion had disappeared, but the French shore question, which concerned French fishing rights on a long stretch of Newfoundland coast, lingered as a bitterly fought issue and prevented an easing of anti-French sentiments in Newfoundland.[15] This prejudice had disseminated to all things French, including French Canada, and consequently led many Newfoundlanders to oppose Confederation.

The issue of Confederation arose on a number of occasions between 1864 and 1934 and was never far from the surface at any time. In 1864 two members of the Newfoundland assembly, F.T.B. Carter and Ambrose Shea, attended the Quebec Conference with the blessing of the governor, but with no authority to commit Newfoundland. Five years later, in 1869, terms were negotiated and agreed to between Ottawa and the Newfoundland delegation, but in the ensuing election in Newfoundland both Carter and Confederation went down to defeat. The anti-Confederates were led by Charles Fox Bennett, who waged a vigorous campaign which played on all the old fears. But there were other factors in the 1860s that precluded Confederation: Newfoundland had experienced no Fenian raids and felt secure under the protection of the Royal Navy and consequently had few defence motives for union; moreover, the colony had relatively few economic links with Canada, Confederation offered no solution to the French shore problem, and Newfoundland would receive no benefits from the Intercolonial Railway. In Ottawa, meanwhile, Newfoundland was not viewed as an essential participant in Confederation and was at times taken for granted and overlooked in favour of more important areas.[16]

The defeat of Confederation in 1869 in Newfoundland did not lay the issue to rest. Discussion was merely postponed temporarily; it would be reopened time and again. In the late 1880s the Confederation issue again came to the fore, this time as a possible solution to hard economic times in Newfoundland. Sir John A. Macdonald had always supported the idea and was ready to negotiate at virtually any time. In 1888 Charles Tupper, the Canadian high commissioner in London, visited Newfoundland to informally open negotiations, but renewed interest in Confederation dwindled as the Newfoundland government stalled and local politicians showed their reluctance to publicly support a cause that had previously aroused so much antagonism.[17]

Sir John Thompson and Mackenzie Bowell opened the question again in 1892 at the Halifax Conference. This conference was called to ease the dispute between Canada and Newfoundland arising from the Bond Blaine Convention, a Newfoundland–United States fisheries agreement negotiated independently of Canada. As was so often the case during this period, Canadian interest in Newfoundland was aroused only when the latter threatened to achieve a competitive edge over Canada in its trade relations with the United States. But at this point the two nations viewed each other more as competitors than as potential partners, and Confederation was placed on a back burner in favour of the more pressing fishery question.

Three years later, however, the situation had shifted dramatically. The bank crash of 1894 sparked a severe financial crisis in Newfoundland and the government was confronted with the problem of being unable to meet its interest payments. Rather than accepting the British government's proposal for a royal commission, the Whiteway government asked that negotiations be opened with Ottawa. The result was a conference in Ottawa during April 1895 to negotiate possible terms for Confederation.

The major snag in these talks was financial. Newfoundland's

proposals followed the lines of those discussed in 1888, with consideration given to the country's immediate needs, but Mackenzie Bowell felt that he could not be too generous because of the deleterious effect this might have on other provinces such as Prince Edward Island. Efforts made to have the British government bridge the gap between the two sides failed and the talks collapsed, leaving a legacy of bad feelings on all sides and solidifying a strong resentment towards Canada on the part of many Newfoundlanders.[18]

Something of a pattern emerged from the discussions on Confederation in these years. In Newfoundland, Confederation was viewed as a possible solution to economic problems at home and tended to be brought up in times of economic hardship, or when it was seen as politically expedient by the ruling party. Likewise, when these conditions eased or disappeared, interest dropped and the talks were allowed to lapse. Popular support for Confederation was never solid. Had the Maritime provinces appeared to have clearly benefited from joining Confederation opinion might have been swayed in Newfoundland, but as it stood there were few firm inducements to advocate union. On the Canadian side, the federal government generally favoured union, but in negotiations tended to be somewhat parsimonious so as not to appear to be giving better terms to Newfoundland than those already accepted by other provinces. Furthermore, because Newfoundland was often negotiating from an economically weak position the Canadians tried to drive a harder bargain. And, in the 1890s, Canada had economic problems of its own and could ill afford to be overly generous towards Newfoundland.[19]

The party system in Newfoundland became more fully developed at the turn of the century, with the emergence of the Liberal party of Sir Robert Bond. The political scene during these years was relatively stable; the government operated on a surplus, and the French shore question, which had troubled Newfoundland politics for more than a century, was finally settled. In 1908, Bond was defeated by Sir Edward Morris and his 'People's party.' Despite its name, the People's party was conservative in nature and relied on the support of Newfoundland's Catholic population.

The only major challenge to the merchant-dominated political system came from William Coaker and his Fisherman's Protective Union, an organization consisting mainly of outport fishermen. Coaker's movement mounted a significant challenge for a short period of time, but it began to crumble during the First World War and eventually merged with the Liberal party.[20]

Politics during the post-war decade were, as one author put it, 'a merry, anarchic muddle.'[21] Patronage and corruption were prevalent, and attention was focused more on leadership than on issues. It was at this time that Sir Richard Squires and his revitalized Liberal party rose to a dominant position in Newfoundland politics. Squires was elected prime minister in 1919, but a political scandal forced him to resign less than four years later. Nevertheless, he returned as prime minister in 1928, with the help of a young Liberal and ambitious worker, J.R. Smallwood. It was Squires's misfortune to be in office when the depression began.

The depression had a very severe effect on Newfoundland's economy and ultimately brought it to the verge of collapse. Throughout the 1920s the government operated with a continuous budget deficit and survived only by yearly borrowing. By 1933 the national debt stood at approximately $100 million at an average interest rate of 5 per cent. Of total government expenditures, close to 50 per cent was directed to interest payments on this debt; consequently, new borrowing was necessary to fulfil all the government's obligations. For example, in the year 1932–3 the total government revenue was $8,085,666 while expenditures were $11,553,774, leaving a deficit of $3,468,108. Included in government expenditures were interest payments which amounted to $5,113,000.[22]

The government's economic predicament was exacerbated by the catastrophic falling off of international trade. The total value of Newfoundland's exports dropped from $40 million to $23.2 million between 1930 and 1933. The fishery was hit especially hard as fish prices dropped to their lowest levels since 1913.[23] The ramifications for Newfoundland's economy were enormous. Lower prices and decreased trade led directly to lower incomes for the large segment of the population involved in the primary industries. In turn, the demand for imports fell, and, because of the government's reliance on import duties, its revenue diminished. At the same time domestic wages were cut and unemployment increased rapidly. Moreover, the traditional escape-release of emigration was closed as the number of job opportunities on the mainland decreased. By 1932 25 per cent of the population was on relief, receiving a modest sum of six cents per day. The result was pressure on the government for more borrowing at a time of increased demand for government services.

The years from 1930 to 1933 were ones of political turmoil in Newfoundland. Finding fewer and fewer potential lenders, the government of Sir Richard Squires found it increasingly difficult to avoid defaulting on its interest payments. Various attempts were made to raise funds, including an offer to sell Labrador to Canada which the Canadians refused.[24] Moreover, on the streets of St John's there was a growing restlessness that was threatening to escalate into violence. In February 1932, a mob stormed the House of Assembly trapping Squires (and Smallwood) inside. Squires escaped without injury but his government was in a desperate condition.[25]

In June 1932 Squire's government went down to defeat at the hands of Frederick C. Alderdice and his United Newfoundland party. One of Alderdice's campaign promises was to look into the feasibility of establishing a commission of government for a brief period. In the meantime, Alderdice continued the search for loans to cover the interest payments that came due every six months.

The Canadian government and several Canadian banks had come in with short-term help, but by late 1932 their benevolence was wearing thin. Compelled to come to Newfoundland's rescue, Canadian Prime Minister Bennett and British Chancellor of the Exchequer Neville Chamberlain offered a joint loan to tide Newfoundland over, but only on condition that Newfoundland accept a royal commission 'to examine into the future of Newfoundland and in particular to report on the financial situation and prospects of the Dominion and what measures may be necessary to secure its financial security.' As one historian has noted, Newfoundland 'had no counter-proposals, nor was there time to make any.'[26] The government of Newfoundland issued a request for a royal commission and it was appointed by the UK government on 17 February 1933.

The Royal Commission under the leadership of Lord Amulree began its study in St John's on 13 March 1933. Over the next ten weeks, more than one hundred formal sittings were convened and 260 witnesses were interviewed. The three commissioners travelled extensively across Newfoundland and managed a trip to Canada to discuss the situation with Prime Minister Bennett in Ottawa and officials of the Bank of Montreal in Montreal.

The report presented by the commissioners was an extensive study of Newfoundland's economy and history. Their conclusions were not optimistic. It was argued that Newfoundland's financial and economic problems were the result of not only present difficulties but also long-term disorders and mismanagement. Moreover, Newfoundland could be set on the right foot again only with outside help and guidance. It found 'first, that the difficulties with which the country is faced, while accentuated by the effects of the world depression, are in reality the result of persistent extravagance and neglect of proper financial principles on the part of successive Governments prior to 1931; secondly, that conditions are now such that it is beyond the powers of the people to make any effective recovery unaided or without some relief from the present burden of the public debt.'[27]

Various solutions were examined. The sale of Labrador was discussed, but the idea was dismissed because the commissioners felt that Labrador would be valuable some day and that it would be unfair to future generations to dispose of it at this time. A proposal for Confederation was mentioned and rejected as being too unpopular, even though the commissioners thought this the best and most logical solution. The possibility that Newfoundland should be allowed to default on its debts was rejected as an idea that 'could only be approached with the gravest apprehension.' Such action would have repercussions far beyond Newfoundland because 'default by a British community would be without precedent, and such a step would at once retard the general recovery and tarnish the good name of the British Commonwealth.'[28]

The major recommendations of the commissioners were twofold. First, the United Kingdom would have to carry Newfoundland financially because the 'burden of the public debt is wholly beyond the country's capacity to pay and it is essential that it should be lightened if the Island is to be saved from the imminent peril of financial collapse.' Second, Newfoundland's difficulties were long-term ones and financial support without fundamental change would not provide a solution, especially 'since those difficulties are largely due to the reckless waste and extravagance, and to the absence of constructive and efficient administration, engendered by a political system which for a generation has been abused and exploited for personal or party ends.' The solution was to change the government sufficiently to 'promote the rehabilitation of the Island on sound principles.'[29] In the commissioners' view, 'the country should be given a rest from party politics for a period of years.' In the place of party politics a 'Government by Commission' would be instituted which would take the necessary steps to put Newfoundland's house back in order. This change would not be a permanent one, for 'as soon as the Island's difficulties are overcome and the country is again self-supporting, responsible government, on request from the people of Newfoundland, would be restored.'[30] Other recommendations included the rehabilitation and expansion of the fishing industry, tariff revision, increased grants for education and public health, reorganization of the civil service, and a series of investigations into the uses and potential value of Newfoundland's resources.

The British government accepted the main recommendations of the report, feeling it was 'impossible to dissent from the main conclusions and recommendations at which that Commission has unanimously arrived.' A commission of government would be established with far-reaching powers and an essentially open-ended mandate. Less concern was given to the future return to responsible government and to the process by which it would be done, except that the Commission of Government would rule 'until such time as the Island may become self-supporting again.'[31]

With this caveat the Commission of Government took office in St John's on 16 February 1934. The suspension of responsible government and the etablishment of the Commission of Government were of enormous importance in the future development of Newfoundland. In the course of Canadian-Newfoundland relations over the next fifteen years contact between the two countries and decisions on the role to be played by Newfoundland were channelled through the Commission of Government which was responsible to the Dominions Office, and ultimately to the British government and taxpayers. Not until 1946 would the people of Newfoundland have the opportunity to exercise a degree of influence in the future of their government. Consequently, decisions affecting Newfoundland were made by the British government with British interests in mind, often with more consideration given to the Canadian government than to the people of Newfoundland.

The establishment of the Commission of Government was met with little concentrated opposition in Newfoundland. On the contrary, many welcomed the Commission of Government and were willing to offer support. One contemporary author countered the suspicions and fears over the loss of responsible government this way: 'Now, there are some who lament our lost liberties, instead of regretting that the crisis did not occur when our public debt was half its present amount; these people fear the evils of an autocratic dictatorship. We need not fear this, as we are assured we can have back what we have surrendered as soon as we become self-supporting again. That should not take long, if that is all we want.'[32] In 1934, if the Commission of Government could improve the economic condition of Newfoundland, most Newfoundlanders would have agreed that it was worth the sacrifice of the old political system.

But some criticism of the Royal Commission *Report* did erupt immediately and has continued through the years. In London, members of the Labour party questioned the precedent that might be set by the withdrawal of dominion status, believing that there was too much unemployment at home for British taxpayers to support another country. Moreover, it was pointed out that instituting the Commission of Government and accepting the responsibility for Newfoundland's national debt was protection for the bondholders only and did nothing to change Newfoundland's economy in any fundamental way. In the words of Clement Attlee, the *Report* focused on the corrupt actions of the politicians but had 'nothing whatever to say about those corrupt capitalists and the whole degrading situation of the economic system in Newfoundland.'[33] These sentiments were echoed in Ottawa by J.S. Woodsworth: 'I think there is no member of any of the self-governing dominions who was not very decidedly perturbed by the fate of our sister dominion, Newfoundland, where they have given up even the forms of democracy. Responsible Government has been replaced by administration by a commission with what amounts to practically dictatorial powers, and I would say that this change has been made primarily not in the interests of the people of Newfoundland but in the interests of the bondholders.'[34]

In a similar vein many Newfoundlanders were bitter over the surrender of responsible government. Sir William Coaker called the Royal Commission *Report* degrading and said that those who accepted it 'would be remembered in history as traitors to the land that bore them.'[35] Likewise, in a letter to the Toronto *Globe*, Alfred B. Morine, a former Leader of the Opposition in Newfoundland, wrote that Newfoundlanders were being reduced to a position of 'quasi-slavery' under the new system for the sake of those who had invested in Newfoundland.[36]

Of course the British government was trying to protect the bondholders, but it was also trying to secure its own position. The commissioners recognized that if one dominion defaulted the recovery of all the rest would be that much more difficult. The question that remains is whether it was necessary to eliminate responsible government altogether in order to achieve economic stability. Newfoundland's economy was in distress and could not have continued without outside help. Moreover, there was widespread corruption in the political system and parts of the economy had been badly mismanaged. But these were not unique characteristics in the world of 1933.

The Commission of Government consisted of six appointed members, three from Newfoundland and three from the United Kingdom. Under the Letters Patent and Royal Instructions, which in effect became Newfoundland's new constitution, the appointed governor presided over the commission and acted on the advice of his commissioners. Overall policy was still directed from London, and policy-making on the local level was usually under the direction of the various commissioners. Thus, the governor acted as something of a chairman, with a vote that was critical only in the event of a deadlock among the commissioners.[37] Each commissioner was given a portfolio, such as Finance or Justice, over which he was responsible. As has often been noted these men were bureaucrats rather than politicians and tended to work in isolation, unable to gauge or placate public opinion. The commission closed the Newfoundland Museum, ignoring the possible detrimental effects this action might have on the local population, and in a cavalier fashion converted the Newfoundland Parliament building into office space for use by the commission. Consequently, the goodwill that had initially welcomed the new government dissipated, especially as economic recovery failed to materialize.

Despite these drawbacks the Commission of Government made a considerable number of reforms in its first five years of existence. First, the Newfoundland debt was converted into new sterling stock guaranteed by the British government at a 3 per cent rate of interest. This cut Newfoundland's annual payments by more than $2 million. The commission's goals were similar to those of previous governments in that it tried to increase the efficiency of old industries and encourage new ones to develop. Fishermen were given rebates on purchases of salt and loans to establish cold-storage depots for bait. Loans were also extended to help build and renovate schooners – more than seventy during the winter of 1934–5 alone. In 1936 the Newfoundland Fisheries Board was established to improve the quality and price of Newfoundland fish through inspection and organization to prevent price-cutting.[38]

A land-resettlement scheme was instigated, largely under the direction of British commissioner Thomas Lodge. This plan to improve the state of agriculture in Newfoundland through a system of land and cash bonuses largely backfired and, as one historian has noted, acted as a drain on revenue that could have been put to better use elseswhere, especially in the reorganization of the fisheries.[39] The inadequacy of Newfoundland's soil and the difficulty of turning fishermen into farmers virtually doomed the plan to failure.

In other areas the Commission of Government had more success. The civil service, which had received severe criticism in the Royal Commission *Report,* was reorganized on the British model; a system of tenure was introduced and new blood was brought in.[40] Expenditures on public welfare, health, and education were increased; the system of railways and steamship services were made more efficient; a geological survey was undertaken; and slowly some of the tariffs on essential goods such as fruit, flour, and evaporated milk were reduced.

The verdict on the Commission of Government has been harsh. 'By 1939,' wrote Frederick W. Rowe, 'it was clear that there had been no economic development of any size or scale. No basic change had taken place in Newfoundland's financial position: there were still as many unemployed and seeking relief as there had been in 1933. There had been no attempt whatever to provide political education or training for the Newfoundland people; such education had been one of the objectives outlined by the Royal Commission's Report. Economically and politically, Commission of Government had been almost a total failure.'[41] The Commission of Government was impartial and efficient, but, limited as it was in action by the Dominions Office and the lack of funds, it was forced to address short-term problems rather than long-term goals. Thomas Lodge, a commissioner but later one of the Commission of Government's most severe critics, condemned the lack of an 'effective head or a directing brain' in the commission.[42] Moreover, he attacked the attitude of the Dominions Office in not showing more concern for Newfoundland: 'all the Dominions Office really wanted was to accumulate nice tidy files of official papers and minutes, in which nobody ever said anything unkind about anybody else and never differed seriously from the previous writer.'[43]

Lodge himself is evidence of the shortcomings of the Commission of Government. As a commissioner he continued to support his land-resettlement plan long after it had become apparent that it was not working. Working more in competition than in co-operation with his fellow commissioners, Lodge became as much a part of the problem as a solution. Furthermore, his analysis of the root problem in Newfoundland mirrored that of the Royal Commission *Report,* focusing more on personal character than on economic forces. 'The problem of Newfoundland,' he wrote in 1939, 'is more moral than material. It is a function of the character of the people. Had the island been colonized by dour Lowland Scots, instead of West countrymen and Irishmen of charm, there would never have been a problem. As it is, the Newfoundlander has had already too much experience of gifts handed out by Government.'[44]

Political corruption, sectarianism, and the system of patronage in Newfoundland had received severe criticism in the Royal Commission *Report*, and from men like Lodge, as if these problems were unique to Newfoundland rather than endemic to most nations of the world. And, despite these strong words, the Commission of Government did not solve these problems; in fact it perpetuated them in many ways. For example, civil-service jobs and the post of Newfoundland commissioner continued to be awarded along sectarian lines, with proportional representation from the Anglican, United, and Roman Catholic churches.[45]

Perhaps the gravest defect of the Commission of Government was its inability to restore Newfoundland politically. As one author has noted, the Commission of Government 'markedly improved the bureaucratic structures of Newfoundland and instituted new administrative practices; but in contrast, it made only a feeble effort to provide training in self-government.'[46] Some effort had been made in the direction of municipal government, but little had been achieved in the field of political re-education, and Newfoundland's constitutional and economic future looked as uncertain as it had in the spring of 1934. Many critics would agree with Lodge's conclusion in *Dictatorship in Newfoundland*: 'To have abandoned the principle of democracy without accomplishing economic rehabilitation is surely the unforgivable sin.'[47]

II

The Royal Commission and Newfoundland's financial collapse in the 1930s reawakened the issue of Confederation with Canada. Since the turn of the century union between Canada and Newfoundland had rarely been discussed; in 1908 the idea was studied by the British government and then dismissed, and between 1913 and 1916 unofficial negotiations were undertaken by Sir Edward Morris and Arthur Meighen but no agreement was reached. As a popular issue, Confederation was in limbo. During the 1920s the most salient irritation in the relations between the two countries was the disagreement over the Labrador boundary – a long-smouldering dispute settled in Newfoundland's favour by the decision of the Judicial Committee of the Privy Council in 1927.

But two of the three members of the Royal Commission, Sir William Stavert and Charles A. Magrath, were Canadians (the latter was chosen by Britain in consultation with the Canadian government), and both favoured Confederation. In a letter to Prime Minister Bennett, Magrath wrote that he believed that 'Newfoundland must become in time part of our Dominion.' In order to ensure this the Canadian government must be generous and pursue a policy 'of active cooperation and assistance.'[48]

In Ottawa the situation was viewed somewhat differently. Bennett was faced by two conflicting views: on the one hand, hard domestic conditions made offering generous terms or financial help to Newfoundland difficult at best, while on the other, it was not in Canada's best interests to have Newfoundland go under financially. O.D. Skelton, the under secretary of state for external affairs, outlined part of the problem in a letter to W.D. Herridge, the Canadian minister in the United States. Skelton suggested that the Royal Commission *Report* 'may increase the misunderstanding that exists abroad as to the relations between the several members of the British Commonwealth of Nations, and make foreign observers consider that the much-boasted Dominion status is a very fragile and temporary development.'[49] The collapse of one dominion reflected on all the others, and a tarnished foreign image could only hinder the recovery of Canada's economy.

Within this framework there were severe limitations on the actions that the Canadian government could take. Bennett favoured union with Newfoundland and the issue was discussed at the cabinet level, but to offer acceptable terms of union to Newfoundland was seen as financially impossible and politically reckless. Bennett hoped that Confederation would be an issue in the next Newfoundland election, but beyond this he could not be very optimistic about the chances for success.[50]

In the House of Commons criticism of the government was not directed at its reluctance to help a sister dominion or its failure to bring about union, but rather at the loans and guarantees given and the steps taken to ensure their security. As Leader of the Opposition Mackenzie King put it in the House of Commons: 'A guarantee was given to Newfoundland as a means of aiding unemployment in the Dominion of Canada.'[51]

On the Canadian side there was a distinct lack of interest in union with Newfoundland. While criticizing the government's role in aiding

Newfoundland, the Liberal MP from Temiscouata said, 'We are not interested in the welfare of Newfoundland any more than that there are human beings there.'[52] This was not an uncommon view; Canadians had too many troubles of their own to be overly concerned or to show much sympathy with the financial predicament of Newfoundland.

Public lack of interest, however, did not preclude closer relations between Canada and Newfoundland. Since the turn of the century the Canadian dollar had been legal tender in Newfoundland, and four Canadian banks had opened branches there, with the Bank of Montreal playing a major role in the finances of the Newfoundland government. Economically, Newfoundland increasingly looked to Canada for its imports, while the development of the fresh/frozen fish industry under the supervision of the Commission of Government was directed more to the North American market than the older, traditional ones. Moreover, the development of resource industries in Newfoundland needed much foreign investment, a growing proportion of which was furnished by North America.

Socially, too, the ties between Newfoundland and the mainland were growing stronger. The creation of the United Church of Canada in 1926 included the Methodist Church in Newfoundland. In an era of improved transportation and communications, Newfoundland's cultural ties with the mainland were strengthened somewhat through the influx of North American newspapers, magazines, and radio, while bonds established through emigration to Canada remained a significant force. Politically, Canada and Newfoundland remained far apart, but economically, culturally, and, in a sense, geographically, Newfoundland was becoming increasingly 'North American.' Although the transition was slow it was significant none the less.

In 1939 Newfoundland's deficit was still being paid by the British government; no new industries had been created; and 50,000 Newfoundlanders were still on relief. World conditions were not much better than they had been in 1933 and Newfoundland's overseas markets had not expanded; in fact they had been hurt by such events as the Spanish Civil War. The Commission of Government cannot be blamed for being unable to counter these forces – no form of government could have had much effect. On the eve of the Second World War, Newfoundland remained a poor and weak country, a dominion in 'suspended status' swaying on the tide of world forces, unable to control its environment either economically or politically.

The Confederation issue was safely buried, but with the coming of war immense forces were unleashed that radically altered the relationship between Canada and Newfoundland. The Canadian government could no longer take a passive stance in relations with Newfoundland; self-interest, shared concerns, and common goals made closer contact and a more active role necessary for Canada. The crisis of war and the reshaping of peace would fundamentally restructure both Canadian-Newfoundland relations and the North Atlantic Triangle as a whole.

2

Who defends Newfoundland?

In 1939 the European powers had embarked on a collision course that would soon lead to war. In contrast to a world that was rearming and preparing for war, defence remained a low priority for Newfoundland's Commission of Government. Faced with a domestic crisis of unemployment, poverty, and economic stagnation that was almost insurmountable, the Newfoundland authorities had little time or resources to give to defence problems. Foreign affairs were safely in the hands of the British government and the problems of the Europeans appeared remote indeed. At the outbreak of hostilities in 1939 Newfoundland's defences were virtually non-existent.

Defence planning never passed beyond the preliminary stages during the 1930s, and the coming of war in 1939 produced only minor changes. The Canadians, who would seem to have had the greatest stake in Newfoundland, were reluctant at all times to enter into defence agreements with either Newfoundland or the United Kingdom. Consequently, from September 1939 to June 1940 defence relations with Newfoundland were tenuous at best. For the most part the British and the Canadians appeared to be unwilling participants in a game they would have preferred not to play. The result was an interesting episode in Canadian-Newfoundland relations that was important not only in itself, but also in contrast to the dramatic events that followed in the summer of 1940.

Soon after the Commission of Government took office it was instructed by the Dominions Office to undertake a study of the state of defence in Newfoundland. This study was produced by a committee chaired by E.N.R. Trentham, the commissioner for finance, and was completed in May 1936. The Newfoundland Defence Scheme, 1936, was a survey of existing defence needs and objectives, examining vulnerable areas and presenting a reasoned discussion of how best to protect these areas in time of war.

That Newfoundland should be defended was unquestioned: 'The possession of any part of it [Newfoundland], especially the South-West and North-West parts, by enemy forces would constitute a serious menace to the Dominion of Canada, and might result in the stoppage of the sea channels between the St. Lawrence and the Atlantic.'[1] Furthermore, Newfoundland was an important link in transatlantic communications as it was a terminal for a large number of Atlantic cables: St John's was the terminal for four and Bay Roberts, five; other cables went to Harbour Grace, Heart's Content, Arnold's Cove, Placentia, and Port-aux-Basques.

The study also looked to the future and predicted an increased role for Newfoundland in the field of aviation: '[at present], the importance of Newfoundland as an air centre is small,' but 'its potentialities from the point of view of trans-Atlantic service are great, and there is every possibility of its developing into an important air base in the not far distant future.'

For these reasons, it was obvious that Newfoundland should be adequately defended, but as to the country's ability to undertake this, the Newfoundland Defence Scheme was blunt: 'The Island is entirely undefended,' it said, adding that 'as there are at present no defences, vessels armed with modern guns of any size could carry out bombardment of St. John's or of practically any other place in the Island by direct observation.' St John's, the main centre of population, commercial operations, communications, and government, was especially vulnerable. The city was constructed mainly of wood and had suffered catastrophic fires in the past; in war it would be susceptible to such things again. The results of a major fire in St John's would be disastrous: 'If a conflagration were to be brought about by enemy action, the money loss would run into many millions of dollars, while the affairs of the Island would be very largely disorganized.' Like St John's, the Bell Island mine, the coastal industries, the cable terminals and wireless stations, and the other population centres were without defences and open to attack.

Despite the apparent vulnerabilities of Newfoundland, the defence scheme showed no sense of urgency regarding the need to improve defences. Full-scale invasion was ruled out as unlikely, and the geographical location of Newfoundland precluded anything but a minor enemy attack. From the air, the 'distance of the Island from all possible centres of aggression is such that hostile bombing operations from a land base could not in the present state of the science be carried out, nor would the value of any military objectives in the Island warrant the employment of aircraft on any but the smallest scale.' Similarly, from a naval standpoint, 'It is considered that the scale of attack would not be likely to exceed a raid such as could be conducted by one or two cruisers, with a maximum landing force of 200–300 men.' As a result, little action was taken in the wake of this study. Faced with the overwhelming task of economic recovery and working with limited funds, the Commission of Government did not look on defence as a major priority. The Newfoundland Defence Scheme was duly signed and transmitted to the Dominions Office, which in turn referred it to the Overseas Defence Committee for its comments, and there the matter rested.

The British made few preparations to defend Newfoundland, aside from earmarking a number of minesweepers to patrol the harbours and coast. The likelihood of an air attack was dismissed. The Goverment of Newfoundland had only two aircraft of its own and no mention was made of providing any additional aircraft for reconnaissance purposes.[2]

Considerably more concern was shown for the defence of Newfoundland by various circles within the Canadian military and government. The strategic importance of Newfoundland in the defence of Canada was obvious to all concerned. This fact alone necessitated action on Canada's part to ensure its own security, independent of the measures undertaken by Britain. In addition, the ore extracted from the Wabana mines on Bell Island was of vital importance to the Canadian steel industry, and the loss of this supply of ore would seriously limit Canadian production of steel.

A 1937 memorandum by the Joint Staff Committee (JSC), an inter-service committee established in 1927 and the forerunner of the Chiefs of Staff Committee, underlined the need for concern in the defence of Newfoundland. It was noted that the Dominion Steel and Coal Corporation and its Sydney blast furnaces were responsible for almost one-third of Canada's steel production. The defence of Sydney was therefore essential, but not sufficient to ensure the continuous operation of the blast furnaces since the necessary ore and limestone were brought in from Newfoundland. Moreover, there were no alternative sources of supply. The implications for Canadian defence plans were straightforward enough: 'Canada has undertaken to make provision for her own local defence and insofar as her Atlantic coast is concerned that defence is intimately bound up with the defence of Newfoundland. The two problems are really one and no good purpose can be served by treating them separately.[3]

Efforts on the part of the JSC to include the defence of Newfoundland as a topic of discussion at the 1937 Imperial Conference proved futile. The policy of 'no commitments' applied to Newfoundland as well as other defence topics, and as such was a subject to be approached with extreme caution. Years later General H.D.G. Crerar recalled being 'carefully instructed' by O.D. Skelton not to appear to commit Canada to anything, and this included discussing the defence of Newfoundland with his British counterparts.[4]

But the British government was not insensitive to Canadian needs and recognized the importance of Newfoundland in Canadian defence. On the advice of Sir Francis Floud, the British high commissioner, copies of the Newfoundland Defence Scheme were made available to the Canadian government. In turn, copies were distributed to various departments in the Canadian armed forces for their examination.[5]

The Joint Staff Committee was critical not only of the lack of defences in Newfoundland, but also of the lack of action on the part of the Canadian government to address the issue. In a memorandum dated 5 April 1938, it was noted that the previous suggestions of the JSC had not been acted on because of the 'absence of specific authority to proceed to this end.'[6] This new memorandum reinforced ideas previously outlined and urged immediate action to correct the situation before an emergency arose.

The JSC also found the state of preparedness in Newfoundland extremely unsatisfactory: 'it would appear from the text of the "Newfoundland Defence Scheme" that the defence preparations contemplated by the British Government in conjunction with the Administration of Newfoundland are of a somewhat superficial nature. In particular, the means allotted for air and naval reconnaissance of its coast line appear dangerously inadequate from the point of view of possible enemy plans for attack on Canadian objectives.'[7] Finally, the committee noted that Sir Humphrey Walwyn, the governor of Newfoundland, and his secretary, Captain C.M.R. Schwerdt, RN, would be visiting Ottawa over Easter on other business and suggested that informal discussions be held with them concerning the defence of Newfoundland. This suggestion was relayed through Skelton to the prime minister who agreed to the discussions, providing they were 'purely exploratory.'[8]

The proposed meeting between Captain Schwerdt and members of the three Canadian services took place on 22 April 1938, at the Canadian Naval Service Headquarters. The discussion was informal and friendly and it was clear from the start that no commitments to either side could or would result. Schwerdt told the Canadians that, ultimately, responsibility for Newfoundland's defence rested with the British government, but that on the local level Newfoundland would do all that it could to provide for its own defence. Unfortunately, he added, Newfoundland's 'financial resources available for defence were very limited.'[9]

The discussion revolved around mutual defence problems and the need to secure the continent against air or naval attack. At one point the Canadians noted that under wartime conditions Canada would seek permission to base a certain number of aircraft at Gander for the reconnaissance of Newfoundland waters and the Gulf of St Lawrence in order to protect Atlantic shipping routes. But, because of the nature of this meeting, defence co-operation and planning remained suspended on a primitive level.[10]

The Joint Staff Committee reviewed the problem of Newfoundland's defence in light of the April meeting. The JSC recognized that Newfoundland was an essential component in the defence of Canada's Atlantic coast and for this reason it was important to know what defensive measures would be taken by the British if war broke out. Moreover, the JSC believed that it would be impossible to make a 'proper appreciation' of Canada's own defence needs in the east without Britain's plans concerning Newfoundland.[11]

In a memo to Ian Mackenzie, the minister of national defence, the JSC recommended that the Canadian government discuss this matter with the UK authorities. Despite the potentially critical nature of the situation, this request was followed by weeks of inaction and confusion. On 13 June Colonel L.R. LaFlèche, the deputy minister, wrote Skelton, asking if 'a decision has been reached' on the request of the JSC.[12] Skelton replied that there seemed 'to be some confusion'; he could not remember receiving a copy of the JSC report, and wrote: 'I have made enquiries of the Prime Minister's Office, and I was informed yesterday that the Prime Minister does not appear to have received any copy of the report.' Skelton finished by asking LaFlèche to forward two copies, one for the prime minister and one for himself, assuring LaFlèche that he would then 'be glad to try to expedite its consideration.'[13]

An interesting comment on this situation was made by Major-General E.C. Ashton, the chief of the general staff; he wrote that, while it was 'most desirable' that Skelton receive a copy of the report, action on the JSC request 'can hardly be taken without reference to the Minister,' in this case, Mackenzie King.[14] If anything, Skelton and the Department of External Affairs appeared to the military planners to be more of a hindrance than a help to British-Canadian military co-operation. Skelton's isolationism and the government's policy of no commitments were quickly becoming a severe handicap to the military in their efforts to prepare Canada for war. The question of Newfoundland's defence was an obvious example of this.

The difficulties were ironed out over the next few weeks, and the JSC memo was considered by the Defence Committee of cabinet in late July. On 27 July a telegram signed by Mackenzie King was sent to the Dominions Office, officially requesting information on the United Kingdom's position. The meeting with Schwerdt was reviewed and it was pointed out how the defence needs of Canada and Newfoundland overlapped in some important areas. For these reasons the Canadian government wished to know 'what measures, naval and air, for the defence of Newfoundland are contemplated in the event of war.'[15]

The reply to the July telegram was not sent until 21 October 1938, but its message was brief. The Dominions Office informed the Canadians that the United Kingdom had 'no specific measures' planned for local defence in Newfoundland, other than sending six auxiliary minesweepers and three auxiliary anti-submarine vessels to St John's after the war had begun. On a more reassuring note it was added 'that the general defence of the territory would rest on the cover provided by the Royal Navy.'[16]

Moreover, the reply stated that 'trade protection units of the Royal Navy' would be centred at Halifax, rather than St John's, and that an air squadron would be stationed there as well. Being based approximately two hours' flying time from St John's, this squadron would also offer increased protection for Newfoundland. Unfortunately, 'No squadron of the peace time Royal Air Force ... is earmarked for this purpose and, in order to carry out the above plans the necessary Squadron would either have to be raised as a new unit in the United Kingdom after the outbreak of war or be provided from some other source in the British Commonwealth.'[17]

There was little doubt whom the UK authorities felt the 'other source' should be. As H.F. Batterbee, the assistant under secretary of state in the Dominions Office, wrote to Sir Gerald Campbell, Britain's high commissioner in Canada: 'What we should hope would be that Canada herself would be prepared to provide this squadron, but we thought it wiser not to say this in terms in the despatch.' Batterbee added that Campbell would 'no doubt be able to let the Department of Defence know informally that this is in fact what we had in mind.'[18]

To this end, Stephen Holmes, a Dominions Office official, met privately with Colonel Maurice Pope on 18 November. Holmes informed Pope of the British government's feelings in this matter. Pope, who earlier had gone 'out of his way' in telling Holmes that he was pleased with the reply of the British government to the Canadian enquiry, assured Holmes 'that there would be no misunderstanding on the part of the Canadian authorities as to the source from which we naturally hoped the air squadron for Newfoundland would be forthcoming.'[19]

The British hoped that the Canadians, having expressed some interest in the defence of Newfoundland, would now open direct talks with the Commission of Government on mutual defence questions.[20] Pope had agreed with this suggestion, but the British authorities knew that everything depended on the reaction of the Canadian government, and the reluctance of the Canadians to commit themselves was well understood. As Campbell noted, the fact that the Canadians had actually made an official enquiry 'itself represented a considerable triumph on the part of those defence authorities here who are anxious for co-operation between Canada and the United Kingdom on such matters.'[21]

Despite the lack of official discussions and defence commitments, it is clear that an informal understanding over Newfoundland defence was emerging. The British had let it be known that they would defend Newfoundland only in a general way, under the umbrella of the Royal Navy, and informally had expressed the wish that the Canadians would assume the remainder of the responsibility. For the JSC the no-commitments policy was a serious obstacle, but not an insurmountable one. Recognizing both Britain's position and the vital importance of Newfoundland in Canadian defence, the JSC took measures that inevitably included Newfoundland in Canadian defence plans. For example, under the JSC's plan for the defence of Canada several RCAF sqadrons were to be stationed in Halifax and in this way would fulfil Britain's needs as well as provide additional protection for Newfoundland. Moreover, the protection of Canada's Atlantic coast necessarily included defending parts of Newfoundland's coastal waters.[22]

All things considered, the British could expect no more. Assuming that the Canadians would enter the war along with the United Kingdom it could be expected that they would contribute to the defence of Newfoundland as a part of the general defence of Canada. Problems that arose could be discussed and resolved on an informal basis, and in the meantime, in the words of Sir Gerald Campbell: 'I think that we may therefore take it that the whole of Newfoundland would be regarded as a Canadian defence "commitment" in the technical sense and that plans will be made accordingly.'[23]

As war in Europe approached during the spring and summer of 1939, defence planning for Newfoundland remained stalled at the preliminary stages. In June, permission was given to the RCAF to undertake reconnaissance flights over the coast of Labrador, but by September there had still been no talks between Britain, Canada, and Newfoundland concerning Canada's actions if and when war broke out. For Mackenzie King, political considerations and the preservation of national unity were the paramount concerns, and this view was reflected in a government stance which emphasized avoidance of war rather than preparation for it. Under these circumstances it was considered dangerous to make any explicit arrangements that could potentially commit Canada to participation in a European war.[24] Hence, even though the military planners had taken a few steps towards an informal defence understanding, on the eve of the Second World War the questions concerning Newfoundland's defence remained unanswered.

II

The entrance of Canada into the Second World War on 10 September 1939 brought a shift in attitude towards the defence of Newfoundland. No longer was it necessary to avoid public acknowledgment of Canadian interests there; once the question of Canadian involvement was settled, Newfoundland could be included within the framework of Canadian wartime policy. In his speech to the House of Commons on 8 September, Prime Minister King gave clear expression to Canadian war aims: 'The primary task and responsibility of the people of Canada is the defence and security of Canada.' But, he continued, the

safety of Canada depends upon the adequate safeguarding of our coastal regions and the great avenues of approach to the heart of this country. Foremost among these is the St. Lawrence river and gulf. At the entrance to the St. Lawrence stands the neighbouring British territory of Newfoundland and Labrador. The integrity of Newfoundland and Labrador is essential to the security of Canada. By contributing as far as we are able to the defence of Newfoundland and the other British and French territories in this hemisphere, we will not only be defending Canada but we will also be assisting Great Britain and France by enabling them to concentrate their own energies more in that part of the world in which their own immediate security is at stake.

Clearly, King had acknowledged not only the need to defend Newfoundland, but also that its protection was an integral part of the defence of Canada itself. 'Once an enemy is permitted to take possession of Newfoundland or the islands of St. Pierre and Miquelon, and use those islands as a base for their operations,' he asked the House of Commons, 'what real security is left for our Canadian Atlantic coast?'[25]

But this new attitude towards Newfoundland was more a matter of style than content. During the final hectic days of peace, permission was granted to the RCAF to fly over Newfoundland and Labrador and to use the country's airport facilities if the Canadians wished.[26] Beyond this, however, the Canadians were ill prepared to assume or undertake a large-scale scheme to build and maintain defence facilities in Newfoundland. Nor did they appear to feel that such action was necessary. Not surprisingly, uneasiness over the lack of concrete action was most strongly felt in Newfoundland itself.

King's statement in the House of Commons had lifted the hopes of the Newfoundland Commission of Government. In 1939, 50,000 Newfoundlanders remained on government relief, and the country lay undefended and without sufficient financial resources to protect itself. Perhaps now, it seemed, the Canadians would be willing to step in and underwrite the costs for defence, relieving the Commission of Government of that responsibility.

Already the Canadians had been of help. The Newfoundland Defence Scheme recommended the organization of a local militia, mainly for the protection of St John's and other vital areas. In 1938 measures were taken to create the Newfoundland Defence Force, but it was noted that the estimated cost of $275,000 per year to arm, feed, and clothe a force of four hundred men would have to be borne by the British government.[27] Over the next year these estimates were pruned to more realistic levels but at the end of August 1939 the Newfoundland Defence Force remained in disarray, without heavy equipment, rifles, ammunition, or the material to make uniforms. With the outbreak of war the Commission of Government turned to the Canadians to fill these needs. After a hastily organized meeting in Ottawa the Canadians agreed to 'lend' the Newfoundlanders the arms they required.[28]

By the end of September, twenty-two men had been recruited, and they were paid at the rate of one dollar per day. The force continued to expand and in 1941 it was placed on active service and incorporated into the Canadian forces in Newfoundland. In 1943 the Newfoundland Defence Force became the Newfoundland Regiment; at its peak it comprised 27 officers and 543 other ranks.[29]

Canadian aid to the fledgling Newfoundland Defence Force was welcomed by the Newfoundland government, but did not remove the deep concern over the sorry state of defence in Newfoundland. In mid-September the Commission of Government suggested to the Dominions Office that, in light of King's House of Commons speech, the Canadians should be invited to assume control of both the Gander airport and the Botwood seaplane base.[30] This plan, it was felt, would not only enhance local defence, but would also relieve Newfoundland of a large financial burden.

The Commission of Government's suggestion fell on deaf ears in London. After six weeks had passed with no reply, a second appeal was made to the Dominions Office on 31 October. Although sympathetic to the difficulties faced by Newfoundland, the Dominions Office did not share the concerns for the vulnerability of Newfoundland's position. In the autumn of 1939 no large-scale attack against Newfoundland was anticipated and it appeared unnecessary to hand over two airports to the Canadians. More to the point, the United Kingdom had already spent considerable sums of money developing these airports, and the Dominions Office recognized that Gander and Botwood would have a valuable role to play in future transatlantic aviation. As J.J.W. Herbertson of the Air Ministry wrote, he believed that it was government policy that Newfoundland 'should remain a separate entity and that anything tending to increase Canadian domination should be avoided as far as possible.' The motivation behind this policy was not a reluctance to accept Canadian offers of help, but a desire to maintain Britain's long-term rights in Newfoundland. 'It is one thing to let them in,' wrote Herbertson of the Canadians, 'but it would be quite another thing to get them out.'[31]

This reasoning was embodied in the Dominions Office response sent to the Newfoundland government on 5 November. Reminding the commissioners of the future importance of Gander and Botwood, the Dominions Office ruled out handing them over to the Canadians because 'it would be undesirable to allow these airports, which are such an important factor in our bargaining position vis-à-vis Pan American Airways and the United States, to pass out of our control even temporarily.'[32] This did not mean that the Canadians were to be discouraged from aiding Newfoundland; indeed, the RCAF would be welcome to use these facilities if the need arose, but the responsibility for the airports would remain with the United Kingdom. In conclusion, the Dominions Office suggested letting the whole matter drop and advised against bringing it up with the Canadian authorities.

Two interesting points emerge from this episode. First, it was the Commission of Government which introduced the idea of transferring the control of these sites to the Canadians. Behind this action lay the fear on the part of the Commission of Government that Newfoundland could not defend itself and would need outside help. Clearly, therefore, the eventual establishment of foreign bases in Newfoundland cannot be viewed as a 'scramble' by Canada, Britain, and the United States to divide the spoils in Newfoundland. Second, it becomes apparent that with the war less than two months old post-war rights in Newfoundland had already become a major concern of the British government. Indeed, the value of Newfoundland in civil aviation had been clear from the beginnings of transatlantic flight. The war had interrupted and changed the circumstances somewhat, but British aviation policy for the duration of the war remained consistent with that established in 1939–40.

The other major area of concern in Canadian-Newfoundland defence relations for the Commission of Government was Bell Island, which, despite its importance, remained undefended. The defence of Bell Island came up for discussion at the meeting of the Commission of Government in St John's, on 27 October 1939. The situation was reviewed and it was agreed that the Canadians should be approached on this matter to see if they would assume the responsibility for its defence.[33] On the advice of the Dominions Office the matter was turned over to Sir Gerald Campbell, the British high commissioner in Canada.[34]

The High Commissioner's Office provided O.D. Skelton with a long memorandum outlining the existing situation. In the view of the Commission of Government the possibility of an air attack was unlikely but could not be ruled out entirely. While it would prove too costly to build sufficient defences for such a slight risk it was believed that adequate protection could be provided by air patrols based at Botwood. The 'chief source of danger' according to the commissioners was the submarine. Rising to the surface, a submarine could easily shell important installations on Bell Island, including the loading piers and electrical transformer. Furthermore, if a ship was sunk while loading it could interrupt exports for a considerable period of time. The Commission of Government recommended setting up two four-inch guns and two searchlights at key locations on the island. In their estimation these defensive precautions would be adequate to prevent submarines from surfacing in the vicinity of the island mine.[35]

Skelton was reminded that the Sydney steel industry depended on Bell Island ore and would increasingly do so for the duration of the war as the need for Canadian steel rose. Moreover, it was noted that the Dominion Steel and Coal Corporation was a Canadian, not a Newfoundland, company, and that Canada had a genuine interest in seeing its Bell Island mines well protected. And, because the Newfoundland government was unable to meet the costs for the defence of Bell Island, the Newfoundlanders 'felt that it would not be inappropriate' to enquire if the Canadians would do so.[36]

The process through which the Canadians responded to this problem was an agonizingly slow one. On 25 November Skelton informed the Department of National Defence of the issue and included a copy of the memo he had received from Campbell.[37] When no reply came over the following weeks the High Commissioner's Office contacted Skelton a second time, reminding him that they were waiting for a reply. In the meantime Skelton wrote to the president of Dosco to find out what defence precautions the company had undertaken to protect its interests in Newfoundland. The reply was received late in January 1940 and contained the same points that had earlier been mentioned by the Department of External Affairs: namely, that the kind of defence needed on Bell Island was beyond the capacity or authority of Dosco to provide.[38]

Still having received no reply, the High Commissioner's Office again reminded Skelton that they would like to inform the Newfoundland government of the Canadians' decision 'as early as may be practicable.'[39] Shortly thereafter, Sir Edward Emerson, the Newfoundland commissioner for justice, travelled to Ottawa to discuss the defence question. In a 29 February 1940 meeting with J.E. Read, the legal adviser of the Department of External Affairs, he stressed the need for action on the Bell Island matter. Emerson emphasized that the Newfoundland government was 'anxious to get a decision' and unofficially suggested that the RCAF establish an airbase for reconnaissance flights at St John's.[40]

Read's memorandum of this meeting was passed from Skelton to Mackenzie King and early in March it was discussed by the Cabinet War Committee. Finally a decision was reached: Canada would undertake 'such measures as are approved by the Department of National Defence' to defend Bell Island.[41] After 'careful consideration' the Department of National Defence had arrived at conclusions similar to those made earlier by the Commission of Government. Two 4.7-inch mobile guns would be installed on Bell Island, along with two searchlights (which it was believed would become available in the near future). The Canadians also offered to provide an officer and two instructors for up to six months to train local crews.[42]

Another problem dealt with by the Canadians at this time was the use of airbases in Newfoundland. In January the Canadian government had asked for and received permission to establish a base at Red Bay on the southern Labrador coast. The main purpose for this base was the protection of the Strait of Belle Isle. Apart from this they showed little interest in using – let alone maintaining – bases in Newfoundland. The need to establish an RCAF base at St John's was brushed aside because the long-range aircraft stationed at Dartmouth, Nova Scotia, could be in the vicinity of St John's within two hours. In addition, if the need to use bases in Newfoundland arose, the Canadians preferred to have Newfoundland furnish and operate these facilities.[43]

The Newfoundland government was only too eager to co-operate with the Canadians. On 25 March the governor informed the high commissioner that the Canadian proposals concerning Bell Island were 'quite acceptable.' He also stated that the Canadians were welcome to use Gander or Botwood if they saw fit, and noted that the Commission of Government would 'be very glad' to discuss the overall air defence of Newfoundland with the Canadians.[44]

This last statement only partially reveals the growing uneasiness of the Commission of Government over the state of Newfoundland's defences. Emerson had returned from his talks in Ottawa disturbed by the apparent absence of any co-ordinated plan to defend Newfoundland. In a memorandum for the Commission of Government he wrote:

I also had an interview with the Counsellor to the Department of External Affairs and I inferred from my conversation with him that some two years ago correspondence took place between the United Kingdom Government and the Canadian Government in which it was suggested that the defence of Newfoundland should in the case of war be looked upon as part of the burden to be borne by

Canada. Nothing however was done to finalize matters ... It would appear also that since the declaration of war by Canada the Prime Minister, who is also Minister of External Affairs, has been so occupied that no such instructions have been issued to the military, naval or air branches to consider Newfoundland as part of the territory which they are to defend.[45]

To the commissioners it appeared that the British and Canadians were willing to undertake defensive measures in Newfoundland only in so far as they were deemed necessary for their own security. The United Kingdom had offered protection under the cover of the Royal Navy, but little else. On the other side, the Canadians had agreed to protect only those areas of vital interest to the Canadians – Bell Island and the Labrador coast. This left large segments of Newfoundland completely undefended, with St John's being particularly vulnerable. And, as the situation in Europe deteriorated during the spring of 1940, this problem became critical.

The apprehension felt by the Commission of Government explains why they had, on several occasions, offered the use of Newfoundland airports to the Canadians. Long-term questions of control were less of a problem to the commissioners than the immediate defence of the island and Labrador. These concerns were echoed by Governor Walwyn in a telegram to the Dominions Office. After again suggesting that the Canadians be invited to establish a base on the Avalon Peninsula he wrote: 'The Newfoundland Government is uncertain at the moment as to whether the provision for the defence of Newfoundland is to come from the United Kingdom or from Canada and would like this uncertainty to be resolved.'[46]

Before a reply had come from the Dominions Office the Canadians notified the Newfoundland authorities that they were sending Colonel C.S. Craig and two others to St John's to discuss and make the necessary arrangements for the defence of Bell Island. Unofficially, too, several Canadians had exhibited more concern. J.H. Penson, the commissioner for finance, reported that while in Ottawa he had met privately with C.D. Howe, the minister of transport, who told him that he thought that Canada should assume the control of Newfoundland's airports for the duration of the war.[47]

Responding to these developments, Governor Walwyn again called on the Dominions Office for action. Stressing the urgency of the situation he recommended that the Dominions Office reconsider the question of inviting the Canadians to assume control of Newfoundland's airports. If they were to do so, he reminded London, Newfoundland's security would be greatly improved and Newfoundland and the United Kingdom would be relieved of large financial expenditures.[48]

The response from Anthony Eden, the Dominions secretary, was an unsatisfactory one for the Commission of Government. Regarding the general defence of Newfoundland, Eden wrote that 'there is no doubt that responsibility for defence of Newfoundland, in so far as this cannot be provided from Newfoundland's own resources, is that of the United Kingdom.' Within this framework, aid from the Canadians 'would on general grounds be welcome.' But clearly the Dominions Office did not share the fears of the Commission of Government: 'At the present time the naval authorities consider the risk of attack upon Newfoundland, either by naval base raider or by submarine, to be remote and in view of other urgent requirements it would not be practicable for them to provide special Naval or Air Forces for patrol purposes ... for the same reasons it is felt that provision of guns for St. John's or placing of mines could not be justified.'[49]

Eden's telegram did little to relieve the apprehension of the Commission of Government. In fact, their anxiety was heightened because the Dominions Office did not directly deal with the suggestion that the Canadians take over Newfoundland's airports. The commissioners believed that it was necessary to have this settled with the Dominions Office before opening any talks with the Canadians. And, as the 'phony' war in Europe became a very real one, the chances of an enemy attack on Newfoundland became an alarming possibility for the commissioners. Moreover, the Canadians appeared to be unwilling to give more than verbal assurances to the Newfoundlanders. By late May the commissioners felt themselves to be in a desperate situation. Governor Walwyn voiced their concerns in a telegram to the Dominions Office:

The defenceless condition of this country causes public alarm in view of occurrences of recent days. The Prime Minister of Canada is reported to have stated on Parliament on May 20th that Canadian Troops are assisting in guardianship of Newfoundland but we have received no information along these lines or any other. If the Newfoundland Airports are to be used as part of the defence of this country by Canadian Government it is probable that they will require to plan substantial erections and installations to be completed at earliest moment after negotiations have been finalized. We urge therefore a very early reply in this matter and venture to suggest that at this stage post war problems should not be a decisive factor.[50]

Unfortunately for the Newfoundlanders, the latter was an essential factor. Many of the arguments used the previous autumn against handing Gander and Botwood over to the Canadians were resurrected. In a letter to Eric Machtig of the Dominions Office, A.W. Street outlined the position of the Air Ministry. Because the British government had invested large sums of money in developing these airports, they were 'not anxious' to let the Canadians in. More important, Gander and Botwood were considered 'valuable assets in the control of the North Atlantic air route,' and thus should be held on to at all costs. Street continued with an interesting illumination of British policy: 'we have always fought hard,' he wrote, 'to keep the Canadians from controlling the Newfoundland stepping stone.'[51]

Nevertheless, the British could not ignore the implications of an Allied collapse in Europe. The rush of events in the spring of 1940 forced the United Kingdom to weigh the pros and cons of this matter under completely new circumstances. Canadian control would, after all, increase the security of Newfoundland, and the Canadians would have to assume the maintenance costs of the airports, relieving the United Kingdom of this responsibility. After considerable discussion the British government decided that the short-term gains outweighed the long-term risks.

On 5 June, the Dominions Office gave its consent to the Newfoundland government, allowing the Canadians to assume control of Gander and Botwood, providing the Canadians agreed to certain conditions. First, the Canadians would pay maintenance costs and for any damage done to the airports. Second, no alterations to the present layout of the airports would be tolerated. Finally, and perhaps most important, a definite date must be set for the return of the bases at the end of the war.[52]

A tremendous hurdle in the defence of Newfoundland had been overcome, but once again the action of the Canadians, British, and Newfoundlanders had been overtaken by events. The questions surrounding the defence of Newfoundland had been answered only in the vaguest sense by June 1940; the Newfoundlanders were financially incapable of undertaking it, and the British and Canadians resisted going any further than was necessary for their own protection. But during the summer of 1940 outside events dramatically reversed these positions. The fall of France and the emergence of the United States as an active participant in Atlantic defence forced a rethinking of Newfoundland policy in Ottawa, London, and St John's. The question 'Who defends Newfoundland?' would never be completely settled, but after June 1940 the old answers were discarded and new revolutionary ones were being offered.

3

Bases, boards, and bureaucrats

The fall of France and the evacuation of the Allied forces from Europe unnerved many Canadians, including Mackenzie King. In his diary, King wrote of the need for unity among British peoples, in order to 'save the world.' A more immediate concern was the 'real possibility of invasion of our shores, an effort will be made to seize this country as a prize of war.' In an effort to counteract this threat, a change of policy was required; Canadians must perforce come 'to the stage where defence of this land becomes our most important duty. It will involve far-reaching measures. We shall have to take them by stages and with care.'[1]

For Mackenzie King's government, or for any Canadian who took the time to look at a map of the North Atlantic, it was clear that the defence of Canada could not be separated from the defence of Newfoundland. As one historian wrote in 1940: 'No potential invader could fail to note the possibilities of this territory, the only piece of North America that can be said to lie within the probable operating range of a European fleet.' Moreover, the 'possession of Newfoundland by an invader as an advanced base would, of course, change the whole strategic situation in North America; it would be disastrous to Canada and most dangerous to the United States.'[2] The continued existence of the British and American navies precluded the possibility of a full-scale Axis invasion, but minor operations by sea or air could not be ruled out. Furthermore, as the Canadian military planners were quick to point out, the destruction inflicted by a single cruiser or aircraft could be extensive.

In the year following the fall of France, Newfoundland was turned into a bulwark in the defence of North America. Compelled into action by world events, the Canadian government assumed considerable responsibilities in Newfoundland, including the control of Gander airport and the seaplane bases at Botwood and Gleneagles. By August 1940 one Toronto newspaper could report that Newfoundland was 'no longer ... an unguarded outpost, easy prey to the first air-raider who thought of coming over.'[3]

Equally important was the emergence of the United States as a significant participant in Newfoundland, brought about through the base-destroyer deal of Septempber 1940. Under the terms of this agreement the United States would ultimately send more materiel and troops, and spend more money in Newfoundland than Canada would. As a result, Canada's relationship with, and perception of, Newfoundland was fundamentally altered. Once the Canadians realized they could no longer take for granted any part of their relationship with Newfoundland, they began to play a more determined role in the events that shaped its future. The stationing of men and equipment on Newfoundland, the numerous conferences, and the signing of a Canada-Newfoundland agreement for the control of the airports were all evidence of this change. So too was the establishment of the High Commissioner's Office in St John's in September 1941 – an appointment made equally as a recognition of present needs and as a portent for the future.

I

Rising in Parliament on 18 June 1940, Mackenzie King informed the House that Canadian troops were now stationed in Newfoundland and indicated how this was a part of the growing Canadian responsibility there. 'In light of recent events,' he said, 'additional responsibiity has been assumed for the military defence of strategic areas there.'[4] A few days earlier the Canadian government had approached the Newfoundland authorities for the go-ahead to station additional men and equipment on the island. The Canadian plan included one flight of bomber reconnaissance aircraft, one flight of fighters, and one battalion of infantry.[5]

For Mackenzie King and the Canadian government the war had taken on a new complexion. Allied collapse in Europe stiffened the resolve of most Canadians to do their utmost to prevent an Axis victory over Britain. At home, the election of 26 March 1940 had maintained the Liberals in power, giving them a mandate to direct Canada's war effort. Riding the crest of electoral victory and a strong sense of national purpose, the Liberal government was now in a position to take a freer hand in the implementation of Canada's foreign and military policies.

It was no coincidence that, on the same day that Mackenzie King spoke to the House of Commons on Canadian actions in Newfoundland, the Canadian government introduced its National Resources Mobilization Act for home defence. The defence of Canada had been proclaimed as a major priority of Canada's war effort. Within this framework it was readily noted that the protection of Canada's eastern seaboard was directly related to the security of the northwest Atlantic region, including Newfoundland, Greenland, and Iceland.

Evidence of concern had surfaced a few weeks earlier in the shape of a Canadian plan to occupy Greenland. The motives were not only strategic; the cryolite mine at Ivigtut was important to both Canada's and the United States' production of aluminum, and the fear for its security increased sharply following the German occupation of Denmark on 9 April 1940.

The scheme was aborted after objections from the Americans based on the claim that Canadian action of this sort would set a precedent for the Japanese to follow in other colonies of occupied nations.[6] Moreover, action by Canada – a British nation – could be construed as a violation of the Monroe Doctrine, and therefore was to be avoided. This stance did not mean that the United States advocated a 'hands off' policy towards Greenland; on the contrary, within a year the Hull-Kauffman Agreement had been signed in which the United States guaranteed the defence of Greenland in return for the right to construct and maintain bases on the island.[7]

The diplomatic flare-up over Greenland had produced a certain amount of bitterness between some Canadian officials and their neutral American neighbours, but on the whole the Canadians acquiesced to the wishes of the Americans. Indeed, King felt that the 'position taken by the Americans was wise,' while some on the Canadian side 'had been a little over-zealous in preparing for a little war on Canada's own part.'[8] But this was not the case for Newfoundland. The reasoning applied to Greenland by the Americans could not be applied to Newfoundland; as Newfoundland was already within the British Empire no precedent could be set, nor did the country come under the umbrella of the Monroe Doctrine. More important, Newfoundland-Labrador was contiguous to Canada and, consequently, was an immediate and vital concern in Canadian defence. Under these circumstances Canadian action in Newfoundland was essential and beyond reproach. Moreover, neither the United States nor the United Kingdom ever suggested that the Canadians should not act with regard to Newfoundland. In fact, both tacitly accepted that Canada had a 'natural interest' in Newfoundland, an opinion reflected in their policies. Over the course of the years this acceptance would resurface time and again, unquestionably reinforcing Canada's position in Newfoundland.

The immediate concern for the Canadian government in June 1940 was not to secure long-term points for the control of Newfoundland, but rather to find ways to shore up local defences and to prepare for the anticipated aggression. C.G. 'Chubby' Power, the minister of national defence for air, reviewed the situation in Newfoundland for the other members of the Cabinet War Committee (cwc) on 14 June. Power began with a reminder of the strategic importance of Newfoundland and then noted that, although no large-scale attack was anticipated, it was imperative to protect Newfoundland from smaller raids. Gander and Botwood were singled out as being particularly vulnerable targets. In conclusion, Power suggested two courses of action with which the cwc agreed: 1 / that talks with the American Armed Services concerning the defence of the Atlantic coast be started immediately; and 2 / that permission to send a party to Newfoundland to discuss the country's defence needs be sought from the British and Newfoundland governments.[9]

The problem that remained was that it was unclear during these turbulent months just what defence measures were needed in New-foundland. What kind of conflict should Canada prepare for, and, ultimately, could Canada undertake the necessary steps or provide the necessary materiel? Early in July the Chiefs of Staff Committee (csc) studied these questions as part of their larger plan for the defence of Canada. The csc plan recognized that the Canadian navy could not withstand attack by the combined naval forces of Germany and Italy and would need the help of the British navy to properly defend Canada. Implicit in its overview was the judgment that should the British fleet be destroyed – which at this time appeared to be a distinct possibility – then the American navy would have to be relied upon.[10]

One infantry battalion (the 1st Battalion Black Watch [Royal High-land Regiment]) had already been stationed in Newfoundland, but the Canadians were finding it difficult to meet the materiel requirements. For example, the two guns promised for Bell Island were still unavail-able in July 1940. And this kind of problem was not unique to Newfoundland. Increasingly the Canadian authorities looked to the

United States for some kind of arrangement through which these problems could be overcome. Efforts to schedule staff talks with the Americans achieved some success, and late in June, Power and J.L. Ralston, the minister of national defence, met with J.P. Moffat, the American minister in Canada, to discuss the salient issues. Moffat recorded in his diary the concern shown by Ralston and Power for the defence of Newfoundland: 'The Canadians are definitely worried about the possibility of an air raid. They understand that Germany has a vessel capable of carrying about forty aircraft, and if this should escape the British blockade, particularly if accompanied by a cruiser, she could do great damage. The most important and vulnerable point is of course the great airfield in Newfoundland [Gander]. The Canadians have troops there, but they have no artillery and no anti-aircraft guns ... The Canadians will want to discuss the whole Newfoundland situation in Washington.'[11]

Under the strain of wartime emergency the two Canadians were willing to involve the United States further. Ralston and Power suggested to Moffat that the Americans undertake long-range reconnaissance flights 'perhaps nominally to Greenland' with 'forced stops' in Nova Scotia and other bases. In addition, they prompted the Americans to 'rent, acquire, or purchase land in the West Indies or Newfoundland and develop them as American air bases.'[12] Mackenzie King concurred on this point[13] and had earlier told Moffat that 'if anything went wrong' and the British fleet (including what Canada had sent over) was destroyed then Canada would be unable to prevent the Nazis from moving into bases in the western Atlantic. The acquisition of Atlantic bases by the United States was already under discussion at this time and, equally, it was clear that the Canadian authorities favoured the idea – including the establishment of an American base in Newfoundland.

The first joint staff talks were held in secret in Washington on 11 July, and although the Canadians had moderate success in securing the release of some American equipment for use by Canada, the talks focused primarily on the exchange of information.[14] The acquisition of bases in Newfoundland by the United States was discussed and the idea was again generally welcomed by the Canadians. From the Canadian point of view, any help from the Americans would be welcome. As Captain L.W. Murray put it, the RCN considered that its role in Newfoundland was to 'provide ourselves with suitable operational bases in order to enable us to play host to either the British Navy or the

United States Navy.'[15] Some groundwork had been covered during these discussions, but until American policy took a more clearly defined direction, little more could be expected.

On the Canadian side some action could be taken. On 7 August, C.G. Power informed the cwc that he was planning a trip to Newfoundland to discuss defence questions with the Newfoundland authorities. Power was one of the first Canadians to recognize the somewhat schizophrenic characteristics of Canadian policy concerning the American role in Newfoundland. On the one hand, an increased American presence was welcomed because it would directly enhance the security of Canada's Atlantic region. But on the other, the Canadians were more reluctant to accept the implications that this presence would have for local defence in Newfoundland and overall command and strategic direction. Like the British before them, the Canadians were willing to let the Americans in but were less eager to see their own role diminished. Consequently, the strategies required to achieve both short-term needs and long-term goals often proved to be somewhat contradictory.[16] Still, action on Canada's part to solidify its own position in Newfoundland before the Americans had moved in could put the Canadians on a stronger footing for future dealings with their American allies. It is not unreasonable to assume that Power had this thought in mind when he met with his Newfoundland counterparts in St John's on 20 August 1940.

Power began with a broad statement of Canadian aims and expressed the hope that Canada and Newfoundland could freely co-operate without infringing on each other's autonomies. He continued by asking 'if the principle could be admitted that Canada should be in charge of Newfoundland defence without any modification.'[17] He received no definite answer to this question, only an assurance that it would be discussed by the Newfoundland government.

On a more practical level, several routine problems were dealt with. It was agreed that the Newfoundland services (naval, air, and military) would all come under the command of their Canadian counterparts, and that Newfoundland would not appoint officers above the rank of colonel. Also agreed to in principle was the recruitment of Newfoundland soldiers into the Canadian forces.[18]

The Canadians put forward their plans for the immediate defence of Newfoundland and Labrador. The headquarters for the RCAF would naturally be at Gander, while the army and navy would have theirs at St John's. Quarters for a battalion of troops in the vicinity of St John's would be required and the Canadians promised to strengthen coastal defences nearby. Naval plans included the establishment of an advanced naval base at St John's and probably a summer base at Botwood. As for the RCAF, it was considered necessary to enlarge the Canadian force at Gander and the required buildings were already under construction. In addition, the possibility of establishing a fighter base near St John's was to be examined shortly.[19]

The Newfoundland authorities concurred with these plans and thanked the Canadians for their generosity. But, added J.H. Penson, the commissioner for finance, Newfoundland could not pay for these developments, though the Newfoundlanders would be willing to make a considerable contribution. In response to this point, Power noted that he had no authority to decide this issue, but that he personally felt that 'it would be repugnant to the ideas of both countries that Newfoundland should, as it were, pay tribute to Canada and thus appear in a somewhat servient role.[20] Instead, he suggested that Newfoundland make its contribution through services and concessions to the Canadians.

The final topic dealt with was relations with the United States. Power began by informing the Newfoundlanders of Canada's position with respect to the Americans: although willing to have the Americans make use of facilities in Canada, under no circumstances would Canadians transfer the sovereignty of Canadian soil into American hands. Newfoundland, Power felt, would wish to do the same. The Newfoundlanders offered no comment on this suggestion but did insist that when Newfoundland was the topic of discussion between Canada and the United States the country had the right to be represented.[21]

Power returned to Ottawa after inspecting Gander airport and receiving the assurances of Governor Walwyn of Newfoundland's 'desire to co-operate to the fullest extent in the common effort.'[22] His talks with the Newfoundlanders had been a success, though some problems remained unsolved; and in Newfoundland the aid proposed by the Canadians was welcomed as a generous offer. Shortly thereafter the Commission of Government passed the Visiting Forces Act to cover the problems arising from the presence of Canadian troops in Newfoundland.

While Power was in Newfoundland the other major area of concern for the Canadian – relations with the United States – also underwent a significant change. Travelling by car to Ogdensburg, New York, on 17 August, Mackenzie King met privately with President Roosevelt to discuss mutual defence problems and the possible exchange of American destroyers for British bases. Emerging the next day, King and

Roosevelt announced the creation of the Permanent Joint Board on Defence (PJBD). This new board was to consist of four or five representatives from each country and its purpose was to 'consider in the broad sense the defence of the north half of the Western Hemisphere.'[23] The board had no specific authority of its own; it could only recommend a course of action to the two governments. Rarely, however, did either government reject the proposals the PJBD had arrived at by unanimous decision.[24]

It is illustrative of the seriousness with which Canada and the United States viewed the defence of Newfoundland that during its first year of existence approximately one-half of the PJBD's recommendations dealt with Newfoundland. And, not surprisingly, at its first meeting, held in Ottawa, on 26 August, Newfoundland headed the list of topics to be discussed.[25] After a few formalities and introductory remarks, the members reviewed the extent of Canadian action in Newfoundland up to this date, and after some discussion decided that more was called for. Their recommendations began with a recognition of the vital nature of their task: 'The island of Newfoundland occupies a commanding position at the entrance to the St. Lawrence–Great Lakes waterway and on the flank of the sea route between the Atlantic seaboard of North America and Northern Europe. It is on the direct air route between the East Coast of the United States and Northern Europe. It is the point in North America, nearest to Europe, from which, if occupied by an enemy, further operations against the North American continent might be effectively initiated. As such it should be adequately defended.'[26]

On a more concrete level, the board made several specific recommendations: more Canadian troops should be stationed on the island to enhance the strength of existing garrisons; efforts should be made to establish a force of fighters for patrolling Newfoundland's coastal waters and the area near Botwood; the necessary construction should be undertaken by Canada to adequately play host to several squadrons of American aircraft if the need arose; and Canada should complete, by April 1941 at the latest, the defensive measures already decided upon.[27]

These proposals, which were embodied in the 2nd Recommendation of the PJBD, were significant ones in that they called for a large increase in the Canadian presence in Newfoundland, and, of course, a concomitant increase in Canadian expenditures to this end. The PJBD recommendations were discussed in the CWC on 5 September 1940. There was no apparent opposition and the recommendations (which also included action with regard to the Maritimes) were given speedy approval.[28]

With the creation of the PJBD a permanent channel of communication had been established between Canada and the United States. And, although not created specifically with Newfoundland in mind, the PJBD provided the machinery through which the ever-increasing number of problems in the defence of Newfoundland could be dealt with. Canadian-American defence relations had been enhanced through the creation of the PJBD, as had the security of Newfoundland. And it could not have come at a better time: the announcement of the base-destroyer deal in September had introduced a new set of circumstances for the members of the North Atlantic Triangle to deal with.

II

Within days of succeeding Neville Chamberlain as prime minister on 10 May 1940, Winston Churchill wrote President Roosevelt asking for American help with 'everything short of actually engaging armed forces.' One of Britain's immediate needs, he noted, was 'the loan of forty or fifty of your oldest destroyers to bridge the gap between what we have and the large new construction we put in hand at the beginning of the war.'[29] Churchill's goals were twofold: first, Britain suffered from a real shortage that could not be overcome for several months and therefore needed American help, and second, any commitment by the United States would draw the Americans closer to the conflict and send a clear message to Germany.[30]

The mounting crisis in Europe did not go unnoticed in Washington; on the contrary, it had had a profound effect on Roosevelt and American policy-makers. Immediate concern was for the security of the British fleet and, following the fall of France, the security of the western hemisphere. But, however sympathetic Roosevelt was to Britain's plight, there were serious obstacles in his way preventing him from transferring the destroyers. The primary one was a recalcitrant Congress which had earlier forbidden the transfer of any materiel unless it was certified as unessential to American defence.[31]

Over the summer of 1940 a deal was struck. As noted above, the Americans had expressed on several occasions an interest in obtaining bases on Britain's Atlantic possessions; now the offer was made to exchange the destroyers for the right to establish these bases. Thus, Roosevelt could mute congressional criticism by presenting the American people with a deal which appeared to favour the United States.[32] Likewise, Churchill could present the exchange as a victory: not only would Britain receive fifty destroyers, the agreement itself marked a step by the Americans towards active participation in the war.

The inclusion of Newfoundland as a possible site for an American base naturally produced a keen interest in the base-destroyer deal in St John's and Ottawa. For the Canadians it had come as no surprise; indeed, they had been kept informed throughout the summer of 1940. Nor did it provoke any concerted opposition. As mentioned above, Ralston and Power had both suggested to Moffat that the United States should utilize Newfoundland as a base site, as did the Canadian representatives at the July joint staff talks. King agreed as well. Writing to Churchill on 16 June, while Allied resistance was collapsing in France, King 'gave it as my opinion that the United States should be afforded opportunity to get bases at Iceland, Greenland, Newfoundland and the West Indies and supply the inadequacy of the defence of our own coasts, etc.'[33]

As the deal evolved, King was kept informed on the progress of the negotiations by Sir Gerald Campbell, the British high commissioner in Ottawa, and Loring Christie in Washington, but played no part himself. This well suited King who appeared to be willing to keep out of the discussions altogether. When approached by Lord Lothian through Christie to put in a good word on the destroyer issue, King hesitated to publicly appeal to Roosevelt, feeling it 'would be in the nature of "coercion",' and that it would 'help to undo for the future any influence I may have.'[34]

Rather than pressing the issue publicly, King preferred to rely on personal contact and the co-operation of Canada's allies. On the latter issue King was fortunate that both Roosevelt and Churchill agreed that Canada had a special interest in Newfoundland and therefore should at least be informed of developments concerning it. For example, when the British War Cabinet discussed the base deal, the special relationship between Canada and Newfoundland was recognized: 'It was pointed out that, while the West Indian Islands, the Bahamas and Bermudas, were the outposts of the United States, Newfoundland was the outpost of Canada, which had special interests in the Botwood aerodrome. It would be necessary that Canada and Newfoundland be consulted before we were finally committed to the present proposal.'[35] The following day Roosevelt was informed of this decision, and within twenty-four hours he had invited King down to Ogdensburg.[36]

Roosevelt read King the telegram that referred to Canada and told him. 'This is where you come in.' King replied that 'we were wholly agreeable to the United States being given bases on the islands of the

Atlantic.' With respect to Newfoundland, King recorded: 'I said both the British and our Government would probably have to do with that matter as well as the United States.'[37] Later King emphasized this point a second time when Roosevelt mentioned that he would take up the issue of the colonies directly with Churchill. King agreed, but reminded Roosevelt that 'as we had undertaken protection of Newfoundland and were spending money there, the British Government would probably want our Government to co-operate in that part.'[38] Roosevelt's concern for the security of Newfoundland was apparent and it was discussed a number of times during King's short visit. It was also clear that one of the major reasons behind the meeting at Ogdensburg was Roosevelt's desire to ensure Canadian compliance in the agreements.

With the announcement of the base-destroyer deal only a few days away there was an increasing interest in examining its possible consequences on the part of the Canadians. The Chiefs of Staff Committee reported that they were concerned that the Americans would try to lease Botwood or even Gander, where the Canadians had already established themselves. Since these bases were crucial in Canadian defence and the Americans were still neutral, they suggested that overtures be made to the British to ensure co-user rights for Canada. As it turned out the Americans made no attempt to lease Gander or Botwood but nevertheless it is indicative of the growing apprehension in Canadian military circles that the Canadian position in Newfoundland would shortly be usurped by the Americans.[39]

O.D. Skelton, too, was sensitive to the implications of the agreement. In a far-sighted memorandum for the prime minister he noted that while Canada had decided against leasing any territory to the Americans, this was not to be the case in Newfoundland. For the time being this arrangement was acceptable, but, he wrote: 'In view of the definite possibility of a movement on the part of Newfoundland to enter Confederation, the question arises whether we should seek to have any arrangement made by the United States as regards Newfoundland brought into harmony (in the event of Newfoundland becoming part of Canada) with the Canadian arrangements. Possibly we can take a chance on that being settled satisfactorily when the day comes but it might be well at least to issue a caveat.' King agreed with Skelton's analysis; underneath the final statement he noted: 'This I should think all that is necessary at present.'[40]

On this particular issue King and Skelton may have been willing to 'take a chance' on a satisfactory settlement, but this willingness could not last much longer. If nothing else, the American acquisition of bases in Newfoundland helped crystallize the realization that Canada's position in Newfoundland was not as secure as many Canadians felt that it should be. Power had returned from St John's and spoken of Canada's assuming the responsibility for the defence of Newfoundland – but this had never been agreed to by either the Commission of Government or the Dominions Office. Moreover, Canadian money and troops were being utilized there on bases which the Canadians had taken over; but again no agreement had been reached. Furthermore, the Canadians had to be out of Newfoundland when the war was over while the Americans would be there for ninety-nine years. Despite the deference displayed by the Americans and British to Canada's 'natural interest' in Newfoundland, it was clear that Canada's grasp on that country was extremely tenuous. What emerged was a dichotomy that would plague Canadian policy-makers for several years: while the Canadians recognized their reliance on their allies and were willing to co-operate to the fullest extent, they also felt the need to guard their interests jealously against the encroachment of these same allies. And the problem of co-operation among friends often proved more complicated and required more delicate treatment than the conflict with the enemy.

On 27 August the cwc discussed a number of questions, including the exchange of destroyers for bases, the PJBD, and Atlantic defence. Mackenzie King read a letter from Sir Gerald Campbell containing an outline of the proposed agreement and he mentioned that he 'had had no hesitation' in giving his approval. These proposals were accepted without question by the ministers present; indeed, Angus Macdonald, the minister of national defence for naval services, even suggested that the establishment of an American base in Newfoundland might make further Canadian action in this area unnecessary. But mention was made of the fact that Canada had undertaken to spend in the neighbourhood of $1.5 million in Newfoundland – presumably with Britain's consent. How would the intervention of the Americans affect this investment? For the time being there could be no answer to this question, and the cwc agreed that the problem should be studied in an effort to better defend Canadian rights and objectives in Newfoundland.[41]

The exchange of notes and the public announcement of the base-destroyer deal on 2 September 1940 met with general acceptance across North America. Two days later, in a letter to Skelton, Campbell outlined the procedure to be followed for the negotiation of the final agreement. Both the United Kingdom and the United States would undertake preliminary examinations immediately, and before the final talks commenced in London, both the Newfoundlanders and the Canadians would have a chance to comment on the British proposals as far as Newfoundland was concerned. Consultation was a concession that was easy to give; as for Canadian participation, that was a different matter. Lord Caldecote, the dominions secretary, suggested that Newfoundland and Canadian representatives should attend the London meetings, but no reference was made to the nature or extent of their role. This problem, like so many others, was left to be settled later.[42]

The Canadians did not have long to wait for Britain's preliminary report. On 6 September, in a telegram sent to both Ottawa and St John's, the Dominions Office outlined the 'maximum concessions' to be offered the Americans. It was considered unnecessary to restrict the use of any part of the southern coast of Newfoundland,and, although not specifically mentioned, this probably included the Avalon Peninsula.[43] Cable stations, St John's, and Conception Bay (i.e., Bell Island) were singled out as areas from which the Americans should be excluded, but even here the Dominions Office warned that it might not be able to resist American pressure.[44] In effect, the Dominions Office had given the Americans a fairly free hand to choose the sites they pleased.

All the developments of August–September 1940 were carefully scrutinized from St John's, but scrutiny was about all St John's could manage. Although Newfoundland was directly affected by the decisions made, the Commission of Government was completely excluded from any involvement in the negotiations. Rumours of a deal between Britain and the United States circulated in St John's for several weeks prior to the announcement, but no concerted opposition arose. Harold B. Quarton, the American consul-general in St John's, surveyed the press reaction and reported to the State Department that the little that had appeared in the press was on the whole favourable.[45]

The editorial opinion of the two major newspapers generally accepted and welcomed the deal, seeing it as an effective contribution to the war effort and as a way to improve Newfoundland's security. Beyond accepting the *idea* of bases, however, there were two major concerns: sovereignty and compensation. The *Evening Telegram* noted that Newfoundland must maintain the sovereignty of its soil: the country should 'be assured that it will not be parting with any of the powers formerly vested in its Legislature and that no part of the country will be subject to the control of a foreign state.'[46] The *Daily News* echoed these concerns and noted that because these bases were so important to the war effort, in return, 'America might be very well satisfied to grant us certain economic concessions as compensation.'[47] No economic concessions were offered by the Americans, and over the years this statement became something of a shibboleth, used in criticizing the Commission of Government for failing to safeguard Newfoundland's integrity.

The Commission of Government, including the British members, had a genuine interest in securing for Newfoundland the best deal possible. Unfortunately they had little freedom of action and were severely limited in their ability to control Newfoundland's destiny. There was considerable apprehension among the commissioners over the possible adverse public opinion that might result from leasing bases to the Amricans despite the general goodwill of the Newfoundland people towards the idea. It was believed that such a reaction would be avoided if the Americans made certain concessions in return. Consequently, they suggested that the Americans be approached to 'give favourable and sympathetic consideration to certain compensating advantages to Newfoundland in such matters as Customs tariffs and immigration arrangements.'[48] But the Commission of Government had no effective means to press this point, except to insist on Newfoundland representation during future negotiations.

The Commission of Government received assurances of representation similar to those given to the Canadians. This rankled a few commissioners, who openly questioned the role played by the Canadians in the past and present. On 12 September the Commission of Government expressed its criticism to the Dominions Office: 'We are not quite happy about the apparent assumption that Governments of Newfoundland and Canada have equal interests in regard to the question of America with a view to bases in Newfoundland. Our view is that this is a matter which primarily concerns Newfoundland and we hope you will do everything possible to disabuse the Canadians of any idea that they are in a position to settle the destinies of Newfoundland in negotiations with the United States.'[49]

It was in their relations with the Canadians that the Newfoundlanders could exercise the greatest leverage, and one way to enhance their influence was to have direct input in the planning of projects for Newfoundland. Usually this responsibility fell to the PJBD. The Newfoundlanders had informed Power that they desired representation of some kind on the board, and after the announcement of the base-destroyer deal, this request was made with an increased sense of urgency. Neither the Canadians nor the Americans saw any reason for excluding the Newfoundlanders from discussions that concerned them, and after the matter was discussed by the PJBD an invitation was sent to Newfoundland to send a representative to the meetings in Halifax in early October.[50]

The base-destroyer deal produced immediate and concrete results in Newfoundland. Within days, American officials had ventured there to investigate, survey, and report on their findings. According to the official American historians, the War Department had undertaken no preliminary work before the base deal had been announced. In late August a 'Board of Experts' consisting of army and navy personnel was created. This board was headed by Rear Admiral John W. Greenslade, USN, and its purpose was to examine the base locations and determine the needs for defence. The board made several excursions to sites in the West Indies and on 14 September 1940, left for Newfoundland.[51]

During the course of its stay the Greenslade Mission, as it came to be called, met with the Commission of Government on two occasions, on 16 and 21 September. The Americans put forward a number of requests: the establishment of major naval and air bases on the Avalon Peninsula; an area in St John's harbour for supplies, repairs, and refuge; a landing field on the west coast; an area near St John's for the establishment of a permanent army base; and joint user rights to the airbase the Canadians were contemplating building in the vicinity of St John's. If the Canadians failed to build it then the Americans asked for the right to construct it themselves.[52]

Overall the Americans did not anticipate a major attack on New-foundland, especially as long as the British fleet controlled the Western Atlantic. Consequently, their report recommended the establishment of small garrisons that could quickly be expanded in case of need.[53] The Greenslade Mission returned to Washington and a copy of their report was given to the U.S. section of the PJBD.

While the Greenslade Mission investigated the situation in New-foundland, the Canadians did not sit idly by. On 5 September the CWC reviewed the situation regarding Newfoundland in light of recent developments. Power's report of his Newfoundland talks was read to the meeting and afterwards he made a few additional comments. He told the members that: 'Action taken by Canada, so far, for the defence of Newfoundland had been on an emergency basis, and no attempt had been made to make arrangements with the Newfoundland government for the determination of Canadian rights by lease or otherwise. This matter, however, should now receive consideration.' There was general agreement on this point and Mackenzie King added that Canada 'should arrange to secure terms which would be of permanent value for strategical purposes in the future. The defence of Newfoundland would always be primary Canadian interest.' He also reviewed the telegrams he had received on the matter and explained that Canada would receive full information from the United Kingdom and would be permitted to appoint a representative to the upcoming London negotiations.[54]

Power believed that it was time to reopen the thorny problem of control of Gander Airport. During August the OK was given in St John's to expand the airport beyond the original plan; the new plan called for the stationing of one squadron of fighters and two bomber reconnaissance squadrons.[55] This, of course, increased Canadian expenditures there and in turn heightened the desire for a more concrete agreement. Power's initiative received approval from Mackenzie King, and in a telephone conversation with Sir Edward Emerson, the commissioner for justice and defence, on 7 September, Power suggested that the Canadians would like to pursue this matter further. A more formal request followed a few days later on 13 September. The Canadians argued that it was 'in the interest of all concerned for Canada to assume control of the Newfoundland Airport,' and requested that negotiations to this end be started.[56]

This was the first time that this question had been raised since the early spring, but there had been no change in the British position over the summer months. The Newfoundland government informed the Canadians that they were willing to partake in talks concerning Gander, Botwood, and Gleneagles, but warned the Canadians that the same provisos (concerning control, alterations, and termination date) would apply.[57] In addition, the British added a few extra conditions, mainly for the protection of their civil-aviation rights.[58] Neither side was explicit about the form that this agreement should take.

At any rate, the two sides had agreed to talk and negotiations got under way late in November 1940. A number of lesser problems dealing with recruitment, the acquisition of property, and the financial arrangements between governments were dealt with, but on the much more difficult question of the control of the airports, little progress was made. Although the Canadians gave their consent to the provisos set out by the United Kingdom in September, two points remained in dispute. First, the Newfoundlanders were willing to give the Canadians permanent title to any buildings or hangars they might construct, although they were willing to discuss leasing them 'for a substantial period.' The second point read: 'No alterations to be made to existing lay-out of bases without prior consent of Newfoundland Government.' The Commission of Government considered this point essential because Gander had originally been constructed for transatlantic civil aviation and the Newfoundland government felt it necessary to maintain a veto over anything that might prevent it from remaining so in the future.[59]

The Canadians were not in much of a mood for a fight. With the London negotiations to settle the American bases looming in the future, the Canadians were anxious to get some kind of agreement over Gander. More important perhaps, Canadian policy-makers increasingly recognized just how fragile Canada's hold on Gander was, and when rumours circulated that the Americans were seeking a lease at or near the airport, the Canadians reacted strongly. This possibility was discussed at a CWC meeting on 13 December and all agreed that 'it would be a mistake' to let the Americans in. The minutes of the CWC meeting expressed, perhaps unintentionally, the paradox facing the Canadian government: 'Such a site was not ours to grant, but we should not consent to any such proposal.'[60]

The Canadians had two possible courses of action, both of which they chose to follow: first, they decided to press the Newfoundlanders for a quick agreement, and second, they would block the idea of the Americans leasing an area near Gander when it came up for discussion at the meetings of the PJBD. On the latter issue the Canadians achieved a degree of success, largely by providing for American needs at Gander at Canadian expense. This way American use of the airport could increase while the control of the base stayed in British and Canadian hands. On the former issue, the Canadian government informed the Commission of Government late in January 1941 that they were willing to accept the conditions that Newfoundland had set out, noting: 'All your fundamental points have now been acceded to.'[61]

Unfortunately for the Canadians, no agreement had been reached before the British-American talks opened in London on 28 January 1941. For several months talks between the United States and the United Kingdom had been proceeding on the unofficial level. Considerable disagreement had erupted over the 'Knox draft' which had originated in the U.S. Navy Department. This draft agreement was comprehensive in scope and gave sweeping powers to the United States with regards to jurisdiction, customs, and the right to assume additional authority in times of emergency.[62]

The Knox draft was eventually withdrawn, but not before the Commission of Government began to have second thoughts.[63] Increasingly the Commission of Government came to see some kind of economic concessions from the United States as a quid pro quo for permission to establish bases in Newfoundland. Sir Edward Emerson, one of the Newfoundland delegates, realized that there would be no authority to discuss economic questions at the negotiations in London and suggested sending a delegation to Washington before the talks began, to see if some arrangement could be made.[64] This course was not followed, but a committee was established under Dr Raymond Gushue, chairman of the Newfoundland Fisheries Board, to investigate possible concessions that could be secured from the United States.[65]

The Canadian government believed it essential for Canada to have a representative at the London talks, but had taken little action to ensure it. Consequently, there was considerable alarm on 27 January when the government was informed by the Dominions Office that the official negotiations were to commence the following day. Accompanying this information was an invitation to send an observer to the talks. King replied to Vincent Massey, the Canadian high commissioner in London, that Canada had 'intended to be represented at discussions but had no intimation they were to begin tomorrow.'[66] He asked Massey to act as the Canadian delegate for the time being until he could be replaced by Lester B. Pearson and Commodore L.W. Murray.

The Canadians and Newfoundlanders approached the London talks with differing points of view – both from each other and from the British and the Americans. The major point of dispute between the United States and the United Kingdom was over jurisdiction of the leased areas and the extent of American control; but for the Newfoundlanders, it was more a question of concessions sought in return for favours granted. The Canadians, for their part, were eager to avoid having their own role in Newfoundland diminished. Bereft of creative proposals and prompted more by their desire to preserve rights already gained in Newfoundland, the Canadians approached the London talks in an essentially negative manner.

For the first few days of negotiations, Canadian attention was focused on the question of status. The British government was adamant in its position that for the discussions concerning Newfoundland, the Newfoundland authorities should be the principal negotiators. Besides, the talks were to focus on the question of jurisdiction, a topic in which the Canadians were not directly involved. Reluctantly, the Canadians accepted observer status rather than full representation at the talks.[67]

The negotiations for the Leased Bases Agreement were scheduled to last two weeks but ultimately ran for eight. Major differences erupted between the negotiators, and much of the original goodwill evaporated as the talks dragged on. The United Kingdom and the United States split over the question of jurisdiction within the leased areas and the extent of American power in the sea and air adjacent to the leased areas. The Americans asked for extensive powers during a time of emergency but were reluctant to assume the responsibility for the defence of the territory in question. The British felt the defence of the leased areas could not be separated from that of the rest of the territory.[68]

The Newfoundlanders had similar apprehensions: if the United States could assume extensive authority during a crisis, did this mean that they could take over St John's harbour, or, assume control of Gander where the Canadians had already done considerable work? In addition, the Newfoundlanders felt that the Americans were asking for too much in non-emergency situations, especially in the use of roads, bridges, utilities, docks, piers, and public lands outside of the leased areas.[69] Increasingly, the Newfoundland delegation began to clamour for separate talks.

Lester Pearson, the Canadian delegate, sat and watched from the sidelines. His role as observer was ill-defined, as were his instructions from Ottawa. His diary reflected some of the confusion and impotence of the Canadian position:

This conference is not going very well, as the Americans are taking advantage of British necessities and exploiting the situation, so it seems, in order to prepare the way for ultimate acceptance of their sovereignty over the territories in question. Our interest, of course, is restricted to Newfoundland. If the United States makes good its claim to certain rights and powers which it is proposing to exercise over Newfoundland, we would find ourselves in a rather difficult position. Unfortunately we are only observers at the Conference and cannot take a very active part. So far all that I have done ... is to keep the High Commissioner and Ottawa informed of what has been going on and of the difficulties and changes in the situation. In return I have not had a single word from the department: if they are not worried, I don't know why we should be![70]

Those who watched the negotiations from Ottawa were not, however, completely silent. The Chiefs of Staff Committee reported to the three defence ministers that they viewed the talks 'with grave concern,' especially if the end result gave the United States authority to assume complete control of Newfoundland in an emergency. They argued that separate talks for Newfoundland should be held, preferably in Canada.[71] At the CWC meeting the next day, many of these concerns were echoed, and it was agreed that the United Kingdom should be approached with the possibility of holding separate talks dealing exclusively with Newfoundland.[72]

Unfortunately for the Canadians, this decision was too little too late. Before Massey or Pearson was informed of this decision, an outline agreement between Britain and the United States was reached. On most points the Americans had prevailed, including the touchy issue of rights during an emergency. Massey went to speak with Lord Cranborne, the dominions secretary, to express Canada's and Newfoundland's objection on this point. He reminded Cranborne of Canada's actions in Newfoundland and pointed out that this agreement might go against decisions already reached in meetings of the PJBD.[73] Cranborne was sympathetic but felt that it was too late to make any changes, suggesting instead that 'there should be a separate exchange of notes making clear the special interests of Canada under present conditions in regard to defence of Newfoundland, and ensuring that Canada would be brought into consultation on any matters arising under the above article.'[74]

The Canadian response that followed the next day (8 March) did not address this proposal. On the contrary, Ottawa reiterated the CSC recommendations made earlier that month and reviewed the Canadian objections to the agreement as it stood. Newfoundland was Canada's 'first line of defence'; therefore, aspects of the agreement had to be rejected 'if the political integrity of Newfoundland is to be adequately retained and the dominant Canadian interest in the defence of that Island is to be protected.'[75]

Massey's instructions were to press for separate talks to deal with Newfoundland. Even though this proposal had already been rejected by the United Kingdom, on 11 March he and Pearson made the rounds in a an effort to persuade both the British and the Americans of the justness of their cause. Pearson recorded their efforts in his diary: 'We didn't get very far. The High Commissioner and I left the Colonial Office after a very unsatisfactory interview and went straight to the United States Embassy. The High Commissioner put the Canadian case very convincingly and clearly, but the most we could get out of Winant [John G. Winant, American ambassador in London] was the Canadian interests in Newfoundland should be recognized by notes to be exchanged at the time of the signing.'[76] Massey informed Ottawa of this development and noted that both the Americans and the British felt it was too late to start over and that any changes at this stage could upset the whole show.[77]

The Canadian government had no choice but to salvage what it could. The new proposal was discussed at the CWC meeting of 12 March and later the same day Massey was informed that Canada 'reluctantly' accepted. In the same telegram the Canadians outlined what they felt should be included in the notes. First, they should recognize the importance of Newfoundland in Canadian defence and that Canada had 'already in fact assumed responsibility for its defence.' Second, Canada claimed the right to be respresented at all future discussions that arose dealing with Newfoundland. Finally, where this new lease conflicted with decisions already made by the PJBD, 'the recommendations of the Board shall prevail.'[78]

Anticipating this decision, Massey and Pearson had already prepared a draft agreement which they discussed with the British and Newfoundland delegations. Adjustments were made in light of the Canadian telegram and on 14 March Massey sent Ottawa a revised version of the proposed deal. Most of the Canadian claims had been met: Canada's role was recognized, consultation was promised, and the decisions of the PJBD would be respected. Within the Newfoundland delegation there was some uneasiness over the words chosen by Canada, and they asked for a softening of tone in the agreement. They questioned the necessity of referring to Newfoundland as Canada's 'first line of defence' and opposed giving the impression that the PJBD could make decisions regarding Newfoundland without consulting the Newfoundland authorities. The draft sent to Ottawa encompassed their concerns and included reference to Newfoundland in the clauses dealing with consultation and the PJBD, and specified that Canada's role in Newfoundland was one 'of special concern' because the Canadians had 'already assumed certain responsibilities' there.[79]

The Canadians accepted these changes in principle but sent back to Massey new wording for the first paragraph: 'It is recognized that the defence of Newfoundland is an integral feature of the Canadian scheme of defence and as such is a matter of special concern to the Canadian government which has, in fact, already assumed certain responsibilities for such defence.'[80] In his memoirs, Pearson recalled the difficulties he had in getting a final agreement. His diary entry for 19 March read:

Struggled with the Dominions' Office, Service Departments, and the Newfoundland delegation over our draft Agreement on Newfoundland. At times I almost felt that they were more suspicious of Canada in this matter than they were of the United States. Finally I got a bit impatient and put the question to the Newfoundland delegates bluntly as follows: 'After all, it is a very simple matter, whether you prefer to be raped by the United States or married to Canada.' Emerson replied that they would prefer the latter if they didn't feel that after the war was over they would be divorced! There is something in what he says.[81]

An agreement on the wording of the draft was reached over the next few days. Minor changes requested by the Americans and the British were accepted by the Canadians and all that remained to be settled was the form the agreement would take. The Canadians had assumed incorrectly that this agreement, although signed the same day, would be independent of the main agreement. On 24 March Ottawa was informed that the British had proposed that the agreement be included as a protocol attached to the main agreement. This proposal was approved by the CWC on 24 March and the green light was given to conclude the agreement.[82]

The Leased Bases Agreement was signed on 27 March 1941, in the Cabinet Room at No. 10 Downing Street. Under this agreement the United States received very wide powers to take the necessary steps to defend the areas involved, including additional power in time of war or emergency. Moreover, the United States received exemptions from income tax and some customs duties, and maintained complete jurisdiction within the leased areas (including over British subjects). Further, additional areas could be leased by common consent, but under the terms of the agreement, the United States was under no obligation to develop them.

The final version of the protocol which Vincent Massey, Lester Pearson, and Commodore Murray signed on Canada's behalf consisted of an introduction and four short paragraphs. The first was essentially the same as that suggested by the Canadians on 18 March recognizing 'that the defence of Newfoundland is an integral feature of the Canadian scheme of defence.' The other paragraphs safeguarded Canadian interests in Newfoundland against possible encroachments by the Americans under various aspects of the Leased Bases Agreement, for example, American activities outside the leased areas under normal circumstances as well as in times of emergency, protection against the Americans using their bases for commercial aviation purposes, and assurances that American actions would not contravene existing PJBD decisions concerning Newfoundland.

While it was a time for celebration and the champagne flowed, it was also a time for reflection. Pearson noted some personal misgivings in his diary: 'No matter how much we may applaud it now, or toast it in champagne, it is a victory for the United States and means the beginning of the end of British rule in the West Indies.'[83] These feelings did not dissipate over the following months. In a letter dated 26 May to Norman Robertson (who had replaced Skelton as under secretary after the latter's death in January) Pearson blamed the British for failing to give the Canadians sufficient warning before the opening of the conference. He also appeared particularly bitter over the role played by the Americans, arguing that 'the main objection' to a separate agreement for New-foundland 'came from the United States and, only secondarily, from the United Kingdom.'[84]

At the root of Pearson's disquiet was the belief that Canada deserved full attendance at the talks dealing with the Newfoundland bases. In response to an earlier suggestion from J.D. Hickerson of the State Department that the Americans would have allowed a separate agree-ment over Newfoundland, Pearson added: 'I must say that I feel somewhat sceptical on that point, but if my scepticism is ill-founded then it is a thousand pities we did not make the suggestion at the very beginning of the conference.'[85] But once the conference was over he began to reflect on where the responsibility for the Canadian failure lay. At the time he was unaware of the ease with which the Canadian government accepted 'observer status' when the talks began in January, and he was surprised to learn of it later. Moreover, why had it taken so long to put forward the Canadian case for separate talks on Newfound-land? The Canadians knew as early as September 1940 that negotiations concerning Newfoundland were to be held, and, even though they were taken by surprise when the talks began abruptly in January 1941, 'no suggestion, so far as I am aware, was made by the Canadian Government until March 8th, 1941, for a separate conference over Newfoundland.'[86] Pearson's questions remained unanswered, but the suggestion was implicit that he held his own government partially accountable for Canada's lack of success.

The protocol attached to the Leased Bases Agreement gave official recognition to Canada's special relationship with Newfoundland, but in no way can it be considered a victory for Canadian diplomacy. Indeed, the Canadians had been slow to act in safeguarding their interests in

Newfoundland, and when they did act they failed to press their case hard. It is questionable how much influence the Canadians could have exercised in any event, but in general Canadian policy-makers reacted to developments rather than initiating them. The negotiations produced a degree of resentment and bitterness in some Canadians such as Lester Pearson, but it also forced the Canadian government to take a more determined and creative role in its future relations with Newfoundland.

III

The Cabinet War Committee discussed the Leased Bases Agreement on 27 March 1941. Mackenzie King read a draft statement he had prepared to deliver to the House of Commons and the cwc gave its approval. C.G. Power brought up the question of the long-stalled negotiations with the Newfoundlanders over the control of their airports and reported that two days earlier a telegram had been received from the Newfoundland government giving the go-ahead to conclude an agreement. Power felt that under the present circumstances Canada should have a representative in Newfoundland to deal with this question and others that might arise between Canada, Newfoundland, and the United States. Ralston agreed and suggested sending Colin Gibson, the minister of national revenue, until a permanent official could be appointed. By this time there was little chance that the negotiations would not be completed successfully because the Canadians had conceded on every major proviso set out over the previous year, including the latest wish of the Air Ministry to maintain control of the existing wireless organizations.

Negotiations finally got under way early in April 1941. Gibson and H.A. Dyde, the secretary to the defence council, flew to Gander on 7 April and were met at the airport by Sir Wilfrid Woods, the commissioner for public utilities. Over the next three days the final arrangements were made and a draft agreement was forwarded to Ottawa. The Air Staff examined the proposals and, with only minor exceptions, found them acceptable, as did the cwc.[87] The necessary changes were made and approval received, and on 17 April the agreement was signed in St John's.

The agreement did not differ in many respects from the proposals made the previous September. Control of Gander, Botwood, and Gleneagles was handed over to the Canadians, attached to a long list of conditions: no alterations would be made without permission; damage to the airports would be paid for by the Canadians; preference would be given to competitively priced Newfoundland material; Newfoundland personnel would be employed as far as possible; facilities were to be maintained for British civil aircraft; and Canada would return control to Newfoundland at the end of the war. The remaining points were of less significance, with the exception of number 18, which read: 'It is understood that it is the intention of the Newfoundland Government when it resumes control of the air bases upon cessation of hostilities that the bases shall be operated primarily as civil airports and in accord with their original purpose fot the development of trans-Atlantic aviation. The extent of the continued use of the bases by the Canadian Forces after such resumption of control shall therefore be the subject of consultation between the two Governments.'[88]

With the signing of the 1941 Airbases Agreement the Canadian government won a largely symbolic victory, but a major one nevertheless. The significance of this was not lost on the Newfoundland negotiator, Sir Wilfrid Woods. A few days before the signing he reflected on how the Leased Bases Agreement and an increased American role in Newfoundland had altered Canadian thinking towards Newfoundland. He reported to the Commission of Government that his talks with Gibson and Dyde 'were dominated by what became a veritable "King Charles' head", the possibility that the U.S.A. would try to obtain a dominating position ... in Newfoundland. It was impossible to find out definitely what was at the bottom of this preoccupation on the part of the Canadians – whether it was mainly a purely professional distaste of being "bossed" by Americans or whether it had a deeper origin in fear that the U.S. will adopt a policy deliberately aimed at drawing Newfoundland out of the British Commonwealth into the orbit of the United States.'[89]

The 1941 agreement was a long time coming, but it did not solve all the outstanding problems in Canadian-Newfoundland relations. For example, American troops had arrived in Newfoundland earlier in the year and their presence had reopened the question of command between the visiting forces. Moreover, there remained a few unsettled problems over communications, customs, and other financial arrangements under the new agreement. Thus, over the following weeks discussions continued in both Ottawa and St John's to iron out existing difficulties.

If nothing else, the meetings in St John's and Ottawa led both Canada and Newfoundland to acknowledge that the problems in the relations between the two countries were so numerous and varied that a more effective method of dealing with them was very much needed. Conferences at various intervals were helpful to a degree, but time and again the representatives came away empty handed – able to agree only on the need for further discussion. The problems between Canada and Newfoundland were now continuous ones that required a more permanent structure in which to seek solutions.

By the spring of 1941 it had become clear to many Canadian officials not only that had Canada undertaken a considerable degree of activity in Newfoundland, but that Canada's role in Newfoundland for the duration of the war would more likely increase than decrease. And, with the Americans entering the scene, it was all the more important to have representation of some kind in St John's to oversee the myriad problems that would arise. H.L.Keenleyside of the Department of External Affairs was very much aware of these factors, and in a memorandum dated the same day that the Leased Bases Agreement was signed, he suggested that perhaps some of the problems in Canadian-Newfoundland relations would have been more easily solved had both Canada and Newfoundland had a representative stationed in each other's capitals.[90]

Norman Robertson held similar views to Keenleyside's, and in a lengthy memorandum for the Cabinet War Committee he outlined the needs for and benefits of posting a permanent representative to Newfoundland. Increased Canadian and American action in Newfoundland would undoubtedly create new problems that would be dealt with more quickly and efficiently by a man on the spot. More important, Newfoundland 'is economically, socially and strategically closer to Canada than to any other part of the British Empire. Inevitably Newfoundland's international position is the resultant of a three-way pull – to the United Kingdom, to the United States and to Canada. Any modification of the present precariously balanced position is of direct interest to this country, and it would seem important that Canada be adequately and directly represented in the Island, particularly during the next year or two, which are likely to see important developments in the Island's relations with the three countries with which it is most closely connected.'[91]

Robertson also pointed out a number of other significant factors: there were difficulties in customs, trade, and fishing relations that predated the war; the Canadian newsprint industry was upset at Newfoundland's price cutting which gave them an edge in the American market; and the existing channels of communications were too cumbersome to be efficient. All these problems could be worked on by a Canadian agent in St John's.[92]

Robertson suggested C.J. Burchell for the post. Burchell, currently Canada's first high commissioner in Australia, was a Maritimer and was familiar with commonwealth and dominion-provincial relations. Over the following years Burchell proved himself to be an able diplomat, and he made a great contribution to the smooth functioning of Canadian-Newfoundland relations.

Robertson's memorandum was distributed to the Cabinet War Committee, and after a brief discussion, approval was given.[93] Burchell was contacted concerning this proposal on 17 July. The telegram emphasized the importance of this position, and in describing his function as high commissioner, two revealing paragraphs were included:

In addition to our immediate military and strategic interest in Newfoundland, we have had to take into account long run trends in the development of Newfoundland relations with Canada which are likely to be accelerated by war developments. The suspension of self-government and the resulting anomalous position of Newfoundland within the Commonwealth are both likely to be transitional phases in the evolution of the Island.

During the next year or two the question of Newfoundland's relation to Confederation is quite likely to become an important issue. In the circumstances, we think it desirable to emphasize Canada's special relationship with Newfoundland and propose to do so by appointing a High Commissioner there.[94]

The Canadians approached the Newfoundland government with their proposal and it was quickly agreed to; on 23 July 1941, C.J. Burchell was appointed Canada's high commissioner in Newfoundland. The Dominions Office was kept informed of these developments, and although not opposed, it did question the title 'high commissioner.' Newfoundland had withdrawn its high commissioner in London when the Commission of Government was established and the Dominions Office felt that setting up a High Commissioner's Office might prove embarrassing.[95] The opposition of the Dominions Office was ill-defined and weak. It did not prevent the Canadians from acting, but over the next few years it did sidetrack the efforts of the Commission of Government to establish an office in Ottawa.[96]

The Canadian high commissioner in Newfoundland performed a wide variety of functions. As a channel of communications the high commission enhanced Canada's ability to respond to problems in

Newfoundland, and in the later years it provided a focus for Canada's efforts in bringing Newfoundland into Confederation. Apart from the larger questions of policy, the high commission also played a significant role in overseeing Canadian trade relations with Newfoundland and was directly concerned with the problems that arose from increasing government regulations and rationing of scarce commodities.[97]

The establishment of the high commission was a recognition of Canada's continuing interest in Newfoundland. Moreover, it was a recognition of past failures in Canadian policy and a symbol of Canada's determination not to repeat the same mistakes. In the year following June 1940 Canada's relationship with Newfoundland had undergone a fundamental change. Initial reluctance on the part of the Canadians to take action in Newfoundland had been swept aside by the fall of France. The introduction of an American presence in Newfoundland after the base-destroyer deal forced a rethinking of Canadian policy: not only would Canada have to act to defend Newfoundland, it would have to act to defend its own position there as well.

In April 1941, Mackenzie King visited President Roosevelt at Hyde Park. During the course of his stay King reminded Roosevelt of Canada's determination to be included in decisions affecting Newfoundland. Roosevelt told King 'that he thought Canada ought to take over Newfoundland ... that would have to come when the war was over.' King agreed, and told Roosevelt that 'Newfoundland had not been brought into Confederation because it was a liability but we would have to turn it into an asset.'[98] By the spring of 1941 this had already been accomplished.

4

Getting along with the Americans: Newfoundland and the Battle of the Atlantic

On 20 January 1941, the *Edmund B. Alexander* put out from New York City, bound for Newfoundland and carrying a crew of nearly 1,000 American officers and men. From the moment of its arrival in St John's, Canadian-American relations in Newfoundland automatically became a concern of major proportions. For the Canadians, the arrival of American forces added a new dimension to the perception of their role on the island, fuelling the continuing re-evaluation of Canada's relationship with Newfoundland.

The establishment of foreign bases on Newfoundland had been undertaken swiftly and without undue concern being shown for the long-term implications. In the atmosphere of crisis following the fall of France, immediate action was urgently required, and many questions were left unanswered. As a result, in addition to the task of defending Newfoundland, the Allies were also burdened with the problems of financial responsibility, jurisdiction, command, and relations with the civil authorities. To their credit, a working arrangement that all sides could accept was hammered out, enabling Canada and the United States to concentrate on fighting the enemy and not each other.

At the same time, Newfoundland's role in the war effort was evolving from a defensive to an offensive one. In 1941–2 the fear that Newfoundland would be used as a stepping-stone to the invasion of North America began to fade, and was replaced by the realization that Newfoundland's location could make a positive contribution to the prosecution of the war effort. The intensified activity of the German U-boats brought the war to the shores of Newfoundland and threatened the shipping lifeline connecting North America with Great Britain. No longer was Newfoundland only the first line of defence in North America; these developments thrust the country into active participation in the Battle of the Atlantic as a base centre for convoy defence.

As the war progressed, more and more of the responsibility for these activities was shouldered by the Canadians, a situation that arose partly as a result of Canada's burgeoning military strength and partly because of government policy to concentrate Canadian efforts on more specific areas of Canadian interest. Over a period of two years the RCN made its most significant contribution to the war effort through convoy defence. Moreover, the Canadians built an airbase at Torbay and a repair base at Bay Bulls, as well as constructing and maintaining a naval base at St John's for the Royal Navy. These major accomplishments enhanced Canada's role in Newfoundland at the same time that the American presence was decreasing. Equally, they were indicative of the firm commitment that Canada had made to maintain its special relationship with Newfoundland.

I

During the first year of the war Canadian naval policy regarding Newfoundland did not differ from Canadian military policy in any marked way. Nor did policy change in any significant manner after the fall of France. No large-scale invasion was anticipated, and defence precautions were confined to patrolling Newfoundland's coastal waters and guarding against attack from enemy surface raiders or submarines.

St John's was the best and most important harbour in Newfoundland and it served as the focal point for Canadian naval operations throughout the war. Outside of St John's, however, the sinuosity of the coast provided a large number of well-protected natural harbours. Similarly, because of the isolation of some parts of the country and the difficulties of communications and transportation, Newfoundland offered numerous potential sites for enemy advanced bases. To counteract this threat, the commanding officer of HMS *Caradoc* suggested utilizing one of Newfoundland's most abundant resources – its fishermen. Although the enemy may attempt to establish a small base on Newfoundland, he noted, 'the large number of fishing boats which abound everywhere would make it extremely difficult for one to do so undetected, provided that it is impressed upon the fishermen that they must remain undetected and report any unusual vessel seen near the coast.'[1]

For the Canadian naval authorities this reliance on the local populace was as much a matter of necessity as design. In the early stages of the war the RCN suffered from a severe shortage of ships and was unable to spare the vessels required for extensive coastal patrols. More important, had the ships been available they would have been assigned to a much more critical theatre of operations overseas. Under the existing war conditions of 1940 the Canadians could no longer depend on Britain's shipyards as they had in the past and they were forced to increase domestic production of ships. But, until ship construction was complete, the RCN performed its duties in Newfoundland waters with a skeleton force.[2]

That this was the case was clear in the 20 August 1940 meeting in St John's between C.G. Power and several Canadian services representatives and the Newfoundland authorities. On the naval issue, the Canadians revealed their plans to establish an advanced naval base at St John's and a summer advanced base at Botwood. These bases would be developed over time and gradually the number of ships stationed there would be increased to between ten and twelve. But, because of the shortage of vessels at that time, 'the best that could be hoped for this fall was one ship.'[3]

Little progress was made over the following months. In November the diesel yacht the HMCS *Ambler* was directed to proceed to St John's and commence operations as an examination vessel, but the establishment of a naval examination service at Botwood was postponed until 1941.[4] Otherwise, the Canadians had a difficult time fulfilling their promises to the Newfoundlanders: not only were naval vessels in short supply, so too were coastal defence guns, lights, and enemy-detection equipment. Not surprisingly, the Commission of Government grew increasingly uneasy as the months of inaction dragged on.

The appearance of the Americans early in 1941 relieved the situation temporarily, but with the coming of spring break-up the fear of enemy activity in Newfoundland waters resurfaced. In sharp contrast to the relatively minor naval activity in 1939–40, the spring of 1941 brought with it the extension of the Battle of the Atlantic into Newfoundland waters. The convoy system had been established only hours after the outbreak of war in 1939, but attacks by U-boats were confined to the waters of the eastern Atlantic. The summer of 1940 came to be called 'The Happy Time' by U-boat commanders because of the ease that the U-boats had in sinking an enormous number of Allied cargo ships. Hunting in wolfpacks and attacking under the cover of darkness proved particularly successful for the U-boats, and by concentrating on unescorted ships they found easy prey and reduced their own risks to a minimum.[5]

The United Kingdom took great pains to strengthen convoy protection and was beginning to achieve a fair degree of success late in 1940. Unfortunately, the wolfpacks responded by moving farther and farther west, attacking ships before they were met by their convoy escorts. The Germans were aided in this effort by longer range U-boats and the acquisition of bases on the French coast after June 1940 which significantly extended the reach of the U-boats.

To counteract these measures the British government devised a plan to extend convoy protection farther to the west. On 10 May 1941 the United Kingdom announced that it had decided to base an escort force at St John's. This force would escort convoys from Halifax and Sydney to the Mid-Ocean Meeting Point where the escort force based in Iceland would take over. The Newfoundland force would transfer to a returning convoy for the voyage home.[6]

St John's was the most logical and suitable site to base an escort force; geographically it was situated in close proximity to the usual convoy route from Halifax, and it was the one harbour that had sufficient facilities to allow the convoy escorts to commence immediately. The creation of the Newfoundland Escort Force revolutionized the role of St John's. Original naval plans confined themselves to local defence – now everything had changed, and St John's was to play a central role in the Battle of the Atlantic.

The Canadian navy promptly volunteered to assume the responsibility for this escort service. The RCN had increased in size since the war began, and by concentrating its ships in this area it felt that Canada could immediately provide the necessary destroyers and corvettes for this force. The Cabinet War Committee discussed the idea on 27 May and gave its approval. Mackenzie King was convinced that this move 'would be in accordance with established principles of Empire defence.' The proposal to assume the responsibility for the Newfoundland Escort Force held several attractions for the Canadians. Here was an opportunity to do a job that was important for the war effort and was also consistent with Canada's policy of giving priority to domestic defence.[7]

The United Kingdom welcomed the Canadian proposal. Both sides agreed on the appointment of Commodore L.M. Murray, RCN, as the commander of the Newfoundland Escort Force, and on 27 May the first convoy left Halifax under the new system.[8] Early in June, Colin Gibson set off for Newfoundland to make the necessary arrangements for acquiring the property rights for the areas in St John's harbour that would be needed for the base.

At the same time the Dominions Office informed the Canadians and the Commission of Government that the original plans for the escort force had to be enlarged and were now to include thirty destroyers, twenty-four corvettes, and nine sloops. The Dominions Office inquired if St John's could handle this increase.[9] The Newfoundland government replied that St John's could make the necessary space but it would 'involve extensive requisitioning of commercial premises on the waterfront, considerable dredging, building or rebuilding of approximately 3,200 lineal feet of wharfage and a building programme covering about 50,000 square feet of floor space on the waterfront apart altogether from magazines, recreational and hospital facilities and housing.'[10]

The Canadians were willing to go along with these alterations, but inevitably the questions of control and financial responsibility were raised. At the CWC meeting on 10 June, Angus Macdonald, the minister of national defence for naval services, informed the members that preliminary estimates put the cost of the St John's base at $10 million. J.L. Ilsley, the minister of finance, questioned why Canada should pay for this development: Canada could provide the necessary dollars, perhaps, but surely, he argued, the ultimate financial responsibility rested with the United Kingdom. King agreed and suggested that it would be unwise to pay for any base in an area that was outside of Canadian control. Ten days later the matter was again discussed and the CWC agreed that the United Kingdom should both control and pay for the base at St John's. Moreover, the Dominions Office should be informed that the Canadians would assume financial responsibility for the base only if they were given title to it as well.[11]

What emerged was a system of joint control. The United Kingdom received title to the base and bore the ultimate financial responsibility, and the Canadians agreed to run the show and pay the administration and maintenance costs. The only condition exacted by the Canadians was a promise from the United Kingdom not to transfer control of the base to any third party without first consulting Canada.[12]

The United Kingdom sent a joint mission (comprising officials in the Admiralty and the Department of War Transport) to St John's and Ottawa to work out the details. A joint committee was established in Ottawa with members of the Naval Service and it was arranged that, in addition to paying the administration and maintenance costs, the Canadians would place and supervise the contracts for the work and would pay for it with Canadian funds. At some later date the debt would be repaid by the United Kingdom.

The contract for the construction (fixed fee plus costs) was given to E.G.M. Cape and Co. of Montreal. The task was considerable: St John's harbour was not especially large and it was crowded with commercial vessels; moreover, the Americans had leased a fair-sized chunk of it as well. Canadian plans included the renovation of the wharves on the south side and the northeast corner, the clearing of some buildings for a dockyard, the construction of barracks, and administration building, hospital, oil-fuel depot, signal stations at Cape Spear and Fort Amherst, and a wireless station farther to the west. Construction began immediately and continued well in to 1942.[13]

In June 1941 the Newfoundland Command was established to oversee the functions of the Newfoundland Escort Force. This command was basically independent until March 1942 when it became a sub-command under the commander-in-chief, east coast defences.[14] Overall strategic command was in British hands in July 1941, but before the summer was over it had been assumed by the United States.

Over the course of 1941 the United States played an increasingly active part in the Battle of the Atlantic. With the passage of Lend Lease in March, the United States became 'the great arsenal of democracy,' but the problem remained to ensure the safe passage of the goods and materials. Roosevelt and his top advisers felt it to be politically unacceptable at that time for the United States to take over the escorting of the convoys, but a way was found to circumvent this obstacle. In April, the defence of Greenland was guaranteed by the United States, and the American security zone was stretched to longitude 25°; this agreement extended the waters of the western hemisphere to the shores of Iceland. In July this boundary was pushed even farther when American troops replaced the British in Iceland and the United States commenced limited convoy duty.[15]

These informal arrangements took more concrete form during the Atlantic Conference between Roosevelt and Churchill off the coast of Newfoundland in August 1941. Churchill was eager to have the Americans participate in convoy duty and he exacted from Roosevelt an agreement dividing the Atlantic into two parts – the eastern half under British direction and the western under American. This arrangement was not put into effect immediately, but it did mean that the Newfoundland Escort Force fell under the strategic direction of the Americans. There was little that the Canadians could do to prevent this and there was resentment in some quarters at being placed under the command of the Americans, who were both inexperienced in convoy protection and nominally neutral.[16]

When a German U-boat fired on the u.s. destroyer *Greer* on 4 September, Roosevelt used the incident as a pretext to fulfil his bargain with Churchill. Calling the attack an act of piracy, he instituted full-scale convoy escorts in the western Atlantic and claimed the right of first strike within the American security zone.[17] In all but name the Americans were now active belligerents in the Battle of the Atlantic.

The ability of the convoy escort forces to protect the shipping lanes was aided considerably by the extensive air patrols covering the convoy routes. In fact, after the initial fear of an Axis invasion of North America had abated, convoy protection became the primary duty of the Eastern Air Command. From the beginning of the Battle of the Atlantic, anti–U-boat patrols had been undertaken by the RCAF from Gander and, to a lesser degree, from Botwood. In addition, Canadian plans to establish an airport near St John's took on new importance; originally planned to service and defend St John's, the base at Torbay quickly came to play a key role in convoy protection.

Canadian interest in establishing an airport near St John's stretched back to the summer of 1940, and Canadian plans to this effect were expressed to the Newfoundland authorities during the August meeting with C.G. Power. In October, the PJBD issued its 'First Report' which also recommended the construction of an airbase at Torbay. A detailed survey of the area was conducted in November, but otherwise little action was undertaken until the spring of 1941.

During the April 1941 meetings in St John's, Colin Gibson discussed the Canadian plans with Sir Wilfrid Woods and asked for written assurances from the Newfoundlanders that they would not oppose the construction of an airport at Torbay. On 17 April, Woods complied; in a letter to Gibson he expressed the Newfoundland government's general acceptance of the Canadians' proposal under the agreed conditions. The area surrounding Torbay was undeveloped and the total financial responsibility for the construction of the base would fall to the Canadians. Crown lands would be freely given or leased (this was to be settled at a later date), but it would be up to the Canadians to acquire the necessary privately owned land. Moreover, the Canadians agreed not to use the airport for civil-aviation purposes without the prior concurrence of the Newfoundland government.[18] Wood's letter to Gibson remained as the sole basis of agreement between Canada and Newfoundland over the construction and use of the Torbay airport.

The agreement to establish Torbay airport was discussed at the CWC meeting on 28 April 1941. Official approval was given and earlier the same day almost $2 million was earmarked for construction of the airport.[19] Construction began shortly thereafter and the airport was in use by the end of the year. The costs involved in construction were considerable: by April 1945 Canada had spent a total of $11,709,431 in building and maintaining the facilities at Torbay. Furthermore, an additional $64,997 was spent in contructing a road linking the airport with St John's. (See table 1 on page 81.)

The airport at Torbay proved to be an extremely valuable asset to the Newfoundland Escort Force. Although often subject to fog, it regularly provided a safe haven for planes from nearby aircraft carriers. Moreover, fighter squadrons and long-range patrol squadrons (after 1943) were maintained there by the RCAF and a vigorous anti–U-boat campaign was undertaken.[20] On the civilian side, Torbay came to be operated as the eastern terminus of TCA, which provided daily passenger flights and airmail service to the mainland. Travel time to Montreal was cut dramatically; what was once a lengthy and often arduous journey by train and boat was shortened to a matter of hours by plane.

The extension of the war into the western Atlantic also gave a sharper edge to a lesser but significant dilemma that emerged over St Pierre and Miquelon. Following the disaster in France, the islands remained under Vichy control, to the dismay of the United Kingdom, Newfoundland, and Canada. The existence of a number of short-wave radio stations on St Pierre presented the possibility that reports on Allied shipping were being transmitted to U-boats in the vicinity.

The three governments felt this situation to be unacceptable but differed in their suggested solutions. The United Kingdom felt that the Allies should allow the Free French to move in and take control of the islands, and they asked the Canadians for their concurrence.[21] The Newfoundlanders felt more strongly about the issue and believed that the islands should be taken over by British forces (i.e., from Newfoundland or Canada), with special care taken to prevent an American presence there. They feared that the Americans might choose to maintain control on a permanent basis, which 'would be truly disastrous.'[22] Their discomfort over this possibility stemmed from a concern that the Americans could establish a fresh-fish industry there and do serious damage to the Newfoundland economy.

For the Canadians, the problem of St Pierre and Miquelon took on different characteristics. In a memorandum for Mackenzie King, Norman Robertson reviewed the Canadian position: the occupation of the islands by the Free French was not to be encouraged because it 'might create misunderstandings in Canada and prejudice the maintenance of our relations with France.' While Robertson disliked the Vichy government, he was aware that there was widespread support for it in Quebec.[23] Moreover, the opposition of the United States to such action also had to be borne in mind. As was the case with Greenland, the Americans opposed the occupation of European colonies in this hemisphere because of the example it might set to others and because, in this case, it could damage relations with France. Robertson's solution was to station a control party at the island wireless station.[24]

The Canadians were willing to sit back and wait, but they were shortly overtaken by events. In mid-December, Ottawa learned that the Free French under Admiral Muselier might occupy the islands; to the Dominions Office this appeared to be 'the most satisfactory solution.'[25] Before doing so, however, Muselier visited Ottawa and promised not to act against the wishes of the Canadians, British, and Americans. Nevertheless, the day before Christmas, 1941, Muselier sailed into St Pierre and claimed the islands for the Free French. The Americans, and in particular Secretary of State Cordell Hull, were enraged over the conduct of the 'so-called' Free French, but Muselier's action effectively ended the problem. And not all the Americans were opposed: A.J. Pick, an official in the Canadian high commission in St John's, remembers drinking a toast to the Free French on Christmas Day with the American vice-consul, who later the same day followed his government's instructions and denounced Muselier's actions.[26] The Canadians, of course, denied any prior knowledge of this venture, and although they had opposed it, would do nothing to force the Free French out. King did wire Massey that 'In view of circumstances of Free French occupation of St Pierre today, do not send Christmas message to General de Gaulle.'[27] After a few days of heated exchange, cooler heads prevailed, and there the matter rested as the attention of the Allies turned to more important developments.

The entrance of the United States into the war in December 1941 had two significant effects on the Battle of the Atlantic. First, now that the United States was an active belligerent, the U-boat wolfpacks began operating directly along the American coast, an area that had previously been immune. Second, the full participation of the Americans enlarged their areas of operations and increasingly they were pressured to concentrate their naval forces elsewhere, particularly in the Pacific.[28] The consequences for the Canadians were profound. Not only would enemy activity likely be stepped up in 1942, but the responsibility shouldered by the Newfoundland Escort Force would also increase. Furthermore, the congestion in St John's harbour was already considerable, and additional construction and expenses would likely be necessary in the future.

These problems were addressed during the CWC meeting on 14 May 1942. Angus Macdonald, the minister of defence for naval services, informed the committee that the Canadian position in St John's, especially in its ability to acquire the necessary property rights, was 'unsatisfactory in many ways' and had resulted in 'serious delays.' To overcome these difficulties and the other urgent matters concerning the expansion of the harbour, he suggested that Canada should take over both the responsibility and the title to the base at St John's. In essence this was a reversal of the policy agreed to the previous year when the Canadians had chosen to leave the title in the hands of the Admiralty. J.L. Ilsley, the minister of finance, although usually reluctant to incur such large expenses, agreed with Macdonald on this issue. As it stood, the United Kingdom was using funds from the billion-dollar gift to pay for the construction, and if Canada took over the title the costs could be tacked on to that gift.[29] Mackenzie King was looking for a more general agreement to settle the whole range of problems between Canada and Newfoundland and was willing to go along on this matter. The request to the Commission of Government was made through C.J. Burchell, the Canadian high commissioner.

The response of the Newfoundland government came as something of a surprise to the Canadians. Burchell reported to Ottawa that the three British commissioners were reluctant to make any decision, especially without first referring to the Dominions Office for advice. As for the three Newfoundland commissioners, they were adamantly opposed. Their first concern was that public opinion in Newfoundland would be unfavourable to the idea, but as Burchell noted, their real fear was that the Canadians would take over large sections of dockyard property and use it for commercial purposes after the war.[30] If they were to do so the Canadians would pose a serious challenge to the commercial interests of St John's.

Despite their failure to assume the title to the St John's base, the Canadians were still faced with the overwhelming problem of congestion in the harbour. Not only was St John's the headquarters for the Newfoundland Escort Force, it was also an important base for repairs and refuge for navy and merchant ships. The congestion at St John's forced some ships to anchor off Bay Bulls, approximately eighteen miles to the south. To deal with this problem the Canadians decided to construct a 'protected anchorage' at Bay Bulls to handle repairs for warships and, they hoped, to relieve the overcrowding at St John's. The cost was estimated at $3 million, which the Canadians were willing to pay, providing they operated and controlled the anchorage, either under a fee simple arrangement or through a ninety-nine-year lease. The Commission of Government agreed to the latter arrangement on 24 August 1942.[31]

The construction of the docks at Bay Bulls alleviated but did not eliminate the crowding at St John's. Consequently, the Canadians decided to renovate the harbour, a plan which included doubling the size of the repair facilities at St John's, erecting more living accommodations (mainly on the south side of the harbour), and building a second 250-bed hospital. These new proposals virtually doubled the cost of the base. The original renovation estimates of nearly $6 million had been increased by $3 million by 1943; this new scheme would increase the cost by an additional $7 million, bringing the total projected cost of the St John's base up to approximately $16 million.[32]

The Battle of the Atlantic continued unabated into 1943. The Canadians and the British continued to view convoy defence as the top priority, but for the Americans there were demands in other parts of the world that increasingly pulled their attention away from the North Atlantic. With too many commitments in the Pacific and Mediterranean, the Americans progressively withdrew themselves from convoy protection in the months following Pearl Harbor.

Gradually the Atlantic convoys were reorganized to reflect the changing circumstances of the war. For example, in 1942 the system was split into two sections: the Mid-Ocean Escort Force and the Western Local Force.[33] Not surprisingly, the role played by Canada was magnified by these developments. But the expansion of the convoy system to cover the complete ocean voyage led to some confusion and complexity in the command structure, and the withdrawal of the Americans only exacerbated the already complicated situation. To deal with these problems, a conference was held in Washington in March 1943, between representatives of Canada, the United States, and Britain.

The Atlantic Convoy Conference produced significant consequences for Canada's role in the Battle of the Atlantic. Because of the decreasing American presence in the area, the responsibility for convoy defence was given to Canada and Britain. A line was drawn near the 47th meridian, about three hundred miles east of St John's, to split the

Canadian and British sections. The area west of the 'Chop Line,' as it was called, and north of the u.s. Eastern Sea Frontier Command fell to the Canadian Naval Service. Overall strategic direction still rested with the United States, but the responsibility for the air and sea-convoy protection now came under Canadian command. Immediately following the conference the Canadian Northwest Atlantic Command was established, and in April the u.s. Commander of Task Force 24 (based at Argentia) turned the responsibility over to the commander-in-chief, Canadian Northwest Atlantic. The commander was Admiral Murray, and all the Canadian sub-commands, including Newfoundland, now came under his control.[34]

The Battle of the Atlantic came to a climax in 1943. U-boat attacks were intensified early in the year, and during March–April Allied losses were enormous. But the days of the U-boats were numbered. From 1942 on, more efficient radar systems were fitted into a large number of ships, providing the convoys with a much-improved system of wolfpack detection. In addition, the radar systems improved the ability of the convoy to stay together and reduced the number of stray ships which had provided such easy targets for U-boat torpedoes. Air protection was extended as far as possible and this enhanced convoy protection, as did new and improved depth charges. Furthermore, years of experience had shown that security at sea depended on the size of the escorts, not on the size of the convoys. Consequently, by increasing the convoy size (which meant fewer convoys and larger escorts), losses could be cut substantially. By May 1943, the number of U-boats destroyed had risen sharply. The U-boat menace continued until the end of the war, but never again did it threaten to isolate the United Kingdom as it had between 1941 and 1943. By the end of 1943 the Battle of the Atlantic had been won.

The Canadian role in the Battle of the Atlantic was their most significant contribution to the war at sea. During the course of the war the Canadian navy had grown into an efficient and powerful force, a fact that was reflected in its presence in Newfoundland. The Canadian personnel at St John's in July 1941 consisted of 150 officers and 750 men. Over the next few years this number increased dramatically, from 2,000 men in November 1942 to 3,600 in December 1943, and 5,000 in December 1944. By 1945 Canada had spent $17,075,000 on the Newfoundland naval bases. Of this total, $14,313,000 was charged to the admiralty, while the $2,141,000 spent on developing Bay Bulls was covered by the Canadians.[35] For the Canadian Naval Service, the protection of the North Atlantic convoys had proved to be not only its heaviest responsibility during the war, but also its greatest achievement.

II

Under the terms of the base-destroyer deal, the United States received base sites in Newfoundland as a 'free gift.' The Americans immediately took advantage of their opportunity; the Greenslade Mission travelled to Newfoundland and investigated American requirements for defence and made the arrangements with the local authorities. During the autumn months surveys were completed, and by the end of the year some construction was under way. Work began at Argentia in December 1940. Months before a final agreement had been reached in London, the Americans were making their presence felt in Newfoundland.

The first American troops arrived in St John's on 29 January 1941. Unfortunately, this first garrison of 919 men and 58 officers was sent before the necessary accommodation facilities were ready, and the men were forced to spend the winter on board their ship. With the coming of spring, Fort Pepperell was established on the leased site near St John's and on 1 May reinforcements arrived, bringing the total number of American officers and enlisted men in Newfoundland up to 1,666. Over the following months the numbers steadily increased; by 1 December 1941, American strength in Newfoundland had risen to 2,383.[36]

The Americans were particularly interested in establishing an air garrison in Newfoundland early in 1941 – before they had time to complete the construction of an airbase. Gander was the logical choice and Roosevelt suggested bringing up the possibility of stationing U.S. forces there at the next PJBD meeting. As noted above, the Canadians were opposed to the leasing of any part of Gander to the Americans, and informal arrangements were drawn up whereby the Canadians made the necessary facilities available for use by the Americans.

Apprehensive about the vulnerability of American installations in Newfoundland, Roosevelt informed Prime Minister Churchill early in April 1941 that the United States was stationing additional forces at St John's. Malcolm MacDonald, the British high commissioner, informed Prime Minister King of this development and explained that Roosevelt felt that under the circumstances the American base construction sites needed extra protection.[37] But, by going straight to Churchill and bypassing the PJBD, Roosevelt upset many within the Canadian government. Like the United Kingdom, Canada welcomed the security benefits gained from additional American forces in Newfoundland, but the slight to Canada's role there could not be overlooked. Coming less than a fortnight after the signing of the protocol, unilateral action such as this appeared to undermine all that Canada had worked for. J.L. Ralston, the minister of defence, was particularly disconcerted, and in a letter to King he argued that 'somehow or other' Roosevelt should be told that 'we are not just non-contributing partners in the Newfoundland situation. We are vitally concerned and we took the initiative and the early effective steps in this business. Consequently, we ought not to be regarded as unreasonable if we suggest there might be consultation with us before a decision is arrived at, or at least, before direct communications are sent to the Prime Minister of the United Kingdom.'[38]

The original American plans for construction in Newfoundland anticipated the need for accommodation for more than 6,000 troops. The cost of these facilities was estimated in 1940 at close to $28 million. Gradually these plans were escalated to include accommodations for up to 16,000 troops. To meet these increasing needs, considerably more negotiating was undertaken with the Newfoundland government following the signing of the Leased Bases Agreement in March 1941. Under Article xxvii of that agreement the United States could acquire additional areas if deemed necessary, and on 14 July 1942 a supplementary lease was signed in St John's to this effect. This agreement added 2,142 acres to the original total of 4,487 acres of land leased to the United States.[39]

The American interests in Newfoundland were centred in three specific areas: on the west coast of the island, Harmon Field was constructed to the south of Corner Brook at Stephenville; in Placentia Bay, on the west side of the Avalon Peninsula, a naval base was built at Argentia, and close by Fort McAndrew was established; the third area was St John's and its vicinity – Fort Pepperell was constructed by Quidi Vidi Lake, an emergency landing strip was built nearby, and several hundred feet of wharfage was leased to the Americans in St John's harbour.

All the construction contracts were given to American firms, and the total cost for base construction was $60,300,212. The number of American forces in Newfoundland continued to increase, peaking in 1943 at 10,882. The implications that these developments had for Newfoundland's economy were profound: millions of dollars were poured into the island through these projects and from free-spending u.s. servicemen. Also, over 80 per cent of the workforce on the construction sites were Newfoundlanders, virtually eliminating unemployment.[40]

As for the Canadians, the list of their responsibilities and achievements in Newfoundland during the war was impressive: Canada assumed the defence of St John's, Bell Island, Botwood, and Gander (significantly expanding the latter), a naval base was constructed for the United Kingdom at St John's, and in 1943 Canada took command of the northwest Atlantic convoy system. On their own, the Canadians constructed a subsidiary repair base at Bay Bulls, an airport at Torbay, and, perhaps their greatest achievement, the Goose Bay airport in Labrador. In addition, there were numerous other installations constructed, including fuel depots, wireless stations, and weather stations.

These projects took large quantities of men and materials, time, energy, and money. In mid-July 1941 Canadian-forces strength in Newfoundland rested at 2,389 men. In September, an additional 1,298 men were sent, and by the end of the year the total reached 3,975.[41] The number of Canadians in Newfoundland continued to increase during 1942–3, although not as rapidly as the number of Americans, and reached a maximum of almost 5,700 in December 1943. In his *Six Years of War* C.P. Stacey lists the major units in 'W' Force, as the Canadian army in Newfoundland was called: two infantry battalions headquartered at St John's and Botwood; two companies of the 1st Airfield Defence Battalion and one of the Veterans' Guard; two anti-aircraft regiments of the Royal Canadian Artillery headquartered at St John's and Gander; three coast batteries of the RCA, one each at St John's, Botwood, and Lewisporte; a company of Atlantic Command signals; and a fortress company of the Royal Canadian Engineers. In addition, there were the 'numerous administration and service units required to maintain the force,' and the Newfoundland Militia (Newfoundland Regiment after 1943) which aided home defence.[42]

The cost of maintaining this force and for the construction of the Canadian facilities in Newfoundland greatly exceeded even the wildest imaginings of 1939. By 1945, the Canadian government had spent almost $40 million on its Newfoundland bases. Add to this the more than $25 million spent on the construction of Goose Bay airport and the total Canadian funds spent in Newfoundland reaches $65,192,468 (see table 1). If nothing else, these sums give clear evidence of the firm commitment that the Canadians had made with regard to Newfoundland – and the unlikelihood of their relinquishing any aspect of their 'special relationship' in the years to come.

The presence of American and Canadian troops on Newfoundland soil forced the three countries to make the best of an inconvenient

TABLE 1
Expenditures for construction and development of airfields and facilities in
Newfoundland and Labrador to 31 March 1945

Botwood seaplane base and facilities	$ 2,808,145
Buchans aerodrome and facilities	1,046,733
Cape Bauld radio detachment	84,752
Donovans fuel depot	82,410
Gander aerodrome, seaplane base, and facilities	20,273,860
Gander radio detachment	8,095
Gander Lake–Lewisporte–Bishop Falls Highway	1,423,200
Holyrood fuel depot	121,705
Lewisporte fuel depot	5,376
Port-aux-Basques radio detachment	66,192
St John's Headquarters	1,831,156
St Andrews radio range	200,389
Torbay aerodrome and facilities	11,709,431
Torbay–St John's road	64,997
Refuelling bases	9,370
Brig Harbour radio detachment	16,239
Goose Airport and facilities	25,382,526
Sandgirt Lake radio weather station	44,107
Spotted Island radio detachment	12,518
Wilson radio range investigation	1,267
TOTAL	$65,192,468

SOURCE: DRCN, Appendix G

situation, but inevitably friction arose. In Argentia, Stephenville, and
Botwood the Canadian and American servicemen were isolated enough
to prevent the eruption of any serious problems of coexistence. This was
not the case, however, in Gander, St John's, and even Goose Bay. Gander
was a constant source of irritation, as it was used by the Canadian,
American, and British airforces. Before the war, Gander had one runway,
a few buildings, and a railway station. In a matter of months it became
something of a boom town and the airport was transformed into one of
the busiest in the world. The RCAF, USAAF, and RAF each built their own
facilities – including mess halls, living quarters, and hospitals.[43] Social
life for the servicemen centred around the Big Dipper Bar. As one author
wrote: 'The Big Dipper Bar stayed open twenty-four hours a day; for-
tunes were won and lost in all-night poker games; men fought for the
privilege of a dance with one of the town's few women; Texas bush pilots
swaggered in ten-gallon hats; RAF officers with handlebar moustaches
drank champagne in toothglasses and bragged of prangs and pieces of
cake.'[44]

Conditions were similar but less severe at Goose Bay. There the Americans were centralized on the 'American side' of the base, located on the southwest corner (the Canadians were on the northeast side).[45] As for St John's, the quarters were not so cramped as they were at the airbases, but contact between the Canadians and the Americans occurred on a regular basis. Both countries maintained large garrisons there, both controlled major sections of the harbour, and both had installed anti-aircraft artillery and harbour-defence guns. Not surprisingly, problems arose from time to time when men from the two garrisons met while out on the town in St John's.

There was friction in other areas as well. Questions over the control of the neighbouring airspace of the airbases arose, as did difficulties in the use of differing air signals. Similarly, in St John's, Canadian aircraft ran the risk of being fired upon by the American-manned anti-aircraft guns if they failed to comply with the American regulations.[46] For the most part, relations between the Canadian and American servicemen were extremely good. Personal differences and other petty squabbles continued throughout the war, but a problem of major proportions never developed. The most serious conflict was over the question of command, an issue that did not concern the average serviceman.

The roots of the command problem in Newfoundland stemmed from the two major defence plans formulated by the PJBD in 1940–1. The PJBD began working on a joint defence plan shortly after its first meeting. By 11 September, a draft plan had been drawn up and after a few amendments the Joint Basic Defence Plan – 1940 (the '1940 plan') was agreed to on 11 October 1940. The aim of the 1940 plan was to 'provide for the most effective use of Canadian and U.S. Naval, Military and Air Forces for the joint direct defense of Canada, Newfoundland and the United States.'[47] It was assumed under this plan that the United Kingdom was no longer a contributing ally and that Canada and the United States must necessarily stand alone against all enemies – in both Europe and Asia.[48]

The 1940 plan was somewhat vague on the matter of command. Responsibility for defence was given with sovereignty: Canadian land and coastal waters fell under Canadian jurisdiction, while the United States was responsible for its own coast, including Alaska. Newfoundland, because of its anomalous position, was 'a case of overlapping responsibilities.'[49] Subsequent discussion over the following months produced a new version of the plan called the 'Montreal Revise' which gave strategic direction to the United States.[50]

It proved unnecessary to be more precise about command because the circumstances envisaged in the plan never materialized, and it was never put into effect. By 1941, the changing war situation had made the fundamental premise of the plan obsolete: Britain had not fallen and would, in fact, continue in the war as an effective ally. Consequently, early in the year the PJBD began work on the Joint Basic Defence Plan No. 2–1941, or ABC-22, in an effort to bring Canadian-American defence planning in line with the changed circumstances.

Joint staff talks between the United States and the United Kingdom produced the ABC-1 plan which saw the British and Americans as allies and laid the framework for co-operation in the event that the United States entered the war. ABC-22, the PJBD plan, was ancillary to ABC-1, and it outlined the various actions to be undertaken by Canada and the United States should the Americans enter the war.[51] ABC-22 was by its very nature more offensive than the 1940 plan. Whereas the 1940 plan centred on the defence of North America alone, ABC-22 envisaged taking offensive action against the Nazis.

ABC-22 sparked a serious controversy over the question of command. Not surprisingly, the Americans assumed that the arrangement made for the 1940 plan would exist under ABC-22 – namely, that strategic direction of the Canadian and American forces would rest with the United States. Newfoundland was included in this plan and it was felt that command would rest with the Canadians until such time as the number of American forces there surpassed the number of Canadians.[52]

This assumption came as something of a shock to many Canadians who saw considerable differences in the intents of the two plans. Strategic direction could be given to the Americans for the defence of North America because of their superior numerical strength and because the plan would obviously be instituted only in a time of extreme crisis. But ABC-22 was altogether different: it focused on the prosecution of the war rather than on home defence, which seemed to make unity of command under the Americans unnecessary. Lieutenant-General Maurice Pope, a Canadian member of the PJBD at this time, later recalled his uneasiness over this issue. He felt that the chances of the Royal Navy being destroyed or Britain collapsing were extremely remote, but should this come about, he 'was cheerfully prepared to concur.' But for this to be the case under ABC-22 was another matter: 'At the time Canada *was* at war ... and we were quite happy about the provision we had made for our own local defence. The Americans, on the other hand, were at peace and their expected entry into the war, rather than complicating matters, would simply make our already satisfactory position the more secure. Why, then, at such a juncture they should wish to take control of our defence measures when at the moment we were serenely managing them for ourselves, was more than I could see.'[53]

The Canadian Chiefs of Staff and the CWC held similar opinions, and Colonel Biggar, the Canadian chairman of the PJBD, was instructed to clarify the situation with the Americans. What followed was a series of tension-filled meetings of the PJBD in Washington in which a suitable understanding was reached.[54] Once the American side realized that the Canadians were unwilling to allow command to slip to the United States, they came to see that a system of co-operation was essential.

The final version of ABC-22, dated 28 July 1941, acknowledged the need for compromise: 'Co-ordination of the military effort of the United States and Canada shall be effected by mutual co-operation and by assigning to the forces of each nation tasks for whose execution such forces shall be primarily responsible.' This scheme of 'mutual co-operation' did not preclude the possibility of instituting a unified command at some future date if both sides consented. As for Newfoundland, the Americans and Canadians agreed to support and assist each other in its defence although neither side was given the overall responsibility.[55] This more acceptable version of ABC-22 was discussed by the CWC on several occasions and received approval on 15 October 1941.[56]

Neither side had been given overall command, and the problem for the Canadians and the Americans in Newfoundland now was to make this arrangement work on a day-to-day basis for the duration of the war. This was not always an easy thing to do, and on different occasions both the Newfoundland and American authorities advocated the unification of command. The Canadians consistently rejected this proposal, not because they opposed the idea of a unified command, but because they could not guarantee that the commander of the unified forces would be a Canadian.[57] As a result they scuttled the whole idea of integration.

The command question in Newfoundland was never completely resolved, but by mid-1942 Canadian-American relations in Newfoundland were marked more by a sense of co-operation than by rivalry. By the end of 1942, a joint-defence plan for Newfoundland was drawn up and approved, meeting both the requirements of ABC-22 and the particulars of mutual co-operation in Newfoundland.[58] Furthermore, joint military exercises were undertaken and efforts were made to facilitate the co-ordination of all the forces in Newfoundland.

The tensions between Canada and the United States in Newfoundland were alleviated by the improving war situation. Victory in the Battle of the Atlantic and optimistic news from Europe produced a significant relaxation of tension in Newfoundland. Under these circumstances, mutual co-operation appeared workable, and the cries for unity of command diminished.

Newfoundland had played a prominent role in the defence of North America. When fears of enemy aggression against this continent ran high, Newfoundland had indeed been the focus of considerable attention. But as these fears dissipated, so too did the perceived threat to Newfoundland. This was particularly true in the eyes of the Americans: as the war progressed, their attention was increasingly pulled away from the North Atlantic to more pressing affairs in Europe and the Pacific. This shift in focus was reflected in the curtailment of the American presence in Newfoundland; American strength never reached early predictions, and after 1943 the u.s. forces were pared down considerably, leaving Newfoundland more and more in Canadian hands.

Canada's role in Newfoundland was strengthened almost by default. The gradual withdrawal of the Americans gave the Canadians the opportunity to augment their own position in Newfoundland. This was not, however, accidental; on the contrary, it was a conscious policy of the Canadian government to maintain its position in Newfoundland. This policy was illustrated in 1944 when the Cabinet War Committee decided to follow the advice of the chiefs of staff not to reduce the Canadian garrison in Newfoundland below the level maintained by the Americans.[59]

Canada gained valuable experience and learned many lessons during the early years of the war. The RCN had matured and stepped into a position of prominence in the Battle of the Atlantic. Moreover, the Canadians had recognized the impracticability of contributing men, money, and material to projects in Newfoundland over which they had no control. In the future they would be more firm in securing Canadian rights. Even on the more negative issue of command, the Canadians had played a more determined role – by refusing to submit to American pressure they prevented the deterioration of their position and could maintain a kind of equilibrium with the Americans. In this sense, the refusal to act could be seen as a minor victory.

It was evident that Canadian interest in Newfoundland would not decline as American interest had. Although the war had shifted away from the North Atlantic, Newfoundland's airports continued to play an important role as bases for the ferrying of aircraft overseas. More important, many Canadians had begun to look to the post-war period and to Newfoundland's ultimate destiny. Too much money and effort had been spent to secure Canada's position in Newfoundland and to prevent any other nation from achieving a dominant influence there. And it was no longer questionable whether Newfoundland would continue to be of primary importance to Canada long after the war had ended. For the Canadians, the realization that this was the case grew clearer every day.

5

Goose Bay: 'A fog of misunderstanding'

The creation of the Atlantic ferry route and the subsequent construction of the airport at Goose Bay, Labrador, underlined the strategic importance of Newfoundland and gave the Canadian government the opportunity to put into action the words of the protocol attached to the Leased Bases Agreement. By the end of the war Goose Bay had become the largest and most costly Canadian project in Newfoundland and had played a central part in the ferrying of aircraft and personnel overseas and back home again. It also proved to be the single most perplexing problem between Britain and Canada over the affairs of Newfoundland during the war.

With the signing of the protocol Canadian interest in Newfoundland received international recognition. The early years of the war had seen a tremendous increase in the Canadian presence in Newfoundland: Canadian troops and ships defended the island and Labrador; Canadian bases at Botwood, Torbay, and elsewhere were fortified and expanded; and the RCAF patrolled and protected the surrounding waters. At a very early stage the PJBD had studied the importance of the defence of Newfoundland and in turn had played a significant role as the mechanism through which defence plans were made. Moreover, formal relations between Canada and Newfoundland were enhanced through the establishment of the high commission in St John's, which furnished a direct link between governments.

The question of command remained unsettled, as did the uncertainty concerning the ultimate responsibility for the defence of Newfoundland, but in general the relations between Canada and Newfoundland, and within the North Atlantic Triangle on the subject of Newfoundland, were good. The crisis of war and the concomitant possibilities of invasion and defeat had smoothed over most of the obstacles to co-operation. There was a willingness on all sides to bypass or postpone the immediate conflicts in an effort to meet the greater challenge.

As the war progressed, however, and the fear of invasion subsided, the nature of defence in Newfoundland and the Canadian role in that defence shifted significantly. The initial focus of foreign activities in Newfoundland was of a defensive nature: Newfoundland was perceived as the front line in the defence of North America and had to be protected against enemy attack, an attitude which had produced the Joint Basic Defence Plan–1940. By 1941 much had changed. The Americans were edging towards war, and it was becoming apparent that Britain would not fall. In an effort to meet these changing circumstances, the second PJBD defence plan (ABC-22) was produced. As noted in Chapter 4, ABC-22 was more offensive than the 1940 plan, and it was aimed at bringing the war to the borders of Germany.[1]

The implications for Newfoundland were immense. Under this new plan Newfoundland would play a major role as 'the first line of outposts from which to catapult the invasion of Europe, or it would at least become one of the piers in a vast bridge of ships and planes leading to Britain.'[2] Although the plan was not to come into effect until the United States entered the war, it was clear early in 1941 that the role of Newfoundland was changing. Nowhere was this more evident that in the Atlantic ferry system.

The idea of an 'Atlantic bridge' to link American aircraft production with Britain's war effort emerged early in the war. The British suffered an acute shortage of planes in 1940 and increasingly came to rely on imports from American manufacturers. Flying rather than shipping them across the Atlantic made sense in several ways: the aircraft would not take up valuable cargo space on ships; the risk of loss because of enemy action was reduced; and travel time was cut dramatically.[3] In July 1940 the British Ministry of Aircraft Production organized the Atlantic Ferry Organization (ATFERO) for transporting medium and heavy u.s. bombers from Canada to Scotland via Gander, Newfoundland. The first shipment of seven Lockheed Hudsons departed for the United Kingdom on 11 November 1940.[4]

Over the following months ATFERO's organizational difficulties were ironed out and plans were drawn up to greatly expand the entire system. The route, as it existed in 1940, had severe drawbacks in that it was suitable for long-range bombers only and was at the mercy of unpredictable weather. Moreover, with the passage of lend-lease in April 1941, the number of available aircraft jumped, and the existing route became increasingly inadequate in the face of the growing American role. A multi-stage ferry route to meet the demands of shorter-range fighter aircraft became the topic of joint British-American staff talks in the spring of 1941.[5]

The framework for the expanded Atlantic ferry route called for bases at key locations in Newfoundland, Greenland, and Iceland, to act as stepping-stones for the transfer of the aircraft. The British had constructed bases in Iceland in 1940 and another hurdle was overcome with the Danish-American agreement of April 1941 permitting the United States to establish bases on Greenland. Surveys were undertaken and construction of two bases began during the summer of 1941. The first, at Narsarssuak (Bluie West 1), was near the southern tip of the island, and the second, at Söndre Strömfjord (Bluie West 8), and 450 miles farther up the coast. From Newfoundland to Bluie 1 was less than 800 miles as was the distance from Bluie 1 to Reykjavik, Iceland. The final leg of the trip, from Reykjavik to Prestwick, was a further 840 miles.[6]

At first, the airport at Gander was the Newfoundland link in the Atlantic ferry chain. But as plans for an expanded system grew in 1941 so, too, did the need for an alternative airport to relieve the congestion at Gander and to provide a more direct route for short-range aircraft. As early as March 1941 talks began between American, Canadian, and British officials concerning the need for a second base in addition to Gander, preferably in Labrador or northern Quebec.[7] As a result of these talks both Canada and the United States agreed to undertake surveys of Labrador and northeastern Canada that spring. The search for a Labrador airbase had begun.[8]

For the Americans, Elliot Roosevelt, the son of the president, was given the job of surveyor. He had put in for overseas duty but had ended up as an intelligence officer in the 21st Reconnaissance Squadron, stationed in Newfoundland. Roosevelt was less than enthusiastic about life in Newfoundland, which he described as 'miserable, muddy, bleak, and woebegone, all rolled into one,' and grabbed at the chance for a change of scenery. As he later described it, 'operating as much as anything on the theory that nothing could be more unpleasant than Newfoundland in March of 1941, I volunteered for a survey job to locate air-force sites in the North Arctic area.'[9]

During the first week of June Roosevelt met with Canadian officers at RCAF Headquarters in Ottawa. After receiving assurances of RCAF co-operation he began his survey along the Labrador coast. His instructions were to survey northern Labrador and Quebec, Baffin Island, and the Northwest River area in Labrador, where it was felt that the most suitable site for a base would be. By August his party had located the sites for what later became the three Crystal weather stations as well as conducting other surveys, including the Northwest River–Goose Bay area.[10]

On the Canadian side the responsibility for surveying the Northwest River area was given to Eric Fry, a dominion land surveyor in the Bureau of Geology and Topography. Fry was aided in his search by information given by F.T. Jenkins, the superintendent of aerial surveys for Canadian Pacific Airlines. Years before, in 1935, Jenkins had undertaken a timber survey for a British pulp and paper company and had mapped the Labrador watershed including the area around Northwest River and Goose Bay. Jenkins had found few spots in Labrador that were both level and free of muskeg and he recommended the Northwest River area as the best possible site. He had surveyed this area on foot and found it to be well drained and level, and felt that it could be easily cleared of trees.[11]

Fry landed at Northwest River on 16 June 1941, after being held up in Newfoundland by bad weather for almost a week. Expecting to be in the area for several months he was surprised to find a sutable site after only a few days. He described what he called the 'Goose Bay' site as a 'large raised bench, over three miles in length and one mile in depth, standing higher than the rest of the surrounding country, its surface being some one hundred and twenty feet above sea-level, and its northeastern or nearest edge just one mile southwest from the western shore of Terrington Basin, the western extremity of Goose Bay.' No other location could match this one and in Fry's words it was 'the only logical site for airport construction in the district'[12] Roosevelt and Fry sent favourable reports to their respective governments, advocating the selection of the Goose Bay site for the new airbase.[13]

While the surveys were being conducted discussions concerning the need for a new base continued. On 29 July the PJBD met in Washington to discuss the need for a new airbase, and it recommended 'that the Canadian government should undertake the construction of an airbase in the vicinity of Northwest River, Labrador.' The board itemized the facilities that would be needed, including two runways (a minimum of 150 by 5,000 feet), storage facilities for 450,000 gallons of gas and 11,250 gallons of oil, a meteorological station and other technical equipment, and housing for the thousands of personnel that would be brought to Goose Bay.[14]

In recognition of Canadian interests in Newfoundland the responsibility for building the airbase had been given to the Canadian government. It seems unlikely that any other possibility had been considered, but it was noted that should the Canadians decline 'for any reason,' then the United States would be 'invited to provided the necessary facilities in the area under reference.'[15]

The recommendation still had to be approved and it was discussed at the cwc meeting on 13 August. There was little chance that a negative decision would result; only a few weeks earlier Prime Minister King had 'agreed that all steps necessary should be taken to keep Newfoundland within the Canadian orbit.'[16] Also, the Americans would build the airport if Canada did not act and they were unwilling to split the responsibility or the cost. In light of this and the previous Canadian actions in Newfoundland, and the aversion for spending on projects without having effective control of them, there could be only one decision. The cwc decided that Canada would build the necessary facilities at Goose Bay, at an estimated cost of $4–5 million, of which, according to C.G. Power, 'not more than one million [dollars] would be needed in the current year.'[17]

The wheels had already been put into motion. Earlier in the month the Newfoundland Commission of Government had granted permission for more extensive surveys of the proposed site.[18] By 26 August the surveys were completed and the Canadian government approached the Commission of Government for formal approval for the use of the site. In response the governor informed Mackenzie King that Newfoundland had no objections in principle to the proposed Canadian actions but reminded the Canadians that 'the question of the control and operation of the Airport during and after the war especially in regard to use for commercial purpose will have to be settled in good time.'[19]

Construction began in September 1941. The contract to build was given to the MacNamara Construction Co. of Toronto which at that time was already doing work at Torbay, near St John's. For William Durrell, the general superintendent of construction, the project was twofold: he was to have temporary facilities ready for use that winter as well as constructing the permanent airbase. Working day and night paid off, for by 3 November three 7,000-foot runways were ready for use.

At the same time as the construction at Goose Bay began the Canadian government gave the United States permission to build meteorological stations on three sites in northern Canada that the Roosevelt party had surveyed earlier that year. The 'Crystal stations,' as they came to be called, were to observe and report the weather, information which would give a tremendous boost to the success of the ferry system. The first station was located at Fort Chimo (Crystal 1) in northern Quebec, the second was on Frobisher Bay (Crystal 2), and the third was across Baffin Island on Padloping Island (Crystasl 3).[20] By the end of 1941 the Crystal stations and the temporary runways at Goose Bay were in operation.

Construction continued in 1942; with the entrance of the United States into the war, the burden on Goose Bay and the Atlantic ferry system was increased dramatically. In response, Canadian plans for Goose Bay were enlarged in an effort to meet the needs of the changing war situation. Two of the permanent runways were widened to 1,100 feet and another was widened to 1,600 feet. All were paved with a 200-foot-wide cement strip. Plans were introduced for five additional hangars and accommodation for 5,000 RCAF and USAAF personnel and up to 3,000 civilians hired for construction purposes. Because of the isolation of Goose Bay, everything needed to survive in a harsh environment had to be built or brought in. The list was extensive and included a bakery, laundry, sewage-disposal plant, wireless and signal station, heating and pumping station, docks for four ocean-going vessels at one time, plus provision for all the administrative needs of a small community, not to mention more than thirty miles of roads.[21]

In April the first small detachment of U.S. personnel was stationed at Goose Bay. Minor frictions with the Canadians erupted and in July the Americans received permission to establish their own accommodation buildings. Each group built its own 150-bed hospital as well. By November the U.S. garrison had moved into new quarters on the opposite side of the field from the Canadians. While accommodations had been built to hold up to 1,000 permanent and 1,200 transient personnel, the U.S. garrison numbered 325 at the end of 1942.[22]

During periods of bad weather the Atlantic flights were delayed, and when the weather cleared there tended to be a surge of planes through the airport. In these times there was an extra crush put on Goose Bay. To deal with this problem and to try to overcome the isolation and boredom of life at the airbase, movie theatres, recreational halls, and bowling alleys were built for use by the troops. One small indication of the size of the task was that 4,500 packs of cigarettes had to be imported every day. Other diversions included hiking and various winter sports, and the occasional USO show. For the more unorthodox there was always ramming trees with a bren-gun carrier or spraying cold water on unsuspecting visitors in the Swedish bath.[23]

On Saturday nights the RCAF mess was transformed into the 'Rat Race,' a weekly dance. There were few women at Goose, and the small number of female nurses were in great demand on these occasions. Trouble sometimes erupted when servicemen became involved with the families of local workers who were employed on the base. Eventually efforts were made to isolate the local population on the base from the servicemen.[24]

Not surprisingly, as the requirements for the base escalated, so did the costs. By the time construction had been completed the bill had far surpassed original estimates. As of 31 March 1945 the Canadian government had invested $25,382,526 in the Goose Bay airbase and its facilities – more than that spent on the Gander airport and the Botwood seaplane base combined.[25] But the numbers for the ferry system were equally impressive: 722 planes were ferried in 1941; 1,163 in 1942; 1,450 in 1943; and 8,641 in 1944.

The construction and operation of the Goose Bay airbase was a magnificent achievement. Against tremendous odds a small city had been transplanted into the wilderness in a matter of months. John Chadwick of the Dominions Office reported to London that the 'airport lies in completely uninhabited territory, and the shock to the traveller in coming upon it must be as great as if he found the Ritz Hotel in the middle of the Kalahari desert.'[26] A.P. Herbert, a member of the British Goodwill Mission sent to investigate conditions in Newfoundland, was also impressed with the base built on a 'vast plateau designed by God.' He could not help but wonder what effect such a large expenditure of money would have on future developments in Newfoundland: 'This is the way to do things – if you have the money. Our dear Treasury would faint if they saw the place ... Our poor Dominions Office may well inquire how they are to teach the virtues of economy and the philosophy of "go slow" to the simple Newfoundlander if these younger countries will fling their money about in this way.'[27] To the traveller arriving at night Goose Bay was no less of a spectacle: 'After five years of black-out in London,' wrote Vincent Massey, 'it was an extraordinary experience to see this brilliantly lit community shining out of the black wilderness below us. All the hangars were blazing with light and the snow was glistening for hundreds of yards around them.'[28]

In many ways Goose Bay was a good example of the ability of nations to submerge national interests in a common effort and for common goals. But the long-term questions remained. Over the next two years Goose Bay continued to be the subject of troublesome squabbling between allies; disputes over long-term control, international usage, and post-war civil-aviation rights steadily eroded the international co-operation so much in evidence during 1940–2. The Atlantic ferry system was a success and the challenges of geography, nature, and war had been met, but the real debate had just begun.

II

The Canadian government's decision to move ahead on the construction of Goose Bay overlooked the long-term effects in favour of expediency; clearly these problems (over the length of the lease, property rights, jurisdiction, use of civil aircraft, etc.) would have to be dealt with eventually. Preliminary conversations had taken place in Newfoundland between Canadian officials and members of the Commission of Government soon after construction had begun. Naturally, little was settled at first, but the framework for future discussions was established. By the spring of 1942 a draft agreement was being circulated to the departments of External Affairs, National Defence, and Transport, and over the next few months discussions continued and various amendments were proposed.

The process was a slow one, and it was not until 16 September 1942 that a draft agreement was presented to the Cabinet War Committee by C.G. Power. The basic outline of the agreement consisted of the following: Canada was to receive a 99-year lease on approximately 160 square miles of territory and the right to construct the necessary buildings and equipment and to use local sources of timber, rock, sand, and water within a determined radius. For the duration of the war 'and for such time thereafter as the Governments may deem necessary or advisable in the interests of common defence,' Goose Bay would be an RCAF base. The base would also be open for use by the RAF and USAAF but they would not be allowed to erect buildings or station troops there without Canadian permission. Civil aviation would be restricted to traffic considered to be 'a necessary part of the war effort,' and Canada would agree not to transfer any of these rights to a third party without Newfoundland's consent.[29]

On the above points there was general agreement in the CWC. The only major objection was made by C.D. Howe, the minister of munitions and supply. Howe was extremely concerned over the question of civil aviation and was already looking to the post-war aviation world and Canada's place in it. Aware of the future potential of Goose Bay, Howe was opposed to any stipulation in the agreement that might preclude Canadian post-war use of Goose Bay for commercial aviation. Thus, after further discussion the CWC agreed to delete or amend the offending clause. The amended version of clause 5 given to the Commission of Government read: 'The question of the continuance after the war of the rights referred to in paragraph 4 [i.e., military and civil-aviation rights] will form the subject of discussion between the Government of Canada and the Government of Newfoundland and this discussion will take place not later than twelve months after the conclusion of the war.'[30]

Post-war rights were also a problem for the Newfoundland Commission of Government. The draft agreement was studied by a committee of four commissioners and they suggested holding a conference with C.J. Burchell, the Canadian high commissioner, to discuss it further. As the delays mounted, the commissioners reflected on what the proposed agreement would mean for Newfoundland. Questions were raised about why the Canadians needed 160 square miles of territory, especially when the base was located in an isolated area in an allied country. Moreover, there was some apprehension that if the Goose Bay site was the only suitable area for a base, then the Newfoundlanders might be giving the Canadians a future monopoly on transatlantic commercial flight.[31]

The meeting proposed in October 1942 did not assemble until 26 January 1943 in St John's. There was general agreement on much of the draft lease concerning construction, use of natural resources, and other arrangements. The Canadians had decreased the requested amount of territory to 120 square miles, and both sides agreed that a 99-year lease would be suitable. As for civil-aviation rights, the Newfoundlanders wanted it more clearly stated that the Canadians could not use Goose Bay for civil-aviation purposes after the war without first consulting the Newfoundland government. A decision on this point was deferred until the Newfoundlanders could work out an acceptable rewording.[32]

A new draft was presented to the Canadians within a week. This draft embodied the agreed points and included a clause protecting Newfoundland's use of the base and postponed a decision on civil-aviation rights until Canadian-Newfoundland talks were held after the war.[33] These changes were made more to reassure the Newfoundland government than to infringe on Canadian rights, and they were accepted by the Canadians. 'It is trusted that in view of the concurrence of the competent Canadian authorities,' Norman Robertson, the under secretary of state for external affairs, wrote to Burchell, 'it will be possible to secure its signature in the near future.'[34] On the surface it appeared that all the problems had been ironed out and that the completion of the agreement was a certainty.

The Commission of Government reported back to London on these developments, but the response of the Dominions Office was not enthusiastic.[35] The Dominions Office suspected that the Canadians were trying to establish themselves at Goose Bay while at the same time excluding all others. Furthermore, even though civil aviation was to be decided at the end of the war, 'possession is nine-tenths of the law, and if when such discussions open Canada is already established with a 99 year lease of the only suitable landing ground in Labrador, even with rights of user limited to defence purposes only, Newfoundland's negotiating position may be so weak as to prejudice seriously prospects of securing satisfactory agreement with Canadians in regard to civil flying.'[36] In their view the Canadians should be allowed a lease on only sixty square miles, the other sixty to revert back to Newfoundland at the end of the war.

After further reflection the Dominions Office added a significant amendment to the proposed draft. Concerning clause 5 they suggested, 'We should like to see this clause extended to include other British as well as Newfoundland aircraft, i.e., we would propose that it should be amended to read: "All British Civil and Military aircraft shall have the right to use the airbase on terms not less favourable than those of the Government of Canada." This would help to safeguard our right to use the airfield after the war.'[37] The Dominions Office recognized the importance of this agreement, a point that was reinforced when it suggested that the negotiations be taken out of the hands of the Canadian high commissioner in Newfoundland and be transferred to Ottawa, where UK officials could directly 'assist.'[38]

In the meantime Squadron-Leader H.A.L. Pattison (RAF), the director of civil aviation in Newfoundland, was sent to Labrador to investigate the situation and report his findings to St John's and then to London. This, of course, led to further delays, which the Canadians found increasingly irritating. In Ottawa, suspicions were growing that the British were using Goose Bay for their own advantage. In a secret letter to Vincent Massey, the Canadian high commissioner in London, Robertson voiced his concerns:

I have an uneasy feeling that somebody in the Dominions Office or the Air Ministry may be toying with the idea that our defective title to the Goose Bay airport may be used for bargaining purposes in the discussion of post-war civil aviation. I am sure this would be a very dangerous card for the United Kingdom to think of playing, given the general relations between our two countries and the special complications introduced by the position in Newfoundland. The suggestion that the United Kingdom is using its control over Newfoundland and indirectly Newfoundland's control over Labrador (which is a fairly recent development) to put pressure on the Canadian Government in the general field of civil aviation, is full of thoroughly mischievous possibilities, which need no elaboration.[39]

Massey was instructed to take the issue of delay up with the British government. Within a week he had met with Clement Attlee, the dominions secretary, but unfortunately the British were less than forthcoming. Attlee reminded the Canadian government that the British and the Commission of Government were 'in the position of trustees for future Governments of Newfoundland,' and as such had to proceed with caution.[40] Furthermore, without a detailed examination of the situation it would be difficult to come to any sure conclusion. The Canadians would just have to be patient.

Fortunately, they did not have long to wait. On 10 July the government of Newfoundland informed the Dominions Office that Pattison had finished his investigation and reported that it would be necessary to give the Canadians both 120 square miles of territory and a 99-year lease. To argue for 60 square miles rather than 120 as the Dominions Office had suggested would have little effect on public opinion in Newfoundland but could jeopardize the negotiations with the Canadians. In addition, Pattison claimed to have seen other suitable sites outside the area under discussion.[41] Interestingly, the Commission of Government had supported the Canadian side over the Dominions Office.

The Dominions Office was convinced by these comments and gave its consent to proceed. The Newfoundland government was informed as was the Canadian high commissioner in London. When Massey wired the news to Ottawa he noted that the agreement would be concluded along the lines agreed to earlier that year. But he also mentioned that there were 'certain drafting points which the Newfoundland Govern-ment will be taking up but these relate for the most part to matters of detail which the U.K. authorities imagine will not give rise to any difficulties.'[42]

These 'certain drafting points' of which Massey was not yet aware were considerably more than 'matters of detail.' The new draft contained those amendments suggested by the Dominions Office to the Commission of Government in May 1943. The most important of these was the inclusion in clause 5 of 'All British civil and military aircraft' in place of just Newfoundland aircraft, giving the use of Goose Bay 'in terms not less favourable than those of the Government of Canada.' Despite their innocuous appearance these changes provoked immediate opposition from the Canadians. In their view British rights for the duration of the war were protected under clause 3 which gave the RAF and USAAF use of the airbase. The only explanation for the change in clause 5 therefore was an attempt by the British to ensure a place for their civil and military aircraft for the whole ninety-nine years of the lease.

The new proposals came before the Cabinet War Committee on 20 August. Secretary of the cabinet A.D.P. Heeney reviewed the situation and noted that to change clause 5 in this manner 'would be a major commitment with regard to postwar aviation which, at an earlier stage, had been agreed should be left to discussions after the war.' In addition, he continued, this 'would open the whole question of postwar access to air bases constructed in Canada by the United States and would create the impression in the United States of an agreed Commonwealth policy.' Finally, the United Kingdom did not appear to be offering anything in return for these concessions. There was no dissent in the War Committee and it was agreed that the change was unacceptable and that the high commissioner in London should 'take the matter up strongly' with the British government.[43]

Massey was informed of the committee's decision and was instructed to act. On 25 August he sent a lengthy letter to Attlee in which he reminded him that the decision to reserve the resolution of post-war rights until after the war had been included on Britain's insistence, and now they wanted to change all this. He reiterated the issues raised in the War Committee and argued that to revise clause 5 would unsettle relations with the United States and could possibly jeopardize the outcome of international discussions on civil aviation.[44]

The response of the Dominions Office was equally firm. There was a willingness to replace the words 'all British' with 'United Kingdom and Newfoundland' which would restrict use by other British countries such as Australia and New Zealand, but otherwise things should stand as they were. Attlee argued that because the United Kingdom controlled Newfoundland 'any lease granted by the Newfoundland Government to

Canada should provide for the equal treatment of United Kingdom with Canadian aircraft in the area to be leased.' As for equivalent rights in return, this 'would seem only to arise if we were seeking equality of treatment with Canadian aircraft on Canadian territory, which of course is not the case.' He also brushed aside Canadian fears that acquiescence to the amended clause would spark American claims for equal treatment in their bases. In his view there could 'hardly be any valid parallel between our seeking these rights in an airfield in territory for which we are responsible, and the United States Government pressing for similar rights at airfields in British territory.'[45]

Canadian concern on this last issue was very real and could not be so easily allayed. Norman Robertson had earlier written Massey that despite Canada's strong position in Newfoundland, its whole case 'would be weakened' if it was publicized that the American-used bases in Canada would be reverting to Canadian control after the war – a situation not desired by Canada vis-à-vis Goose Bay. Consequently he argued for a fast conclusion to the whole affair. Moreover, to seemingly give to the United Kingdom post-war rights that had been denied to the Americans in their bases could only stir up more trouble and delay.[46]

All these factors stiffened the Canadian resistance to the proposed British changes and increased their resolve to come to a swift completion of the lease. Late in September, Vincent Massey, with the support of a long telegram from Ottawa, discussed the situation with Sir Eric Machtig and Alexander Clutterbuck, two senior officials in the Dominions Office. Machtig assured Massey that the British were not looking for special status in civil aviation, but as things stood the United Kingdom did have a special relationship with Newfoundland. Massey gave his opinion that the real problem was over the use of civil aircraft only, not military aircraft, and after discussing it Machtig and Clutterbuck agreed to suggest to the Air Ministry that the amended clause cover only military aircraft. Massey wrongly believed that this would be acceptable to the Canadian government, and reported this development to Ottawa.[47]

On 30 September the cwc rejected both the British proposal to replace 'British' with 'United Kingdom' and the possibility of limiting the wording to only military aircraft, arguing that it left the main Canadian objection unanswered. Mackenzie King had revealed strong feelings since the start of the war about maintaining a hold on Newfoundland and he added that 'the amendment might lead to serious complications if Newfoundland should ultimately decide to enter Confederation, since, in that event, Canada would be faced with long term commitments to the United Kingdom.'[48] In cabinet the possibility of Confederation was a common theme but rarely, if ever, was this sentiment conveyed to the British as an explanation for Canadian moves. But, as long as Newfoundland's future remained uncertain the Canadian government would guard its position jealously, against all encroachments.

Massey was informed of this decision and was told to bring it to the attention of the British authorities. King's instructions were simple: 'Please use your best efforts to bring this matter to an early conclusion.'[49] This was no small order. On 24 September Attlee had been replaced as dominions secretary by Lord Cranborne, but no noticeable change in policy on the topic of Goose Bay was immediately forthcoming. In a letter to Massey, Cranborne expressed his disappointment over the failure to arrive at a settlement, but this did not indicate a softening of Britain's position; it was more a recognition of stalemate. 'As a result of the telegram received from your Government we are now back where we were,' he wrote, 'and I can only suggest that the whole matter should now stand over for personal discussion with Mr Howe when he arrives here for the general Civil Aviation talks.'[50]

Howe was travelling to London for Commonwealth discussions on civil aviation, an attempt by Britain to work out some kind of unified policy before meeting the Americans in a truly international conference. Howe supported a more independent role for Canada and was keenly aware of Canada's unique position and importance in the world of aviation. He would not submit easily to the machinations of the British, including the talks on Goose Bay: to give Britain post-war rights in Newfoundland before anything else was settled could prove harmful to Canada's own plans for transatlantic flight.[51]

A meeting of the two sides was held in Cranborne's office in the House of Lords on 20 October 1943. In addition to Cranborne and Howe, the meeting included Massey, Machtig, Clutterbuck, Sir Arthur Street from the Air Ministry, and Sir Wilfrid Woods, a member of the Newfoundland Commission of Government. The discussion revolved around several 'new' amendments presented to Howe by Cranborne. These proposals reflected little real change of position: clause 5 would pertain solely to UK and Newfoundland military aircraft, and a new clause would be added reserving a decision on UK civil aircraft until post-war talks between the three governments could deal with the issue.[52] Howe left the meeting, agreeing to discuss the proposals with his colleagues.[53]

Howe left the impression in London that the main opposition to the British proposals came from the Department of External Affairs. In many ways this as an accurate observation, for the main drive to settle Goose Bay on Canadian terms came from that department. The central official on the Canadian side was Norman Robertson, and with him a handful of officials, including R.A. MacKay, Arnold Heeney, C.J. Burchell, and Hugh Keenleyside, determined the major thrust of Canadian policy. In the Cabinet War Committee, Robertson or Heeney would outline new developments concerning Goose Bay and then propose the Canadian response. The cwc rarely disagreed or questioned these suggestions, and for the most part agreement was given immediately. Of the cabinet ministers only Howe and Mackenzie King showed a continuing interest in the talks. After the airport had begun to operate, Power's interest in having a signed agreement declined, while the others showed little apparent interest in the negotiations.

Howe's overriding concern was civil aviation, and, although he appeared eager at all times to cut through red tape and to settle the differences with the British, he was extremely reluctant to give them post-war rights. During the London meeting he had 'half seriously' argued that the British were trying to get an airbase for free, with Newfoundland making the land available and Canada paying for it.[54] For those in London it became increasingly clear that Howe was not the best channel through which to put their case. A few weeks later Clutterbuck reflected that the Howe talks may 'have hindered rather than helped us,' and that it appeared 'essential in the first instance to put ourselves right with the Department of External Affairs, who may have felt that we were out to appeal to Canadian Ministers over their heads.'[55]

As both prime minister and minister for external affairs, Mackenzie King was directly connected with the negotiations from their inception. On the surface King appeared cautious and reluctant to force the issue, but with regard to Goose Bay and relations with Newfoundland in general, King, more than any other minister, exhibited a firm determination to secure Canada's position. King was particularly sensitive to the problems in dealing with Newfoundland and was at all times conscious of the long-term implications of Canadian policy. Time and again he reminded the cabinet of the need to keep Newfoundland within the Canadian orbit and to safeguard Canada's interests there. In addition, King and Robertson seemed to understand each other very well on this issue and together they were the overseers of Canada's part in the talks.

On Howe's return to Ottawa the Cranborne proposals were studied and discussed at the CWC meeting on 3 November, but there was little chance that they would be found acceptable. Robertson told the ministers that these new proposals had changed nothing and that the whole affair 'had been further complicated by an enquiry received from the United States as to commitments regarding postwar use of the base.' Howe suggested that Canada take no action, and instead should rely on a general international air agreement to settle the question of civil aviation. No one had a better solution to the deadlock. The War Committee again rejected the British amendments and decided to adopt a wait-and-see attitude.[56]

In the meantime, enquiries had been made by the Americans, in both Ottawa and St John's. The State Department had been left pretty much in the dark during these negotiations, having to be satisfied with promises of a copy of the agreement when it was completed and by assurances from External Affairs that the Canadians were not taking advantage of the situation.[57] In St John's, George D. Hopper, the American consul-general in Newfoundland, put out feelers of his own, and after speaking with a number of members of the Commission of Government, he reported his impressions back to Washington. The Canadians had made a decision, he suggested, probably because of the better weather conditions, to emphasize their role in Goose Bay. 'It is argued that Canada may be quite willing to relinquish rights in Newfoundland after the war,' he wrote, but was 'inclined to press firmly for monopoly in Labrador. Newfoundland should therefore keep her weather-eye on the future of Goose airport which is evidently the big stake for which Canada is playing.'[58]

The stalemate in the talks was unbearable for the Canadians, especially in light of the increasing uneasiness of the Americans. Perhaps, suggested Burchell, it would be better to reopen the talks through St John's and the Commission of Government again, since direct talks with the Dominions Office had ended in failure. More important, Burchell had reported a conversation with Sir Wilfrid Woods in which Woods mentioned that he had reason to believe that the Dominions Office had changed its position somewhat and was now willing to allow both military- and civil-aviation decisions to be put off until the end of the war, provided that the United Kingdom be included in these talks.[59] Also, Woods and most of the other commissioners were in agreement with the Canadian position. Burchell's idea seemed to be a good one and he was instructed by Ottawa to start up talks with Woods as soon as possible.[60]

Meanwhile in London, Vincent Massey was growing impatient. Following the October meeting with Cranborne he had informed Ottawa and 'had since awaited information as to whether the amendments then suggested were acceptable.' No instructions arrived from Ottawa and everything had ground to a halt: 'Unfortunately a fog of misunderstanding seems to have enveloped the discussion of this question and I feel every effort should be made to dissipate it as soon as possible.'[61]

The fog appeared to be thickest around Canada House. Both Massey and Cranborne put the blame for the delay on the Canadian government, and in many ways they were correct. Following the CWC meeting on 3 December, Massey was not informed of any decision. As Hugh Keenleyside put it, 'you should have been informed at the time, but I find that unfortunately you were not.'[62] It was early January 1944 before Massey was brought up to date on the latest developments. But Massey's disquiet stemmed from a deeper source. On 10 June he recorded in his diary: 'We seem to be pedantic, suspicious, legalistic and even uncivil in our approach to the Government here on this subject ... I don't see what will break the impasse which turns on our unwillingness to allow for the use of the aerodrome by British military aircraft for the duration of the lease, on the ground that the Americans might claim the same privilege.'[63]

He later reflected that a solution would be found following a 'return to reasonableness' on Canada's part.[64] Massey never seemed to fully appreciate his government's stand on Goose Bay and tended to view Canadian forcefulness as intransigence. In his memoirs he used Goose Bay as an example of what he called the 'Anglo-Canadian problem,' a needless set of circumstances sparked by 'a compound of supicion and querulousness' in Ottawa.[65] Lack of information undoubtedly hindered the effectiveness of his role, but apart from this he often appeared more in tune with the British authorities, especially on the key issue of post-war rights.

The resumption of the old channel of discussion through St John's proved to be no faster. By the end of February 1944 no new developments had surfaced and Hugh Keenleyside, who had replaced Burchell as acting high commissioner, became increasingly concerned over the deteriorating situation in St John's. In a dispatch to Ottawa he noted that Woods was at a loss to explain the lack of action by the Dominions Office, and he explained the effects of the delay: 'In the meantime the situation here is deteriorating. In the press, but even more in private discussions, it is hinted and in some quarters even taken for granted that the Commission of Government has given way to Canadian pressure, has sold out Newfoundland rights, and is afraid to make the terms public because they are so detrimental to Newfoundland interests ... there is a tendency here to think that the United Kingdom is attempting to defend Newfoundland rights against the complacency of the Commission of Government and the avarice of Canada.' His advice was to apply 'whatever pressure is necessary' on London to find a solution.[66]

Burchell had been assigned as the new Canadian high commissioner in South Africa, but before taking up his new position he met with Cranborne in London on 1 March 1944. Burchell brought up Goose Bay but could get no response from Cranborne who appeared to be more interested in the effects of the speech made in Toronto by Lord Halifax, the British ambassador in Washington. Cranborne gave no sign of changing policy along the lines hinted at by Woods a few weeks earlier.[67] Burchell also met with Beaverbrook while in London and left with the impression that he and Cranborne were the ones responsible for blocking the lease.[68]

The view from London was, of course, different. The Dominions Office had a genuine interest in doing its best for Newfoundland and naturally looked out for its own interests as well. In the case of Goose Bay it was important not to allow the Canadians too much control because once in they would never get out – and this, it was felt, was not in the interests of either Newfoundland or the United Kingdom. John Chadwick of the Dominions Office expressed this feeling after seeing Goose Bay first hand. The Canadians, he wrote, were obviously 'thinking very hard about post war aviation,' and added that they 'have not merely sent men up here for the good of their health or to fly bombers across the Atlantic. They know that Goose Bay may be the controlling factor in Trans/Atlantic flying, and they are determined to sweep the board with Gander if they can. What is of cardinal importance is that we safeguard our own – and Newfoundland's – post war civilian interest to the uttermost.'[69]

The British position on Goose Bay evolved from discussions between the Dominions Office and the Air Ministry, and was fairly straightforward. P.A. Clutterbuck outlined the three basic goals of the United Kingdom in a lengthy departmental memo, dated 27 January 1944. The first was to secure military rights for the United Kingdom for the length of the lease, the second was to ensure that British civil aircraft receive equal rights with the Canadians after the war, and the third was to obtain complete equality between Newfoundland's and Canada's military and civil aircraft for the duration of the lease. In Clutterbuck's view these objectives were 'inherently reasonable' but because the efforts to secure them had reached an impasse, he suggested that 'our aim should now be to thrash matters out by friendly discussion, through which our case could be fully put to the right quarters in Ottawa.'[70] By 'right quarters' Clutterbuck meant the Department of External Affairs in general and Normal Robertson in particular.

The Dominions Office reflected this view, under both Attlee and Cranborne. And then there was Beaverbrook, back in the War Cabinet as Lord Privy Seal. More than anyone else in the British government, Beaverbrook fought to maintain the British position on the Goose Bay issue. In November 1943 the reports of the Goodwill Mission came up for discussion in the British War Cabinet, and dominion status for Newfoundland had found a new champion in Beaverbrook. In a memorandum prepared for the cabinet Beaverbrook argued that Newfoundland was again self-supporting and should be offered back its dominion status. This, he noted, 'would be a protection against Canada's unjust claim over Goose Bay and the pretensions which the United States will advance to civil air bases in Newfoundland.' He concluded: 'With Dominion status, Newfoundland will safeguard our Imperial interests in the Western Atlantic against any "ganging up" by Canada and the United States, always a possibility under a different Government.'[71]

Beaverbrook proposed this line at the meeting of the War Cabinet on 19 November 1943 but was overruled by Cranborne who felt that a decision on the future of Newfoundland should be left until after the war.[72] In a letter to Cranbone a few days after the cabinet meeting Beaverbrook argued that only Newfoundland could give away civil-aviation rights.[73] Cranborne was more flexible than Beaverbrook, feeling that Newfoundland would be better off as a part of Canada.[74] After a further attempt by Beaverbrook to have the discussions postponed until after responsible government had been reinstated in Newfoundland, Cranborne replied to Beaverbrook that he did not think he could keep the Canadians waiting very much longer. Further delays of this nature, Cranborne wrote to Beaverbrook, could only aggravate relations with the Canadians and might lead them to feel that, 'having received the benefits of the hard work and hard cash they [the Canadians] have put into the project, we are now seeking to stall on the fulfillment of our part of the bargain.' The result of such action would be pressure from the Canadians for an immediate conclusion of the agreement, 'which is the last thing that either of us want.'[75] The best they could hope for, he felt, was a postponement of the talks until after the war had ended. Beaverbrook gave his concurrence to this plan and the Dominions Office instructed High Commissioner Malcolm MacDonald to take this up with the Canadians.

On 10 March MacDonald left a memorandum for Norman Robertson containing the new initiative. The old wording was gone; instead there was the proposal that the talks be scrapped until the end of the war, to be taken up by the governments of Canada, Newfoundland, and the United Kingdom. It was hoped that by then many of the civil-aviation questions would have been cleared up, facilitating a quick completion of the lease.

This was a new proposition, but it was equally unacceptable to the Canadian government. R.A. MacKay noted that this new course would probably intensify the already strong suspicions of Canadian policy harboured by many Newfoundlanders. It might also lead to questions in the House of Commons and press concerning Goose Bay and the failure to obtain a lease, which would be embarrassing. Moreover, not having a lease would put Canada in a very weak position once the war was over. In fact, no confirming acts had been passed in St John's dealing with the Canadian bases, and as it stood, Canada had no titles to anything in Newfoundland.[76]

The Canadian position was further elaborated on by MacKay in a second memorandum. To postpone a decision could possibly seriously harm Canadian-Newfoundland relations and lead to embarrassing questions in Canada. The new proposal was unfair because Canada had invested millions of dollars in the airbase and had agreed to safeguard Newfoundland's interests from the start. Second, it was against Canadian policy to make commitments to anyone else concerning post-war rights in bases in Canada, and although Goose Bay was not actually in Canada it was 'no less vital to Canada's defence arrangements than air bases in Canadian territory.' Third, Canada was willing to have the United Kingdom be a party to the post-war discussions on civil aviation but refused to permit post-war military rights to be written into the lease. Essentially, the United Kingdom could receive post-war rights, both civil and military, but only through the post-war discussions, after a lease had been signed.[77] Finally, the Commission of Government was eager to pass a confirming act to deal with all the properties obtained by Canada in Newfoundland. It was felt that a single act rather than several would be less likely to spark public criticism against the commission, and therefore, it had become imperative to have the Goose Bay question settled immediately, before the act went through.[78]

The Cabinet War Committee agreed with the thrust of MacKay's memos. These points formed the basis of a note given to Malcolm MacDonald with the Canadian government's response to the British suggestion to put off signing a lease until after the war was over. A meeting between Robertson, Massey, and Cranborne during the Prime Minister's Conference later that spring had failed to produce anything but now the Canadians made a new offer to postpone the question of post-war military and civil use of the airport until after the war. Two new clauses were proposed: first, a new clause to follow number 5: 'The right of the United Kingdom to use the base for military aircraft shall be the subject of consultation and agreement between the Governments of Canada, the United Kingdom and Newfoundland after the war, and in the meantime the rights of the United Kingdom under Article 3 of this Agreement shall continue unimpaired.' Second, a new last sentence to clause 10 to read: 'The question of its use for civil and commercial operations after the war, and all matters incidental thereto, will form the subject of discussion between the Governments of Canada, the United Kingdom and Newfoundland, and this discussion will take place not later than twelve months after the war.'[79] This way the Canadians would get their lease without making promises to the United Kingdom about post-war rights, while assuring the British that they would be consulted before any decisions were made.

The Canadians did not let the matter drop; on the contrary, they intensified their pressure on the British. On 3 July Robertson and Heeney met with MacDonald and again stressed the Canadian position. In addition, Robertson said that the Canadian ministers were becoming impatient over the delays, and regretted that it had come up for discussion in the Cabinet War Committee at this time, 'when several Ministers were critical of the United Kingdom Government's attitude on Mutual Aid.' Robertson's point and tacit warning were well taken and MacDonald in turn reiterated the important role that Goose Bay played in Britain's defence. Robertson confided to MacDonald that he saw no difficulty in securing military rights for the British in the post-war talks, and even suggested a possible trade-off of rights with the United Kingdom at some future date, but the meeting itself produced nothing.[80]

By August 1944 the stalled negotiations over Goose Bay were beginning to affect Canadian-United Kingdom relations in general. As the cwc had earlier warned, the longer the Goose Bay matter remained unsettled the more it would interfere with the normal functioning of British-Canadian relations. And here the Canadians found some leverage to press their case. When C.D. Howe met with Harold Balfour of the Air Ministry to discuss the possibility of holding Commonwealth talks on civil aviation, he assured Balfour that he foresaw no problems in getting Canadian agreement. But, Howe noted, it would be nice to have the Goose Bay mess out of the way; he 'said that this is a sore spot, and is souring relations all round, being a constant irritation to Ministers who see it constantly in their Cabinet agenda, and yet it is never cleared up.' Balfour made no reply, but fully understood Howe's meaning.[81]

For Prime Minister King and the Department of External Affairs the negotiations had gone on long enough, and the arrival of Lord Keynes's mission to settle outstanding financial problems between Canada and the United Kingdom provided a further opportunity to pressure the British government. On the morning of 15 August Robertson met with Sir Patrick Duff, the British deputy high commissioner, and told him 'that Ministers – (and he particularly mentioned the Prime Minister) – could not see their way to conclude the financial negotiations except on the condition that this other matter [Goose Bay], ... was in a fair way of being disposed of.'[82]

Later the same day Duff accompanied Keynes to a meeting with Robertson and Heeney. Robertson repeated to Keynes what he had earlier told Duff, that the Goose Bay lease had to be settled before any conclusion could be reached to the financial negotiations now under way – an ultimatum to which King agreed. Duff recorded his impressions in a long letter back to the Dominions Office:

They were obviously feeling very uncomfortable over the job they had to do: indeed, poor Robertson could hardly this time quite get his tongue round the unfortunate word 'condition.' At the first mention of Goose, Keynes said that he knew nothing about it and that in any case it would be quite improper and altogether outside the terms of his reference to discuss it. Nonetheless, Robertson dealt at length with the Canadian arguments for Canada's concluding the agreement with Newfoundland, emphasizing the impatience on the part of Ministers over the delay in this matter and the soreness which our whole attitude on it caused them: and concluding that, in consequence, Goose should be settled before the financial arrangements could be held to be confirmed.[83]

Following more discussion Robertson agreed that any hint of 'conditions' should be removed and that the two sets of negotiations should remain separate. Duff continued: 'It was obvious that in going as far as this he was entirely departing from his instructions and that he would have to make his peace elsewhere for having done so. But it was plain all along that he himself regarded the attitude which he had been told to adopt as untenable and certainly it was plainly distasteful to him.'

Nevertheless, Robertson had put forward the Canadian case forcefully. Even without a formal ultimatum the intent of the Canadians was clear. In conclusion Duff wrote, 'As you see, this business came very near to dishing the Keynes' talks. Indeed, unless Robertson had withdrawn, Keynes would have found it necessary to go one step further then he actually, in the event, had to do, and say that he must throw up the task altogether. The trouble is that from now on Goose is going more and more to pervade the consideration of all matters at issue between us. Time and again at our interview, Robertson and Heeney emphasized what a spreading and running sore it is in our relationships.'[84]

It is difficult to gauge how much effect this pressure had on the officials in the Dominions Office. Clearly they were aware of the growing Canadian irritation over the lack of a settlement, but there are indications that the Dominions Office might have agreed to the July proposals anyway. The telegram sent by Duff arrived in the Dominions Office on the morning of 18 August, but it made no mention of the 'conditions' which Duff preferred to put in a personal letter to Cranborne. Although it was dated 19 August 1944, it is possible that Cranborne did not read Duff's private account until nearly the end of the month, after the decision had been made to accept the Canadian proposals.[85] Even so, Cranborne was well aware that the Canadians had begun to see the settlement of Goose as a pre-condition to the holding of Commonwealth aviation talks and the conclusion of the financial negotiations.

On 18 August Clutterbuck and Machtig informed Cranborne that the Canadian proposals now seemed to meet most of the wishes of the United Kingdom, and suggested accepting them.[86] Cranborne found the proposals 'a considerable advance in the part of the Canadian Gov't,' and felt an agreement now could be reached, providing the Air Ministry agreed.[87]

Agreement with the Air Ministry was reached over the weekend and on 22 August Cranborne sent the Newfoundland governor the Dominions Office response to the Canadian offer of 3 July. The Canadian offer in civil aviation, he noted, 'corresponds very closely with the suggestion which I made to Mr. Howe in October last and fully meets our position'[88] Cranborne went on to say that he felt that it would be unnecessary to push for further written clarification of Newfoundland's civil air rights because no country was given rights for civil aviation under this lease and it might produce 'a certain awkwardness' to press for this before any rights had been given to Canada. In light of this he suggested that the new lease be accepted essentially as it stood.[89]

One result of the Canadian threats was to hurry the conclusion of the lease once agreement had been reached. After reading Duff's letter Cranborne noted that it was 'really becoming most urgent that this matter should be settled.' Cranborne recognized the need to act but did not fully understand the impatience of the Canadians: 'It seems to me that it is we, if anyone,' he wrote, 'who have the grievance.' But an agreement had been reached and it was now important to see it through as quickly as possible.[90]

Over the next few weeks the final arrangements were put into effect. On 5 September the Commission of Government notified London of its approval and on 8 September Malcolm MacDonald relayed this information to Norman Robertson. Only two insignificant drafting points remained and these were incorporated into the new lease. Permission to sign the lease was sent to St John's, from both Ottawa and London, and on 10 October 1944 the Goose Bay Agreement was signed by Sir Wilfrid Woods and J.S. MacDonald, the new Canadian high commissioner in Newfoundland.[91]

The signed lease gave Canada 120 square miles and listed the rules and regulations to which the Canadians had to adhere. As agreed, wartime rights were given to the United Kingdom and the United States, but post-war civil and military use was to be left undecided until negotiations after the war. More to the point, post-war use by the United Kingdom was not rejected, merely omitted.

In Canada and the United Kingdom the announcement of the Goose Bay Agreement produced little controversy. The *Winnipeg Free Press* called the lease 'a notable coup' for Canada and declared that it marked 'not only a new departure in the foreign policy of this country but an event of the deepest significance.'[92] For the most part it was discussed in the press in conjunction with the Commonwealth aviation meetings then under way in Montreal.[93]

In American circles there was some uneasiness over the lease. The *New York Times* noted the large expense incurred by Canada and openly wondered whether the Canadians were not planning to use the base for peacetime as well as wartime purposes.[94] This concern over Canadian motives was not unique to the *New York Times*. In fact, it was shared by many others, including officials throughout the government. G.D. Hopper, the consul-general in St John's, reported to Washington that the Canadians were looking very much towards a civil-aviation agreement because of the potential importance of Goose Bay and the Canadian money already spent there. Strong Canadian interest was evident: 'A Canadian official in St John's told me in confidence that his Government was compelled to use "forceful language" with the British Government before the latter consented to the leasing of Goose Bay air base to Canada.'[95]

In Washington, L.B. Pearson was keenly aware of the possible American repercussions. He wired Robertson that the American authorities might bring up Canada's rights in Goose Bay as a contrast to the rights given the Americans for their installations in Canada. How should he respond to the difficult questions that might be raised; for example, if Canada could be guaranteed post-war rights on its bases in Labrador why shouldn't the United States receive the same privileges in Canada?[96] Robertson quickly responded to Pearson, assuring him that 'the analogy between Goose Air Base and bases constructed by the United States in Canada is quite unsound.' He continued: 'The ground for continued possession of Goose Air Base by Canada is not the cost but the importance of the air base for the defence of Canada and Newfoundland as part of the western hemisphere. Were Newfoundland able to assume full responsibility for the defence of this region of the continent, there would be no occasion for continued occupation by Canada for reasons of hemisphere defence.'[97]

If this was not also the case for the Americans why had they not offered to return their bases to Newfoundland? The main difference between the American and Canadian situations in Newfoundland was that 'the United States insisted on a formal agreement in advance whereas Canada went immediately to the assistance of Newfoundland relying on the good faith of Newfoundland and United Kingdom to implement agreements made then in principle.'[98] This somewhat angry reply clearly reveals the disturbing effects that the long, drawn-out negotiations had had on Robertson, as well as on many of the other Canadian officials and ministers.

For the Newfoundlanders the effect of Goose Bay was direct and immediate, while their input or control of the negotiations had been non-existent. Not suprisingly, it was here that the protest was the strongest. J.S. Macdonald reviewed the reaction of the St. John's and outport press in a series of telegrams to Ottawa in October and

November 1944. to many editors the Goose Bay lease was one more example of what can happen to a country that is lacking self-government. In their view only a democratic and properly elected Newfoundland government should be allowed to sign a ninety-nine-year lease, not a commisison of government appointed from London.[99]

Although the reaction of the general public was less dramatic than that of the newspapers, there were those outside the press who voiced their concerns. The very influential Newfoundland Board of Trade prepared a long document denouncing the agreement and delivered it to the Commission of Government. Numerous objections were raised: why was so much territory given for such a long period of time, and, would this not put Newfoundland in a position of having to negotiate for the use of its own territory at some future date? Moreover, it was clear that the Canadians' real interest was in securing civil-aviation rights in Labrador, and not merely for defence purposes. In their view the Canadians should trust Newfoundland's 'imperial spirit' which would give Canada access to the base if and when the need arose.[100]

Several prominent Newfoundlanders were also opposed. One such individual was Leonard C. Outerbridge, a leading Water Street merchant and later Newfoundland's lieutenant-governor. In a letter to the governor and in private at a grouse shooting with the Canadian high commissioner he voiced his own particular concerns. He wondered whether Canada could be trusted in the future to use the base or allow others to do so in alliance with the United Kingdom and Newfoundland. He wrote the governor that 'Canada within twenty years is likely to be predominantly French, with the Quebec influence all-prevading, and this means anti-English, anti-Empire, anti-participation in any war, or, in other words, in these respects Canada is likely to be another Erie [sic]. The wonderful war effort of the English-Canadian majority in Canada (swiftly becoming a minority) should not blind any student of Canada to the present and probable future behaviour of the French-Canadian minority (fast becoming the majority).'[101]

J.S. Macdonald noted that Outerbridge was not alone in feeling that Canada had used its influence with the United Kingdom to take advantage of Newfoundland. He went on to add that he did not feel that public displeasure with the lease was strong enough to lead to a 'mass movement' against it, but was saddened by the extent that it had already soured Canadian-Newfoundland relations.[102]

The negotiations for the Goose Bay lease had indeed been long and tiring and had left behind a bitterness between the countries involved.

For many in Ottawa the experience served to reinforce the uniqueness of Canada's relations with Newfoundland. On the one hand Newfoundland was an essential factor in Canadian and hemisphere defence and Canada had made the major contribution to its defence, but on the other Canada's actions were hampered by Newfoundland's uncertain constitutional status, American self-interest, and the machinations of the Dominions Office. It could not have gone unnoticed in Ottawa that all these difficulties would have been bypassed had Newfoundland been a province of Canada.

If nothing else Goose Bay had produced a rethinking of the 'problem of Newfoundland.' For a small number of officials and government members the result was twofold. First, it revealed that the Dominions Office, while not unsympathetic to Canadian interests in Newfoundland and the idea of Confederation, could not be expected to give away rights in Newfoundland – concern for their own interests would continue to dictate their actions there. Second, Goose Bay helped crystallize the recognition of American power and its potential threat to Canada. American influence in Canada and Canadian defence had grown steadily throughout the war, and, with the approach of peace, it became necessary to assert a degree of independence if Canada were to play a significant role in the post-war world. For this reason it was imperative to get the lease signed before the war had ended.[103]

Despite the small role played by the United States in the actual discussions, the American presence in Newfoundland was a consistent factor in the minds of Canadian negotiators. Not only did the Canadians have to protect their own interests in Newfoundland, they had to resist the spreading influence of others as well. For all intents and purposes by 1945 Newfoundland was being treated – at least in defence matters – as if it were Canadian soil. Goose Bay had in some ways shown the evolution of this attitude more clearly than any other development in Newfoundland during the Second World War. Moreover, Goose Bay had given the Department of External Affairs the opportunity to flex its growing muscles and was illustrative of the shift towards a more active foreign policy that characterized these years. Ironically, a good deal of the blame for the delay in the negotiations must lie, if not with the Department of External Affairs alone, then with the Canadian government as a whole.

By war's end the Goose Bay airport had proved successful. Apart from its role as a base for coastal patrols and convoy protection, Goose Bay was a major link in the North Atlantic ferry route, and had been used by thousands of airplanes. Furthermore, these planes carried tons of cargo and thousands of troops overseas and then returned them to North America when the war was over. The Canadian government had invested in the neighbourhood of $25 million in building one of the largest airports in the world, an investment that would continue to pay dividends long after the war had ended.

6

Civil aviation

A Canadian traveller in Newfoundland early in the war was impressed by the scope of the changes that had overtaken the country. Never before had the two peoples been as close as they were now – working in unison for a common cause. To explain this development he pointed to one significant event: 'Perhaps no single incident,' he later wrote, 'apart from the pressure of the war itself, has had so practical an effect on drawing the peoples of Canada and Newfoundland together as the coming of the Trans-Canada Air Lines to Newfoundland.' Now Moncton was 'a bare four hours' away from St John's, while Ottawa and St John's were now 'less than a half-day's run by plane from each other.'[1]

These events produced 'startling and eventful changes' in Canadian-Newfoundland relations as well as profound questions. What effect would these circumstances produce, and what role would they play in the determination of Newfoundland's future constitutional status? To this Canadian visitor, it seemed that Canada must take the initiative, because the choice was clear: 'Either Canada assumes the logical responsibility of a larger, richer, more successful British neighbour toward Newfoundland, or that Island may turn to the United States for some long-term answer to its economic and administrative dilemma.'[2] During the long and complex negotiations over aviation problems, however, it was often difficult to see into the future with such lucidity.

Civil aviation was a relatively new field for the Canadian leaders in the 1940s, but they were quick to realize the advantages it held for Canada. As C.G. Power told one reporter, 'Geographically, Canada is sitting pretty.'[3] More than that, the Canadians were determined to put their advantages to good use: the Canadian government, said Mackenzie King, 'intends to press vigorously for a place in international air transportation consistent with Canada's geographical position and progress in aviation.'[4]

Including Newfoundland within this framework was the natural extension of this policy. It took no leap of imagination to recognize that the pattern set by the Atlantic ferry system would be followed for commercial aviation in the post-war world. And, until technological advances bypassed it, Newfoundland's pivotal position was secure. During the 1940s Canadian civil-aviation policy regarding Newfoundland had two major thrusts: the first was to achieve a dominant position in the service connecting the island with the mainland, and the second was to secure for Canada its rightful share of the traffic that would utilize Newfoundland's airports in transatlantic flight. And, in reaching these goals, a lasting non-military tie was fashioned between Canada and Newfoundland.

I

Civil aviation has had a long but rocky past in Newfoundland. From the earliest days of flight, pilots, daredevils, and adventurers were attracted to the country because of its geographical location. In the spring of 1919, Alcock and Brown used Newfoundland as the starting-point for the first non-stop America-to-Europe flight. There followed over the next few years a succession of imitators and imprudent amateurs adding their names and exploits to the colourful story of aviation in Newfoundland.

Newfoundland's geography, however, also imposed major barriers to aviation. Because of the isolation of many communities and the difficulties in transportation and communication across Newfoundland, the benefits that could be derived from flight were obvious. But, equally, the hazards of cold and fog and the lack of suitable areas for landing-fields made aviation a perilous undertaking at all times. Moreover, Newfoundland's financial circumstances in the inter-war years prevented the Commission of Government from entering the field in any significant manner.[5]

Nevertheless, the lure of aviation caught the imaginations of many Newfoundlanders, and several attempts were made to establish mail and passenger services, either across Newfoundland or connecting the island with the mainland. In 1929, two Newfoundlanders, A.D. Sullivan and D.C. Fraser, formed Newfoundland Airways Ltd to provide a domestic mail service. Limited to a single de Havilland Gipsy Moth, this venture never proved to be successful.[6]

St John's played host to an international aviation conference in 1933 which laid the groundwork for a transatlantic mail service. This conference was followed in November 1935 by a larger one in Ottawa, between Canada, Newfoundland, Britain, and the Irish Free State. Agreement was reached in Ottawa on the formation of a joint operating company, subject to each government's approval, to be responsible for a regular transatlantic passenger and mail service once it became feasible. Canada, as well as Newfoundland, was included in this agreement, and Ottawa promised to pay up to 20 per cent of the annual subsidy. The United Kingdom and its agent, Imperial Airways, maintained a dominant position in the joint operating company by paying up to 75 per cent of the annual subsidy and holding the right to nominate its chairman and managing director.[7] Discussions were also held with the United States at this time, and a reciprocal agreement was reached permitting both Imperial Airways and Pan Am to operate overseas flights.

Subsequent to these developments the UK government began developing an airport in Gander and a seaplane base in Botwood. In 1938 and into 1939 a number of experimental flights were undertaken through the northern circle route – New York to Botwood, Foynes, and ultimately, Southampton. In August 1939, a regular weekly service was inaugurated by both Imperial Airways and Pan Am. The service commenced on 5 August with the flight of the *Caribou* and continued into early October when it closed for the winter season.[8]

Canada was included in these arrangements, not as an independent, but rather as a partner with Britain and Ireland. This may have been an acceptable arrangement in 1935, but by the end of the decade it was no longer so. Trans-Canada Airlines (TCA) had been created and expanded, under the watchful eye of C.D. Howe, to act as the 'chosen instrument' of the Canadian government.[9] And Howe was determined to see TCA play a more independent role – which did not augur well for the 1935 agreement.

Between 1937 and 1939, TCA's regularly scheduled flights expanded into a transcontinental passenger service, stretching from Montreal to Vancouver. By the autumn of 1939, the service had been extended to include Moncton. Newfoundland was the next logical step.

C.D. Howe had made it clear to all who cared to listen that TCA would be the dominant Canadian airline, and in considering extending service to Newfoundland it was only natural that it would be undertaken by TCA. Thus, when rumours circulated that an independent company wished to establish a Newfoundland-Canada service, the Canadians were quick to inform the Newfoundlanders of Canadian policy that 'all main line operations and especially those sevices operated between points in Canada and other countries, should be operated by the nationally owned company.'[10]

As was so often the case in Canadian-Newfoundland relations, the Newfoundlanders could not automatically respond favourably to the wishes of the Canadians. The Newfoundlanders were receptive to the idea of establishing a link to the mainland, but the lines of a controversy were already being drawn. For example, the British Air Ministry believed that transatlantic flight should be in the hands of BOAC (formerly Imperial Airways), and this would include the last leg of the trip between Newfoundland and the mainland.[11] Moreover, an American company, Northeastern Airlines, was also interested in establishing a service to Newfoundland and had begun to make enquiries by the autumn of 1941.

Confronted with these conflicting views, the Newfoundland government approached the Dominions Office for advice. In their view the establishment of a service would be a great asset for Newfoundland, especially in light of the large number of Canadian and American troops on the island. But the Newfoundlanders also expressed the opinion that neither BOAC nor TCA could at that time undertake this service. How, then, they asked, should they deal with an application from the American interests?[12]

The Dominions Office's response followed on 1 October 1941. The British agreed that BOAC was not then in the position to instigate such a service and therefore they had no qualms about an American line coming into service, providing it was 'limited to [the] period of the war and no monopoly or special privileges are granted.' The Canadians should be consulted beforehand, and they may even want to operate the service, but in the eyes of the Dominion Office, 'it would seem to be unwise for Canada to undertake it in view of recent criticism in the United States Press of activity of Canadian air lines in general at a time when United States air lines are being denuded of equipment to meet our military needs.'[13]

This criticism in the American press did not appear to concern the Canadians to any great degree, and in October 1941, C.J. Burchell, the Canadian high commissioner in Newfoundland, approached the Commission of Government for permission to extend TCA service to Newfoundland. Burchell conferred with Sir Wilfrid Woods, the commissioner for public utilities, and an arrangement was worked out. Woods had originally been under the impression that Canada was not interested in the line and consequently had held talks with representatives of Northeastern Airlines. He was surprised to learn differently, but was easily persuaded to accept the Canadian offer.[14]

Thus, on 3 November, Burchell informed Ottawa that he had received formal approval from the Newfoundland government. In addition, Northeastern Airlines was also given permission to establish a non-commercial line to Newfoundland, mainly to service the American bases on the island.[15] Burchell, who was always sensitive to Canada's prestige in Newfoundland, was apprehensive that the actions of his government might be misconstrued. Through mismanagement on its part, Canada appeared to be coming in at the last moment to displace an American rival. And, wrote Burchell, it was unfortunate but Canada would 'not obtain the same credit for the establishment of this service when it becomes known that one of the American lines was the first to offer the service.'[16]

The whole affair provides another example of the rather ambiguous influence of the United States in Canadian-Newfoundland relations during the war. The operation of a Newfoundland-mainland commercial service had obvious benefits for the Canadians, and chances were that eventually a service would have been established. The introduction of an American presence did not bring the Canadians to this way of thinking; it acted more as a catalyst, sparking the Canadians into action. In effect, the American factor tended to reinforce Canadian policy by providing another excellent reason for proceeding, and by forcing the Canadians to move swiftly. In many respects this paralleled the development of the Canadian-American military relationship in Newfoundland.

There remained a number of problems to be ironed out before the service could be started. The Newfoundlanders had offered the Canadians the same conditions that London had felt suitable for the American interests, namely that the service would be limited to the war period and that no special privileges would be given to TCA. Ottawa instructed Burchell to inform the Commission of Government that because of the 'nature of the terrain and climate,' the operation of the service would be more costly than usual runs, and therefore Canada should be granted at least a five-year agreement. In addition, numerous radio stations and other facilities would have to be provided at Canadian expense. How could the Newfoundlanders expect the Canadians and TCA to pay for all this if they were left 'open to unrestricted competition from other sources'?[17]

These obstacles were not insurmountable. On the question of monopoly the Canadians could afford to be flexible; even if competition did arise, any rival would have to turn to the Canadians for permission to use their airports in Newfoundland and Canada. And, as Norman Robertson wrote to Burchell: 'The fact is that Canada would not grant such facilities to any such line.' Furthermore, under the protocol and the 1941 Airbases Agreement, Canada would have to be consulted before any alterations could be made to the existing arrangements. In this way the Canadians believed that they could curtail Canada's request for monopoly rights.[18]

A final agreement was reached early in February 1942, following a number of meetings in St John's between Ira Wild and Sir Edward Emerson, both members of the Commission of Government, Burchell, J.A. Wilson, the director of air services, and representatives from TCA and the Department of Transport. On 5 February the main outline of an agreement was reached and Burchell was asked to draw up a written draft. The Commission of Government gave formal approval on 7 February.[19]

The two sides agreed that the permit to run the services would be renewable on a yearly basis, with either side having the right to cancel after giving six months' notice. No monopoly clause was included but Canada was to be consulted before Newfoundland granted a permit to anyone else that might compete with the Canadian line. In addition, the Canadians were given some exemptions from taxes and duties on much of the necessary equipment. For their part, the Canadians promised to operate the line along the normal standards of rates and conditions set up by TCA.[20]

Burchell was pleased by the outcome of the meetings and sensed that it would have significant long-term effects. He wrote Emerson on 9 February 1942 and suggested to him that 'February 7th may be looked upon as a red letter day because as a result of our conference, Newfoundland has been brought closer to the mainland of America'[21]

The Dominions Office gave its approval on 27 February, and the Canadian government earmarked $600,000 for the operation of the line. On 2 May 1942 the first regularly scheduled flight arrived at Torbay airport and inaugurated the Canada-Newfoundland daily (six days a week) service. People on all sides were excited by the opportunities offered by the route. In the 1 May edition of the *Fishermen-Workers Tribune*, it was reported that mail transportation was 'no longer a matter of days but of hours.' On a more pensive note, the author reflected on the changes taking place in Newfoundland, and he concluded: 'One definite effect of all this will be to make Newfoundland better known to the world,' and it will 'unquestionably serve to bring more and more visitors to our shores. All we need now is some place to put them when they get here.'[22]

II

Civil aviation was of major concern during the Second World War precisely because all parties involved recognized that it would maintain its importance long after the war had ended. Clearly, few long-term arrangements could be worked out during the volatile and uncertain conditions early in the war; but nevertheless preparations were being made from the very beginning, in anticipation of future developments. For the Newfoundlanders, this meant jealously guarding against any attempts by foreign powers to secure long-term civil-aviation rights at Newfoundland's airports. In this respect they were largely successful: at Gander, Torbay, Botwood, and even Goose Bay, civil-aviation rights were withheld and reserved for post-war discussions.

During the first years of the war Canadian civil-aviation policy was cautious in tone. For the most part efforts were made to work within the existing arrangements dating back to 1935. On more than one occasion, however, complaints were raised over the difficulties experienced in securing space on the British and American transatlantic flights for Canadian diplomatic mail and military personnel on urgent business.[23] This problem plagued the Canadian government until July 1943, when an independent transatlantic air service, operated by TCA, was established.

On the specific issue of a transatlantic air service and in the formulation of a general civil-aviation policy, the Canadians exhibited a determination not to be overtaken by outside events. The Interdepartmental Committee on International Civil Aviation (ICICA), which was created in 1942, continued throughout the war to churn out reports on what Canadians should expect and plan for in the future. In its March 1943 'Interim Report on Post-War Policy' the ICICA outlined the need to protect Canadian sovereignty in the air while at the same time being flexible in allowing others to use Canadian airspace. Complete freedom of the air was opposed, noted the report, but Canada should be willing to submit to some degree of international co-operation. Above all, the functional principle should be followed – Canada's importance must be recognized with a large role in any post-war organization.[24]

On the political level, Canadian policy was largely determined by Mackenzie King and C.D. Howe. King's role as a general overseer and forceful defender of Canada's role should not be underestimated, but it was left to Howe to be both the watchdog and architect of Canadian civil-aviation policy. Howe had travelled to London in October 1943 for the Commonwealth discussions on civil aviation determined not to succumb to a single Commonwealth policy, but he was willing to bend in other matters. His concern was to secure for TCA its rightful share of the services connecting the various nations of the Commonwealth. And through formal and informal conversations with Lord Beaverbrook, the Lord Privy Seal, he achieved a fair degree of success.[25]

In March 1944, Howe unveiled a more substantial and detailed Canadian policy to the House of Commons. He presented the House with a draft proposal for the creation of an international civil-aviation authority to oversee and regulate services, rates, and licensing. Under Howe's guidance the Canadian plan was refined and revised over the succeeding months and was used as the basis of Canadian policy at the Commonwealth aviation meetings held in Montreal in October 1944, and at the International Civil Aviation Conference held in Chicago in November.[26]

Although the Chicago conference proved to be largely unfruitful, it did produce an agreement to create an interim civil-aviation organization with limited powers to study and review civil-aviation questions and help settle international aviation disputes.[27] Two other supplementary agreements were issued, completely independent of the main discussions. The first was the International Air Services Transit Agreement (the 'Two Freedoms' agreement) in which the signatories granted the first two freedoms to the other participating nations. These freedoms included the right to fly over each other's territories and to land for non-traffic purposes. The second was the International Air Transport Agreement (the 'Five Freedoms' agreement) which added three more freedoms, dealing with the right to land and take off in foreign territories carrying passengers and cargo.

Newfoundland was not accorded full representation at the Chicago conference and this ruffled a few feathers in St John's. In a rather surprising move the Commission of Government asked the Dominions Office to instruct Lord Swinton, the head of the British delegation, to refrain from giving Newfoundland's concurrence to the Two Freedoms agreement. Again the fear was that such a move would produce a backlash of·public opinion that the Commission of Government was selling out Newfoundland's rights under the direction of the Dominions Office.[28] The British, of course, saw this from a different perspective. The treasury was paying to support Newfoundland and it was only natural that the Newfoundlanders should follow the British lead – to act in contradiction could severely damage Britain's position at the conference.

The Newfoundlanders eventually agreed to go along with the Two Freedoms agreement but not before generating considerable concern. As Winston Churchill put it in an angry letter to Beaverbrook, Newfoundland 'will never be considered as an entity for itself against the general view of the British Empire and against the needs of world society.' He continued: 'Everybody knows that Newfoundland is bankrupt and a pauper and has no power apart from us. Therefore nothing we can say will make the Americans believe that we are not pulling the strings of a puppet.'[29]

Churchill's words, although perhaps unduly harsh, were perfectly true. The Americans did view Newfoundland's policy as directed by the Dominions Office, and when it went against British policy it appeared that the British were scheming to achieve ends through devious means. As Robert Cavanagh in the American consulate in St John's reported to the State Department almost one year later: 'regardless of the statements in the press and to the comments of the man on the street, the fact still remains that any decision concerning civil aviation, so far as it refers to Newfoundland, will come from London. As one Commissioner put it in informal conversaton, "We are a Commission of Government for the Dominions Office and it must be admitted we are tied to its apron strings."'[30]

An understanding had been reached at Chicago with respect to the Two Freedoms agreement, but a number of problems remained, especially for the Canadians who were exploring the possibility of allowing the TCA-operated transatlantic service to take on fare-paying passengers. It still remained to be decided which airports in Newfoundland would be designated for international traffic and who would pay for their maintenance and operation.[31] Moreover, with the end of the war, the time had come to settle the numerous questions dealing with civil aviation that had been postponed over the previous years. Under the terms of the agreements dealing with Goose Bay, Torbay, Gander, and Botwood, the Canadians were left without civil-aviation rights in Newfoundland. The possession of these airports was, of course, a strong bargaining point, but by the summer of 1945 the Department of

National Defence, the RCAF, and others who were concerned were eager to reduce the Canadian military presence in Newfoundland. The question of what to do with the Canadian-built facilities – utilize them for civil-aviation purposes, allow someone else to use them or destroy them to prevent others from using them – now had to be confronted.

To this end, informal talks were held between C.D. Howe and Lord Cranborne, the dominions secretary, during the latter's visit to Ottawa in June 1945. Cranborne recognized the need to settle these matters quickly and agreed with Howe that a formal conference attended by the three governments be held as soon as possible. In September, the Department of External Affairs informed the United Kingdom that Howe was contemplating attending the upcoming conference in Bermuda to discuss telecommunications and wondered if this would be an appropriate time to hold bilateral talks on transatlantic aviation, including matters dealing with Newfoundland and the West Indies. To this the British agreed.[32]

An interdepartmental committee was established in Ottawa to help formulate the Canadian position in the upcoming talks; it included R.A. MacKay from External Affairs, J.R. Baldwin from the Privy Council Office, and other representatives from External Affairs, National Defence, and the Air Transport Board. On at least one occasion H.J. Symington, the president of TCA, was also present.[33] The committee agreed that Canadian needs in Newfoundland could be focused on a few areas. It was believed that only one airport, in addition to Goose Bay, was needed in Newfoundland for transatlantic flight.[34] Gander was the obvious, but not necessarily the best choice. For example, R.A. MacKay noted that Gander was extremely susceptible to fog and because of the terrain could not easily be expanded. MacKay argued for a more comprehensive study of Canadian needs in Newfoundland and would not rule out scrapping Gander in favour of a whole new airport. He also thought that Torbay should be maintained for domestic TCA flights connecting the island with the mainland.[35]

The committee's proposals were embodied in a lengthy memorandum, dated 5 September 1945, for the Cabinet Committee on Reconstruction. Several recommendations were offered: Canada should ask Newfoundland to designate Goose Bay and Gander as their two airports for international traffic; Canada should develop Goose Bay as a civil airport; and Canada should offer to transfer to Newfoundland the other airfields under Canadian control providing Newfoundland operate one airport as an international airport, allow TCA to continue its service, extend the five freedoms to Canada, and promise not to 'make available' these sites to anyone else.[36]

The Bermuda civil-aviation conversations took place at the Belmont Hotel from 17 to 19 December 1945. The discussions were wide-ranging and informal, and they resulted in a broad agreement between the three governments. The United Kingdom gave the Canadians transatlantic rights to British airport facilities, agreeing to give TCA rights at London and Prestwick equal to those given the British carriers. A bilateral agreement was signed giving BOAC and TCA reciprocal rights, equally dividing the transatlantic service. The Newfoundlanders consented to designate Gander as the official airport for international traffic and stated that they were willing to assume complete control of Gander. It was impossible for them to do so at the present time, however, and the United Kingdom agreed to maintain control of the air-traffic-control services, and Canada agreed to provide the meteorological services on an interim basis. In addition, Canada was given the first four freedoms at Goose Bay and was allowed to maintain Torbay as in the past. Finally, it was recommended that Newfoundland give third and fourth freedoms to the United States in exchange for reciprocal rights – with BOAC acting on behalf of the Newfoundlanders.[37]

The Bermuda conversations largely resolved the outstanding questions between Canada and Newfoundland over civil aviation. But there remained the problem of the United States and the use of its airbases in Newfoundland, and over the course of the next few years negotiations were undertaken to put the existing arrangements on a more concrete footing. British-American civil-aviation talks in February 1946 produced the Bermuda Agreement that dealt with the American-leased bases but excluded Newfoundland. Efforts to bring Newfoundland in were made, but they were hampered by Canadian persistence in not allowing the Americans to acquire more rights or freedoms in civil aviation than those already held by Canada.[38]

Newfoundland's turbulent political situation also impeded efforts to achieve a permanent solution. With the country's constitutional future in limbo, the British and Americans agreed in May 1947 that rights granted to the United States dealing with Newfoundland would no longer apply after a change in Newfoundland's constitutional status; at this point new agreements would have to be negotiated by Newfoundland, or whatever state was empowered to act on Newfoundland's behalf. After Confederation in 1949, Newfoundland came under the Canadian-American arrangements dealing with civil aviation, such as the 1949 agreement which included a partial extension of fifth-freedom rights. In June 1949, the matter was settled through an exchange of notes limiting the commercial use of American bases in Newfoundland to emergency purposes.[39]

During the years leading up to Confederation in 1949 the Canadian position in aviation negotiations was consistent but not totally inflexible. Central to this stance was the fact that Canada could bargain from a position of strength. By the end of the war Canada had a strong aircraft industry and a large body of skilled pilots and technicians which enhanced Canada's prestige and influence in the aviation world. By applying this strength, the Canadians established an independent role for Canada in the field of aviation and extended their authority to include Newfoundland. More so than in most aspects of their relationship with Newfoundland, the Canadians were conscious of their goals in civil aviation and they showed the determination to achieve them.

It could be argued that the development of air flight more than any other single factor was responsible for bringing and keeping Newfoundland within the Canadian orbit. This was true for not only the obvious benefits in communications, transportation, and defence, but also on the symbolic level: the establishment of a TCA link to the mainland was an indication of the increasingly important bond between Newfoundland and Canada that had been forged during the war. And the unfolding of a new and dangerous world in 1945 served only to reinforce this bond. As one historian wrote at the time, by the end of the war 'Canada and Newfoundland were locked into the maps of world air strategy whether they wanted to be or not.'[40] The recognition of this reality influenced Canadian policy in both military and civil aviation, awakening an interest in the value not only of Newfoundland but of the whole Canadian north.[41]

7

The problem of Newfoundland

On a number of occasions during 1940, mail delivered to the American consulate in St John's bore the address 'Newfoundland, Canada.' The American officials in St John's found this somewhat embarrassing, and the consul-general, Harold Quarton, requested that this error be remedied. He reminded the State Department that Newfoundland was not now a part of Canada nor would it likely be so in the foreseeable future. In his view, there was 'more talk of Confederation with Canada outside of Newfoundland than in this Island. Even if Canada were to pay Newfoundland's debt, it is not believed that the population of this Island would vote for a union with Canada. Most people think that this Island can do better with British help and by marketing their fish in their own way.'[1]

Confederation and the general question of what to do about Newfoundland were, indeed, more discussed outside Newfoundland than in. For the Dominions Office, the problem of Newfoundland's future came under scrutiny soon after the introduction of government by commission. It was not clear, however, exactly what direction the Dominions Office should take, and it was recognized that there existed no long-term solution that would be universally acceptable.

In 1939, L.S. Amery, the aging British Conservative MP, wrote Sir Thomas Inskip (Lord Caldecote), the dominions secretary, that there 'can be no possible future for Newfoundland unless it is included in one or other larger community, Canada or the United Kingdom.' Consequently Amery proposed that Newfoundland become part of the United Kingdom for a period of ten years, with an option to stay longer, under an 'Ulster Constitution.'[2] Inskip agreed with much of Amery's argument but personally felt 'that union with Canada would be the natural and most likely development in the long run.' According to Inskip, incorporation into the United Kingdom would 'transform the whole Island into a country of "pensioners," content to be provided for indefinitely by the United Kingdom tax payer!' Canadian interest in Newfoundland, he added, 'might be very different if Newfoundland could be restored, if not to prosperity at any rate to something approaching solvency.' As for Confederation, 'we should do nothing in the meanwhile to discourage or interfere with the natural evolution of opinion in the Island in this direction.'[3]

Conversations of this nature were not uncommon within the Dominions Office during the 1930s. And, although it would have seemed inappropriate to introduce sweeping changes before Newfoundland was in fact on its feet again, the main lines of a debate had been drawn by 1939. At that time there was no clear-cut policy or 'conspiracy' within the British government to force Newfoundland into Confederation. On the contrary, there was considerable disagreement within and between different government departments, and a variety of solutions were proposed, ranging from responsible government, to Confederation, to incorporation into the United Kingdom.

The circumstances produced by the war acted as a kind of midwife to a final settlement by clarifying the limits of the discussion. There were a number of reasons for this: the war returned Newfoundland to financial prosperity and reawakened an interest in politics among many Newfoundlanders; the need to defend the island and Labrador and the presence of the Americans there sparked a concern in Ottawa that gradually evolved into a forceful ambition not to 'lose' Newfoundland; and Britain's own financial predicament at the end of the war precluded the maintenance of generous long-term economic support to Newfoundland. The debate continued throughout the war, and by 1945 a decision had, for the most part, been reached.

I

The war did for Newfoundland's economy what the Commission of Government had tried and failed to do – it transformed the country's deficit into a surplus, established full employment, and brought the standard of living of thousands of Newfoundlanders up to a more decent level. This minor miracle was not home grown; rather it was a direct product of the influx of thousands of foreign troops and millions of foreign dollars.

The most immediate effect was in jobs. Enlistment in the armed services of Canada and Britain aided the unemployment situation in Newfoundland, and demand for unskilled construction workers to work on the Canadian and American installations eliminated unemployment altogether. The number of Newfoundlanders employed on construction sites rose to an estimated peak of 19,752 in September 1942,[4] and subsequently tailed off. High wages and steady work sparked a boom that one author compared to the 'frontier days on the American continent.'[5]

Naturally those who lived in the vicinity of the bases or were directly employed there received the greatest benefits, but the impact permeated the whole economy. In 1942, a record year, wholesalers and store-keepers could not keep up with the rise in consumer demand. New-foundlanders had a lot of catching up to do and increasingly their problem was one of shortage of supply, not of cash.

Nowhere was this transformation more clear than in the monthly trade reports and the annual economic reviews sent home to Washington from the American consulate in St John's. Citing the Newfoundland Board of Trade as a source, reports described 1940 as a year 'of progress in all fields of economic endeavor.'[6] Fish was selling at good prices, and lumber and mining output was up. But by September 1941 the impact of the Canadians and Americans had begun to be felt and the economic consequences for Newfoundland far exceeded anything previously imagined. Fred E. Waller, the American vice-consul, reported the good economic news to the State Department: 'Many people who have been living near the bare margin of existence for several years are now in a position to satisfy many wants, to improve their diet, and more adequately to clothe themselves and their families. Repairs, long overdue, are being made, and some things which locally are considered luxuries are beginning to be demanded. The standard of living is definitely rising.'[7] At the turn of the year Waller looked back over 1941 and called it 'the most prosperous year in Newfoundland's history during the past generation.'[8] And economic conditions in Newfoundland continued to improve: more than a year later, in April 1943, the 'Annual Economic and Financial Review' for Newfoundland, prepared in the American consulate, noted that 1942 'was without precedent in the history of the Island.'[9]

Two major indications of the economic impact of the war were imports and government revenue. Increased purchasing power and consumer demand coupled with wartime inflation produced an unparalleled surge in the dollar value of Newfoundland's imports: between 1939–40 and 1941–2 Newfoundland's imports increased from $28,421,897 to $45,198,865. Canada received the greatest part of this increase with a 54 per cent growth in exports to Newfoundland during the same period.[10] Imports from the United States increased as well, but not as rapidly as those from Canada. By 1944–5, Newfoundland's total imports reached $57 million with Canada supplying 61 per cent.[11] (See table 2.)

Newfoundland's exports over this same period did not fare so well. Between 1939–40 and 1941–2 total exports increased by almost $6 million, rising from $33,393,845 to $39,102,557. The increase was largely the result of significantly higher fish prices that boosted the export value of Newfoundland's output by more than $4 million despite a decrease in that output. It is interesting to note that the largest increase was in the fresh/frozen fish industry, which grew to one-third of the total fish exports.[12] Canada was not a major importer of Newfoundland goods in the pre-war era and this did not change during the war, although Newfoundland exports to Canada did rise to more than $7 million. Exports to the United Kingdom, traditionally Newfoundland's best client, dropped significantly from $11,170,637 in 1940–1 to $3.9 million in 1942–3. Only in exports to the United States was there a strong upswing (to $15.9 million in 1941–2), making the United States the single most important customer for Newfoundland products.[13]

The skyrocketting value of imports was good news to a government that depended on customs tariffs as its major source of revenue. Government revenue from this source almost tripled during the war. In 1939–40, government revenue was $12,571,015 while expenditures were $15,688,596, producing an overall deficit of more than $3 million. This was turned around the following year, and for the rest of the war the Newfoundland government experienced a budget surplus. By 1944–5 government revenue had grown to $33,310,014 and expenditures had increased to $21,817,059, leaving a surplus of $11,492,955 – an amount larger than the total government revenue of 1938–9.[14] Ironically, the one-time debtor state and financial drain on the British treasury had been transformed into a creditor of the mother country through interest-free loans. By January 1944, approximately $10.3 million had been loaned to the United Kingdom from the coffers of the Newfoundland government. This had risen to $12.3 million by the end of the war.[15] (See table 3).

TABLE 2
Percentage distribution of Newfoundland imports

	1938/39	1942/43	1944/45
United Kingdom	24	4	4
Canada	37	57	61
United States	32	36	33
Other British sources	2	1	1
Other Foreign sources	5	2	1
	100	100	100

TABLE 3
Revenue and expenditure, ordinary account

Fiscal year	Revenue	Expenditure	Deficit (−) or surplus (+)
1932–1933	$ 8,085,666	$11,553,774	(−) $ 3,468,108
1936–1937	10,995,665	12,095,976	(−) 1,100,311
1939–1940	12,571,015	15,688,596	(−) 3,117,581
1941–1942	23,313,741	14,668,659	(+) 8,645,082
1944–1945	33,310,014	21,817,059	(+) 11,492,955

SOURCE: DO, *Financial and Economic Position of Newfoundland*

On the expenditure side the Commission of Government had proceeded with a cautious but not parsimonious attitude. No large-scale development projects were inaugurated but some new construction was undertaken, more money was spent on building and maintaining roads and bridges, a system of free and compulsory education was introduced in 1942, and bed capacity of hospitals was increased from 1,390 in 1938 to 2,419 in 1945. In general, government revenue was divided along three lines; 1 / maintaining public services; 2 / paying of the public debt; 3 / providing interest-free loans to Britain.[16]

The economic upheaval caused by Canada and the United States, together with the more mundane difficulties of wartime supply, sparked the implementation of a number of controls on Newfoundland's economy. For example, the influx of foreign soldiers and increased civilian demands put a strain on housing, particularly in St John's. In an effort to prevent exorbitant rent hikes, rent controls were put into place in 1941. In 1942, a labour relations officer was appointed to oversee labour problems that arose on the foreign defence projects. Efforts were made to avoid competition for the existing labour forces in Newfoundland and to regulate hours, wages, and working conditions.[17]

Inflation was also a serious concern for the Commission of Government. The Newfoundland Cost of Living Index estimated the rise in prices between 1938 and 1946 at 63 per cent.[18] There were several causes for the severity of the problem: first, increases in the cost of Canadian and American goods were passed directly on to Newfoundland; second, a wartime revenue tax of 7.5 per cent was tacked on to the import tariff (already working on ad valorem basis); third, increased domestic purchasing power confronting supply shortages led some local merchants to charge unusually high prices; and, finally, the higher cost of transportation due to delays, losses at sea, and insurance was in turn added on to the price of the goods.[19]

Food was particularly hard hit, jumping 46 per cent in price between October 1938 and November 1941. And, for those in the outports who did not benefit directly from the new prosperity, but still had to meet the rising costs, life continued much as it had in the past. As William E. Cole, the American vice-consul in St John's, wrote in April 1943: 'A consideration of living costs in Newfoundland presupposes a standard of living which has been attained in the past by only a small proportion of the population. The majority, existing on the subsistence level of a primitive economy, have seldom obtained more than the barest necessities. Only a nucleus of merchants, professional persons, and civil servants maintain a standard of living comparable to that of an average community in the United States.'[20]

To meet this challenge, the Commission of Government appointed a deputy price controller in 1942 to work under the wing of the Commissioner for Public Health and Welfare. His role was to establish the ceiling price for foodstuffs, taking into account transportation costs and import duties. One advantage was that most of Newfoundland's food had to be imported and the deputy price controller could obtain accurate information from the Customs department. Government controls were also placed on specific products like eggs and milk, molasses, potatoes, automobile tires, gasoline, and coal, and the wartime revenue tax was removed from other goods, such as canned meats.[21] As the war progressed these arrangements became more efficient and in 1943 a system of coupon rationing was introduced for coffee, sugar, and tea.[22]

The Commission of Government also quickly recognized that securing the source of supply was equally, if not more, important than controlling the cost. Because of Newfoundland's dependence on Canada and, to a lesser degree, the United States for its imports, any disorders in those countries' ability to export would have immediate and severe repercussions in Newfoundland. Newfoundland did not have the domestic resources or a substitute trading partner to fall back on. Thus the Commission of Government felt the need to keep an eye on the organization and distribution of goods in North America.

To offset some of these potential difficulties the Canadians appointed a trade commissioner to Newfoundland in May 1942. R.P. Bower was nominated to this post and he worked in close connection with the High Commissioner's Office. The function of the trade commissioner was not to act as a salesman for Canada, it was more to endeavour to match Newfoundland's temporary supply needs with the material that Canada could best provide. Working in St John's would give the commissioner first-hand knowledge of Newfoundland's requirements and would better prepare him to advise what goods should be supplied.

Obtaining sufficient food supplies was a constant problem for the Newfoundland government, and they were obliged to approach the British-American Combined Food Board in Washington to meet some of their requirements. An interesting indication of Newfoundland's absorption into the North American economy was the Dominions Office suggestion that Newfoundland s needs would be better presented to the board by Canada than by Britain, even though Canada was not at that time a member of the board. Newfoundland benefited from this connection as a result of the board's purchasing system which helped maintain the demand and the price of Newfoundland fish at relatively high and stable levels.[23]

Because Newfoundland was obtaining supplies from both Canada and the United States, it was important for these countries to co-operate to avoid duplication. This work was largely undertaken by the Wartime Prices and Trade Board (WPTB), created in 1939, which controlled the price, supply, and distribution of goods in Canada, and a similar American organization, the Board of Economic Warfare (BEW). Gradually the WPTB and BEW assumed the control of the total supply of foodstuffs to Newfoundland, whether or not they came under the jurisdiction of the Combined Food Board.[24] A level of supply was established and maintained, based on pre-war rates plus an additional quantity that took into account Newfoundland's wartime prosperity.

These arrangements were put on a more formal basis through an exchange of notes, dated 10 May 1943. Schedules were drawn up indicating the specific supplies Canada and the United States were to provide for Newfoundland, and obligated them to maintain the quantities at consistent levels over the following months.[25] The agreement was to last one year and was renewed in 1944 and again in 1945. Thus an effective system of supply was established that alleviated a potentially critical problem.

The prosperity experienced by Newfoundland continued until the war was over. Defence construction tapered off from the high-water mark of 1942–3, with the number of jobs for Newfoundlanders falling from nearly 20,000 to close to 8,500 by December 1943. But, the reopening of the sea lanes and some foreign markets permitted large numbers of Newfoundlanders to return to fishing, and for others who lost their construction jobs there was the opportunity to work in Canada and the United States. Through various recruitment schemes an estimated 3,600 Newfoundlanders left to work on the mainland. Government revenue, moreover, remained high, and by the end of the war Newfoundland possessed a surplus of approximately $32.5 million.[26]

There were other indications, however, that were not so promising. Social services had been greatly expanded during the war, and the extra burden that this placed on the Newfoundland government would continue into the post-war world. And, although income taxes had increased as a source of government earnings, the Commission of Government still depended on the customs tariff for the major part of its revenue. To meet its financial requirements government revenue from imports would have to remain high – an unlikely occurrence given the decline in purchasing power that would result from the drop in jobs and income following the withdrawal of the Canadians and Americans. In addition, Newfoundland would have to count on a full recovery of its export markets that had been closed by the war.

There was serious concern that Newfoundland was merely experiencing a fleeting prosperity that would evaporate as quickly as it had appeared. This was reasonable thinking because the war had not seriously altered the fundamental structure of Newfoundland's economy; the prosperity induced by the Canadians and Americans was grafted on to Newfoundland's economy and was likely to wither once deprived of the steady flow of foreign dollars. Writing near the end of the war, R.A. MacKay reviewed the outlook for Newfoundland: 'There have been no advances in industrialization comparable with those in Canada and the United States; no new resources as yet proved to be of substantial importance have been brought into production; and no radical changes in the techniques of production appear to have been developed. Except for the improvement in the Government's financial position, and probably in the liquidity of many Newfoundland businesses, Newfoundland will face the immediate post-war era with an economy substantially the same as that of 1939.'[27]

Newfoundland emerged from the war with an economy that remained dependent on world trade and at the mercy of international forces. Unfortunately for the Newfoundlanders, much had changed in the world, and the pre-war pattern of trade was unlikely to revive in the unstable post-war world. This was particularly true for the United Kingdom, which clearly would never return to its former position of prominence.[28]

Nevertheless, a degree of economic prosperity lent itself to a growing interest in Newfoundland's political future. The negotiation of the base deal in 1940–1 revealed to many Newfoundlanders their country's startling inability to control its own destiny. Other incidents grated on the pride of many Newfoundlanders. For example, the introduction of a measure of representative government in Jamaica sparked a new round of calls for the restoration of responsible government in Newfoundland. The American consul-general reported to Washington that as a result of this act, 'considerable healthy discussion is taking place in Newfoundland.'[29] Before too long 'healthy discussion' had produced a degree of anger; in September 1942 the *Daily News* described Newfoundland's position: 'It is the only all-white population within the Empire that is completely void of franchise and of any other symptom of constitutional democracy. In this respect it is inferior to some of the smallest of the West Indian colonies.'

The obvious focus for attack was the Commission of Government, which had consistently failed to implement a system of good public relations with the local population. To many Newfoundlanders the Commission of Government appeared to have made few significant reforms; it had eagerly sold out to the Canadians and Americans with regard to their defence projects, and it had failed to secure for Newfoundland any of the 'obvious' benefits to be had from Newfoundland's airports and unique location: could this government be trusted to lead Newfoundland into the post-war world? For the *Daily News* the answer was no: 'Can we expect constructive policy aimed at the creation of a decent minimum living standard for all the people from a system of Government which has been reluctant to accept new ideas and has placed its reliance on the establishment of a primitive economy which is unsuited to the needs of the people?'[30]

The other major newspaper in St John's, the *Evening Telegram*, echoed many of these concerns. An editorial on 15 September 1942 noted that Newfoundland 'feels not only the humiliation but the disadvantages as well of having no voice in the control of its affairs.' But the *Evening Telegram* was not so sure that the immediate return of responsible government was the best solution, even though government by commission was the antithesis of democracy. The editors were not yet 'convinced that the country as a whole considers the times or the circumstances to be opportune for any immediate change.'[31]

One man who was convinced was Peter Cashin, a former Newfoundland finance minister and early opponent of the Commission of Government. During 1944–5, Cashin conducted a one-man campaign across Newfoundland for the restoration of responsible government, and through his radio broadcasts on VOCM, a St John's radio station, stirred public opinion against the Commission of Government.

The inescapable reality of the situation was that because of wartime prosperity, Newfoundland was 'again self-supporting' and therefore met the preconditions set up by the United Kingdom in 1933. In fact, the tables had turned: Newfoundland had lent millions of dollars to the United Kingdom while the British had come hat-in-hand to North America looking for financial aid. The temptation was too great not to compare Britain's predicament at the end of the Second World War with that of Newfoundland in 1933: 'Just now Great Britain can't pay her way and was forced to raise a large loan in the U.S.A.,' noted the editor of *The Fishermen's Advocate*. 'Just what an almighty squawk would rise to high heaven if it was suggested that in return for financial assistance the U.S.A. would appoint a Commission of Government to rule the British Isles?'[32]

Clearly a decision regarding Newfoundland's future would have to be made. The British were, of course, concerned over Newfoundland's financial viability in the post-war world and the fear that the country would not continue to be self-supporting tended to overshadow the other constitutional niceties. And, although the Dominions Office was reluctant to act while the war continued, the wheels were put in motion during these years to find some workable solution. By the end of 1945 a decision had been reached – but not one that would please all Newfoundlanders.

II

In his book *The Commonwealth Office*, the late Lord Garner wrote that the function of the Dominions Office 'was to further the interests of Britain; the D.O. was not the representative of the Dominions. Its aim was to secure the cooperation of the Dominions where necessary in carrying out British policies.' In doing so the Dominions Office 'sought to present those policies in a manner likely to prove acceptable to Dominion Governments and at the same time make known to British policy-makers any difficulties that Dominion Governments might see and to recommend ways of overcoming these.' Unfortunately this led to difficulties where the views of the two governments remained far apart, leaving the Dominions Office 'in danger of being caught between two fires, exposed to complaints from each side that its case was not being sufficiently pressed.'[33]

Newfoundland's unusual constitutional status singled it out as a unique problem for the Dominions Office. In some ways its job was easier: the direct rule of Newfoundland guaranteed that country's co-operation with the wishes of the United Kingdom. Moreover, the need to interpret Britain's motives was removed because the Newfoundlanders lacked an effective means for opposition. This is not to suggest that the Dominions Office adopted a callous attitude towards Newfoundland – if anything, it did just the opposite. The problem of Newfoundland did not attract much attention or stir much enthusiasm inside the Dominions Office, but among those officials who were involved there was exhibited a dogged willingness to see that the best was done for the Newfoundlanders. At times, however, this appeared something like benevolent paternalism shown to a troublesome colony.

The real trouble lay with the fact that the Dominions Office was forced to take a more active part in its relationship with Newfoundland. More so than in its relations with the other dominions, the Dominions Office played a role in the formulation of policy for Newfoundland, rather than acting to interpret policy between two governments. And only after Newfoundland's present problems had been thoroughly investigated would the DO be in a position to formulate an effective policy for the future.

Throughout the war there were a series of investigative trips to Newfoundland by British politicians and officials from the Dominions Office. Each would stay a short while, travel around the island and talk to the local population, and then return to London to submit a memorandum on the 'Problem of Newfoundland.' Most never returned to the matter, leaving their mass of information in the hands of a few officials in the Dominions Office and, ultimately, the dominions secretary.

Three individuals within the Dominions Office stand out as having played a continuous role in the affairs of Newfoundland: 1 / Sir Eric Machtig, the permanent under secretary of state for dominions, 1940–9; 2 / Alexander Clutterbuck, who had been secretary to the 1933 Royal Commission and was assistant under secretary for dominions during most of the war, before becoming Britain's high commissioner in Canada from 1946 to 1952; and 3 / St John Chadwick, who was the secretary to the Goodwill Mission and author of the 1946 'Report on the Financial and Economic Position of Newfoundland,' and who later wrote *Newfoundland: Island into Province* (1967).

The base-destroyer deal and the beginnings of an economic turn-around in Newfoundland prompted the Dominions Office late in 1941 to initiate an investigation into the changing circumstances in Newfoundland. This included sending two representatives of the Dominions Office to Newfoundland: Geoffrey Shakespeare, the under secretary of state for the dominions office, and Joe Garner, the secretary to Lord Cranborne, the dominions secretary. Their visit to Newfoundland was a side trip of their visit to Canada and lasted only a few days.

On their return both men filed reports in the Dominions Office of their impressions of Newfoundland. Garner in particular believed that the British government had a responsibility to help improve the general economic situation in Newfoundland, which struck him as being a country 'in a thoroughly neglected and dilapidated state.' Long-term reconstruction would be necessary, and, moreover, the time for action was the present – before Newfoundland was allowed to slip back into 'economic chaos.'[34] Shakespeare was in basic agreement with Garner, but his report focused more on Newfoundland's political future. Confederation or union with the United States was immediately dismissed as unacceptable to an intensely loyal population. This left two choices: either restore dominion status or have the British government instigate a large-scale development scheme under the Commission of Government. Dominion status would be returned on its completion – if the Newfoundlanders wanted it. Shakespeare favoured the latter alternative and called for a 'bold, imaginative plan' to see it through.[35]

The Garner and Shakespeare memos were circulated around the department and elicited a number of comments. P.E. Emrys Evans, who followed Shakespeare as under secretary, tried to bring the policy choices into clearer focus. The economic reconstruction of Newfoundland should be Britain's 'immediate aim,' but over the long term, he felt, efforts should be made to enhance Canadian-Newfoundland relations: 'If close and sympathetic co-operation in the development of the Island and of Labrador came from Canada, the possibility of union might come into the realm of practical politics. The ultimate aim of our policy should be to bring Newfoundland into the Confederation.'[36]

Sir Eric Machtig presented Emrys Evans's memo and a summation of his own comments to Clement Attlee, the dominions secretary. Although Machtig disagreed with some of Evans's reasoning, he accepted his conclusions. When the war ended there would be a strong call for change in Newfoundland and it was imperative that Britain take steps now to prepare for the future. As for Confederation, he could not agree more; in the unfolding of the post-war world there would be an increased need for co-operation between nations in defence and economic matters, and smaller nations would likely find it tough going. Britain's goal, therefore, 'should be to bring Newfoundland into the Canadian Federation if by any means this can be accomplished.'[37]

Clement Attlee was the final recipient of this bulk of information, suggestion, and comment. Surprisingly, he found considerable time to devote to the problem of Newfoundland, despite his numerous other duties as dominions secretary and deputy prime minister. St John Chadwick explains that 'it was typical of Mr. Attlee's sympathy with the political underdog and of his keen interest in training the unenfranchised in the arts of politics that their problems and recommendations invariably received his full attention.'[38] But, in addition to his sympathy for the workers and fishermen of Newfoundland, Attlee also brought his own prejudices into play: a strong concern for the establishment of local government, a zeal for the decentralization of authority, and an antipathy for the St John's ruling elite. He raised a number of questions with his officials and, still dissatisfied, decided to see for himself.

In September 1942, Attlee paid a short visit to Newfoundland before travelling on to Canada. He held talks with the governor and a number of commissioners and spoke to the public in a radio broadcast. After praising the Newfoundlanders for their war effort he told them that they could not count on full employment continuing into the post-war world. As for constitutional change, this must be submerged until the war was over. Until that time, the Newfoundlanders must make preparations to solve the problems of reconstruction. Few specifics were mentioned, either on radio or in private, and Attlee refused to commit himself or his government to any future action.

Attlee returned to London with perhaps a fuller understanding of Newfoundland's predicament, but no closer to a solution for it. As long as both Canada and Newfoundland showed no inclination towards union, then Confederation must be ruled out. This, according to Attlee, left three choices: maintain the Commission of Government, restore full dominion status, or find something in between, a kind of 'half-way house' for Newfoundland. Attlee felt that the first choice was impracticable and believed the second would be unpopular in Newfoundland. This left the idea of a half-way-house system in which responsible government would be restored in stages. Yet Attlee also recognized that if the Newfoundlanders demanded the immediate return of self-government, the United Kingdom would be bound to comply.[39]

The Commission of Government made its views clear to Attlee in a rather long but interesting telegram, dated 7 January 1943. The commissioners were adamant in their belief that Newfoundland would not be able to stand on its own economically after the war, and thus the answer might be 'in the political incorporation of this country in a larger unit.' One possibility was to transform Newfoundland into another Northern Ireland; the other was Confederation. The commissioners were not convinced that union with Canada was unacceptable, since no serious attempts had been made for decades. In fact, it might be best to strike while the iron was hot: 'Canada's present and growing interest in this country, her fear of an increase of United States influence, her desire to acquire the Labrador, are all powerful factors. At no time has our bargaining position been so favourable and it is doubtful if it ever will be so again.' Any overt efforts to bring in Confederation would be unwise at that moment, 'but it is one of the alternatives which we consider might be explored in secret between persons in the highest quarters.' What the United Kingdom should do at this time, the Newfoundland government recommended, would be to establish a committee to conduct another investigation, this time concentrating on economic matters.[40]

As deputy prime minister, Attlee was a member of the British War Cabinet, and on 15 March 1943 he brought up the question of Newfoundland. He reviewed Newfoundland's position in a memo distributed to the ministers, noting that the country was experiencing tremendous prosperity, to the point of making sizable loans to the

United Kingdom. He reminded them of Britain's responsibility to return self-government if the Newfoundlanders asked for it, despite the appalling lack of public interest in the machinery and responsibilities of government. Attlee then proposed to send a parliamentary mission to Newfoundland to 'see something of its many activities and the way of life of the people, and form some idea both of the potentialities of the country and of the capacity of the Islanders to take charge of their own affairs.'[41] It would also please the Newfoundlanders and give them a new channel for criticism.

The War Cabinet gave its approval and within a fortnight the Commission of Government had agreed as well.[42] On 5 May Attlee informed the House of Commons of the creation of a 'Goodwill Mission' which would 'have no defined terms of reference,' other than to travel 'amongst the people' and examine the problems of Newfoundland.[43] Moreover, because of its informal nature, the Goodwill Mission would not publish a final report on its return to London. In its place, oral reports would be made to the House by the individual members.

The Goodwill Mission consisted of C.G. (later Lord) Ammon (Labour), A.P. Herbert (later Sir) (Independent), and Sir Derrick Gunston (Conservative), and included St John Chadwick, who accompanied them as secretary. For several months during the summer of 1943 they travelled the island by road, rail, sea, and air, covering as much territory and meeting as many Newfoundlanders as they possibly could. Before too long they had become enthralled by the 'charming folk' in Newfoundland, and Herbert, in particular, was taken by the Newfoundlanders that he met: 'They are gay, good-humoured and generous; tolerant, temperate, tough, God-fearing, sabbath-keeping and law abiding. Fond of holidays but fine workers: politically maddening but personally the salt of the earth.'[44]

Unfortunately, personal differences interfered with the smooth workings of the Goodwill Mission. Ammon, the dour 'old-line' Labour politician, was quite the contrast to A.P. Herbert, the outgoing, ardent drinker and professional humourist. Watching from St John's, George Hopper, the American consul-general, described the clash of personalities this way:

Mr. Ammon is temperamentally quite different from the others, being less sociable, a teetotaller, and reputedly an ardent seeker-out of the clergy class, eagerly accepting all invitations to occupy the pulpit in village churches, whereas the others are extremely gregarious, not adverse to taking a drink, and strong believers that more can be learned from the ordinary man than from one of the clergy class; Mr Ammon is said to be inclined to regard the Mission as his own and that the others, especially Mr Herbert whom he sometimes belittles, are along only to support his views, whereas each of the others believes that all share in the Mission and that Mr Ammon, whom they refer to jokingly as 'der Fuehrer' [sic], should consult with them.[45]

The result of all this was that the Goodwill Mission did not travel as a single unit during the whole of its stay in Newfoundland, and ultimately it failed to submit a unanimous report. Herbert approved of this method and remembers that 'when I saw Derrick Gunston again I found that, in odd corners and moments, he had nearly finished tapping out his version of Newfoundland. And John Chadwick, at the more stately speed of the Civil Service, was drafting a most able report for our leader. This, I think, was a good arrangement. I do not believe very much in the modern technique of artificial unanimity.'[46] This is not surprising, since Herbert saw Ammon as a supporter of Confederation, an idea which was anathema to him. Herbert found the Newfoundlanders 'intensely English. Their names are English, their ancestors were English, and after all these generations their accents are English still. The great go-getting, twanging continent next door has not got the Newfoundlander yet.'[47]

Yet, considering the significant differences in viewpoint, there emerged a rough agreement on some matters. The members of the Goodwill Mission found the Newfoundlanders united only in terms of opposition; few wanted to return to the atmosphere of the pre-commission days, and for reasons of impracticability and unpopularity, Confederation was ruled out. But they agreed that most Newfoundlanders were not sure exactly what they did want. All three members agreed on the holding of a plebiscite after the war to have the Newfoundlanders choose the form of government they would like to have. Ammon and Herbert also recommended a long-term (ten years was usually suggested) redevelopment plan assisted by the United Kingdom, in an effort to put Newfoundland back on its feet. None suggested the removal of dominion status, but Herbert recommended that serious consideration be given to the possibility of bringing Newfoundland into the United Kingdom along the lines of Northern Ireland. A second idea, and one that found a more favourable reception, was to establish a 'national convention' of Newfoundlanders from all walks of life to debate and decide for themselves the kind of future they wanted.[48]

The Goodwill Mission returned to London and the individual reports were filed with the Dominions Office. In the meantime, Lord Cranborne, a Conservative, had replaced Attlee as dominions secretary, with Lord Beaverbrook assuming Cranborne's old office of Lord Privy Seal. Cranborne studied the reports and agreed with Attlee's decision not to publish them, although he saw no problem in the members of the mission expressing their opinions during the upcoming debate on dominion affairs in the House of Commons.[49]

Before this debate took place, Cranborne prepared a memorandum on the Newfoundland question for the War Cabinet. The Goodwill Mission, Attlee's 1942 visit, and the various other voyages of investigation had met with the appreciation of the Newfoundlanders, but they had also added to growing agitation for constitutional reform. For this reason Cranborne believed that some concrete action was called for immediately, even if it was not the ideal time for it from the British point of view. A statement of Britain's intentions, he argued, would 'have a steadying effect' in Newfoundland.[50]

Cranborne's memo was discussed at the War Cabinet meeting held on 19 November 1943. Lord Beaverbrook presented his own memo on Newfoundland to the members, and it was at this meeting that he and Cranborne discussed the Goose Bay situation. At the mention of Confederation, Beaverbrook brusquely dismissed it as impossible; in his view the return of self-government was the one and only answer.[51] Self-government, to him, implied a continuing and close connection with Britain. Though Beaverbrook may have been the most colourful, he was not the only exponent of Newfoundland as a valuable strategic jewel in the Imperial crown.

Cranborne laid out what he proposed to announce to the House in the anticipated debate on dominion affairs. Cranborne himself favoured Confederation, but that solution was unworkable because of its unpopularity in Newfoundland, which was likely to continue 'so long as there is money in the till and no pressing necessity for so drastic a step.' Otherwise, he made five recommendations: 1 / no change in status until after the war; 2 / the provision, at the end of the war, of appropriate 'machinery' for the Newfoundlanders to examine and determine their own future; 3 / a promise to return self-government immediately if the Newfoundlanders asked for it; 4 / a promise to at least examine any proposals for a half-way-house arrangement; 5 / the immediate development of local government to prepare the Newfoundlanders to govern themselves.[52] He was not specific of the nature of the 'machinery' but he did mention that he was impressed with Herbert's idea of holding a national convention. Attlee applauded Cranborne's emphasis on the need for improvements in local government and education, and said he had reached similar conclusions during his tenure as dominions secretary. Then, with the exception of Beaver-brook, the War Cabinet approved Cranborne's proposals.[53]

On 2 December 1943, Emrys Evans rose in the House of Commons and delivered a statement of policy concerning Newfoundland. He told the members that it was understood 'that as soon as the island's difficulties are overcome and the country is again self-supporting, responsible government, on the request from the people of Newfound-land, would be restored.' Yet, he added, because of the 'existing abnormal conditions caused by the war which make it impossible for the Newfoundland people as a whole to come to a considered conclusion as to the Island's future prospects, there should be no change in the present form of Government while the war lasts.' Evans continued with an elaboration of Cranborne's proposals to set up machinery after the war which would enable the Newfoundlanders to decide for themselves, but he was equally vague on the nature of that machinery.[54]

The Commission of Government studied the proposals but its response revealed surprisingly little enthusiasm for the British plans. Questions were raised over the constitutional propriety of setting up 'machinery' that might lead to the establishment of a new system of government in Newfoundland – such a possibility had not been debated in 1933, and if it had, chances were that the Newfoundland government would have refused to agree to the suspension of responsible govern-ment. But the announcement had been made, and the British govern-ment was unlikely to backpeddle on a policy already made public in the House of Commons. The commissioners recognized this and were willing to follow whatever decisions were reached in London.[55] And, in the meantime, they carried on with the formulation of a reconstruction plan for Newfoundland.

III

The developments in London and St John's were watched from Ottawa with an increasingly attentive eye. For a small group of civil servants centred around the Department of External Affairs it was becoming clear that Canada would have to do something about Newfoundland before too long. The island and Labrador had become too important, and the risks of losing a dominant position there had become too great to let the matter rest as it had in the past. Traditionally Canada had been reluctant to pay the high price of union because the return had appeared negligible; now, for official Ottawa at least, the cost had become acceptable and the cause a necessary one.

In his biography of Norman Robertson, J.L. Granatstein notes that Robertson, along with Pearson and Hume Wrong, 'presided over the change in Canada from a timid Dominion to a sometimes aggressive and nationalistic middle power.'[56] Evidence of this was the willingness of the Canadians to exercise their growing strength and the emergence of the functional principle, or the assumption of responsibility equal to the role played by Canada. Equally, the evolution of the concept of middle-power status brought with it new dilemmas: 'The big fellows have power and responsibility,' wrote Lester Pearson in 1944, 'but they also have control. The little fellows have no power and responsibility; therefore are not interested in contol. We "in between" States sometimes get, it seems, the worst of both worlds. We are necessary but not necessary enough!'[57]

The Department of External Affairs (DEA) had grown in size and strength during the 1930s with the recruitment of a strong cadre of young Canadians. In many ways these new men, such as Robertson, Pearson, and Wrong, reflected the 'new mood' in Canada's foreign policy by calling for a larger autonomous role for Canada. This became more evident following the death of O.D. Skelton in 1941 and his replacement as under secretary by Norman Robertson. In his book *The Shaping of Peace*, J.W. Holmes notes the evolution of differing perceptions of the meaning of autonomy: to the senior men it meant being able to keep clear from commitments; to the younger men it indicated an ability to get things done.[58]

Newfoundland was a problem that furnished the DEA with the opportunity to 'get things done.' The fall of France and the base-destroyer deal awakened a keen interest in the problem of Newfoundland, but only among a handful of officials. Lester Pearson was introduced to the question as a spectator during the negotiations of the Leased Bases Agreement in 1941. Similarly, Norman Robertson began to see the American presence in Newfoundland as a serious threat to Canadian interests. As early as May 1941 he told J.P. Moffat, the American ambassador, 'that the United States did not in fact take Canadian interests in Newfoundland seriously as Canada felt they ought to be taken,' and noted that 'the situation deserved better handling and franker interchange than it was getting at present.'[59]

A few weeks later Robertson again discussed Newfoundland with Moffat, and the American recorded that Robertson felt that Canada and Newfoundland would someday 'have to face the problem of confederation.' By the end of 1941 Robertson was warning Prime Minister King of 'the gradual assumption by the United States of hegemony in Newfoundland.' And, in the meantime, Robertson was reading up on Newfoundland history.[60]

Robertson remained at the centre of a small group within the DEA that helped form Canada's policy towards Newfoundland throughout the war. At various times this group included Pearson, Escott Reid, and Hume Wrong, in addition to the Canadian high commissioners in St John's – C.J. Burchell and J.S. Macdonald. Others, such as J.R. Baldwin, touched on Newfoundland issues more indirectly, through their work on related matters, like civil aviation. Two other members of the department also bear mentioning. The first was R.A. MacKay, who was recruited from Dalhousie University early in the war, and was put in charge of the Newfoundland Desk in the DEA. The second was the ubiquitous Hugh Keenleyside, whose contact with Newfoundland affairs during the war ranged from his years as secretary to the Canadian section of the PJBD to his months as acting high commissioner in St John's in 1944.

The question of long-term policy regarding Newfoundland attracted a good deal of attention late in 1941, and on one occasion (29 October 1941) reached the Cabinet War Committee. Yet no long-term goals were carved in stone then or later, other than to keep Newfoundland within the Canadian orbit. For the most part, Canadian policy continued to be predicated on the changing interpretation of Canada's 'national interest' in the western Atlantic area. Canada's role in the Battle of the Atlantic, the negotiations with Newfoundland over the use of Gander and Botwood, the dispute over Goose Bay, and the implementation of the Atlantic ferry and a transatlantic air service were not undertaken with an eye on the possibility of leading Newfoundland into Confederation; rather the Canadians were serving their own interests as best they could. If union ultimately came about, so much the better.

The question of Newfoundland's future was not the kind of problem that inspired much conversation in the halls of the East Block or informally in the cafeteria of the Château Laurier. In the atmosphere of wartime crisis, other, more important topics dominated the Ottawa scene. Slowly, however, the situation began to change. The experiences of those involved in Newfoundland affairs had driven home the importance of Newfoundland in the Canadian scheme of things, and at the same time had shown just how fragile Canada's hold on the country was. The fear of losing Newfoundland to the Americans brought many Canadians who had previously never given Newfoundland much thought to the realization that they wanted to keep it.

Outside of government there was a growing awareness of Newfoundland, or at least that a Newfoundland problem existed. Although Canadian-Newfoundland relations never caught the public imagination, there were at this time a growing number of articles and books dealing with Newfoundland. Under such titles as 'Canada's 10th Province?' and 'Canada and Newfoundland ... The Bonds Grow Tighter,' the pros and cons of Confederation were examined. More often than not, the authors included a warning that if Canada did not act, then the Americans would.[61] To virtually all, Confederation was a good idea; to most, it was inevitable; to some, it was absolutely necessary.

A larger study of Newfoundland was undertaken at this time by R.A. MacKay, who in 1947 became head of the Commonwealth Division in the Department of External Affairs. Under the auspices of the Royal Institute of International Affairs, MacKay produced *Newfoundland: Economic, Diplomatic and Strategic Studies*, an excellent book which included chapters on history, the Commission of Government, external trade, and public finance. This book became the standard work on Newfoundland and it was distributed throughout the Department of External Affairs and later to the National Convention in Newfoundland. Although MacKay's pro-Confederation feelings did not surface in the book, he held out little hope that an independent Newfoundland could flourish in the post-war world.

The revival of the debate over Newfoundland's constitutional future in St John's and London in 1943 sparked an equally sympathetic concern in Ottawa. Informal contacts concerning Newfoundland matters were easily made, given the already established close working relationship of the British and Canadian officials. The atmosphere of wartime Ottawa produced an ample measure of comradeship, shared purpose, and, remembers one participant, an 'extraordinary degree of intimacy and trust.'[62] This was perhaps nowhere more evident than in the relationship between Robertson and Malcolm MacDonald, the British high commissioner. On a number of occasions during 1943 MacDonald found the opportunity to bring up the problem of Newfoundland on an informal basis, knowing he could trust Robertson to keep the matter confidential.

For the last two years of the war dealings between the two governments on the Newfoundland issue became increasingly frequent. Rarely, however, were they undertaken in the public eye. On the contrary, there was a tacit understanding that giving any hint that Canada and the United Kingdom were 'conspiring' to settle Newfoundland's future must be avoided at all costs. Mackenzie King subscribed to this view, and would make public pronouncements concerning Newfoundland only when hard pressed.

Such was the case in July 1943, when J.W. Noseworthy, the MP for York South, delivered a lengthy speech in the House of Commons on Newfoundland and its importance to Canada. Noseworthy, who was born in Newfoundland, argued that the war had made North Americans out of the Newfoundlanders, and that the time would soon be ripe to open negotiations for Confederation. Interestingly, his real concern seemed to be the Americans: 'One cannot wonder that the presence of United States money and the knowledge of United States standards of living are making a significant appeal to some of the people.'

Mackenzie King brushed off the suggestion of opening negotiations suggesting that this was 'not the particular moment at which it would be most advisable to discuss the question.' King followed with the argument that it was up to the Newfoundlanders to make any overtures towards Confederation, and continued by making what would be his final statement on Newfoundland affairs for the duration of the war:

I would say that Canadians like and admire the people of Newfoundland. They are attached to them by bonds of sentiment and by the memory of dangers shared and victories won together. They look forward to a continuation of the friendship and cooperation which have increasingly marked our relations during recent years. Canadians are interested in the defence of Newfoundland which is so vital a part of the defence of the continent and the hemisphere. They hope that the people of Newfoundland will find some wholly satisfactory solution of the political and economic problems which confront them. They will be happy if, in any way, they can contribute to the solution of these problems, many of which are common to both countries.

If the people of Newfoundland should ever decide that they wish to enter the Canadian federation and should make that decision clear beyond all possibility of misunderstanding, Canada would give most sympathetic consideration to the proposal.[63]

King's statement was warmly received in the Dominions Office. Any indication of Canadian interest was to be welcomed and encouraged, and early in August MacDonald brought the issue up over lunch with Robertson. He explained the Dominions Office position and the purpose of the Goodwill Mission, and suggested that the United Kingdom would like to have a 'preliminary exchange of views' with the Canadians before they made any official statement concerning Newfoundland.

Robertson reported this conversation to King, adding: 'My own feeling is that "somehow, sometime" Newfoundland should become part of the Canadian Confederation. I think that, in the long run, both political and strategic considerations make this inevitable.' Yet Robertson was also sensitive to the myriad difficulties hindering the likelihood of union. The entrance of Newfoundland into Confederation would have little effect on the amount of goods exported to Canada from Newfoundland, and before too long Newfoundland 'would very quickly take over as its own all the old Maritime grievances against the Canadian tariff and freight rate structure.' Moreover, the concept of union was a very unpopular one in Newfoundland and, in addition, many Canadians would hesitate before taking on such a financial burden.[64]

Informal conversations continued into the autumn of 1943. For example, on a visit to London in October, Keenleyside discussed Newfoundland with both Lord Cranborne and Sir Eric Machtig, and found the latter strongly in favour of Confederation.[65] Despite the mounting controversy over Goose Bay, important elements within the Dominions Office had not permitted short-term problems to overshadow long-term goals.

Canadian policy underwent a significant re-examination in November 1943, as a result of a seventeen-page memo by R.A. MacKay. MacKay quite likely knew more about Newfoundland than anyone else in the department, and he prepared for Robertson an informed and reasoned overview of Newfoundland's economic position. He included his own views on the country's outlook for the future and what Canada's response should be. It was an ambitious effort to put some flesh onto the skeleton that was Canadian policy regarding Newfoundland.[66]

MacKay began with a discussion of the circumstances surrounding Newfoundland's economic difficulties. If the world experienced a revival in international trade and Newfoundland could re-establish its pre-war trading patterns, then Newfoundland could make it on its own, but this was very much in doubt. Newfoundland's economy remained virtually unchanged, and it was likely that the country would be ill-prepared to survive in the post-war world.

MacKay turned next to Canadian interests in Newfoundland. As it stood, Canada had no post-war rights in either defence or civil aviation and the effort to secure them would have to be the cornerstone of Canada's 'Newfoundland policy.' This left Canada and Newfoundland with three choices: 1 / Confederation; 2 / the continuation of the existing situation, with Canada, the United States, and the United Kingdom jointly defending the country; and 3 / to make Newfoundland a military dependency of Canada. The last choice was straightforward: Canada would secure its own position in Newfoundland without having to shoulder any economic burden. Confederation, however, would safeguard Canadian interests in defence and civil aviation, but as a province Newfoundland would likely become an economic and political liability.[67]

MacKay developed his ideas further in a second memo, dated 21 March 1944. He recommended establishing a joint defence board with Newfoundland and the United Kingdom along the lines of the PJBD. This proposal was rooted in the belief that Canadian policy regarding Newfoundland could not be founded on the assumption that Newfoundland would enter Confederation in the near future. Nevertheless, Newfoundland would remain a high priority for Canadian policy-makers, and, suggested MacKay, Canada should assume the responsibility for the sea, air, and land defence of its territory: If the Newfoundlanders objected, Canada could calm their fears by taking over some of Newfoundland's financial obligations.[68]

MacKay's proposals were examined by other members of the department and they struck a responsive chord with Robertson, who introduced them to the Cabinet War Committee in April 1944. The CWC found the proposals valuable as potential objectives for the future, but was cool to a policy of actively pursuing them. A decision was made to delay any action until the question had received further consideration, but the matter was not returned to and it was allowed to drop.[69] Nevertheless, the Canadian government had been awakened to the need to have a Newfoundland policy. Evidence of this was the appointment of Hugh Keenleyside as acting high commissioner in St John's in January 1944. Keenleyside recalls that Ottawa felt that 'someone should go to the island to review the problems and possibilities of the time when the hurricane of war should have subsided.'[70]

For the British, who saw Keenleyside as a Confederate, his appointment was a signal, showing that the Canadians were 'now taking Newfoundland much more seriously than they have in the past.'[71] Joe

Garner, who was now stationed in the British high commission in Ottawa, believed that it offered the occasion for action: 'If ... there are any seeds which the Dominions Office want to sow,' he wrote Clutterbuck, 'Keenleyside's stay in Newfoundland should present an admirable opportunity for influencing the mind of the Canadian Government.'[72]

Indeed, the evolution of a strong Canadian interest in Newfoundland was, in the eyes of the British government, a development of fundamental importance. As long as Newfoundland remained a strategic bastion in Britain's defence and was a major stepping-stone in the world of civil aviation, there were good reasons to maintain the status quo. Newfoundland had proved to be a valuable asset to Britain during the war. But victory in the Atlantic and the invasion of Europe somewhat lessened the perception of Newfoundland's importance. Moreover, Britain's position in Newfoundland was relatively well protected, regardless of future political developments there: Britain was guaranteed participation in the future talks concerning the civil use of Gander and Botwood; the British could, if they wished, maintain their control of St John's harbour; and by the end of 1944 the Goose Bay Agreement was signed, giving the United Kingdom a right to sit in on the post-war discussions dealing with the military use of Goose Bay.

Not surprisingly, as the strategic value of Newfoundland dropped, more attention was paid to the costs of maintaining it. And, if Newfoundland could not support itself after the war, where would Britain find the necessary dollars to keep the country afloat? Even the most optimistic became sceptical of Britain's ability to continue long-term support, given Britain's acute dollar shortage. Despite the wartime prosperity, by 1945 Newfoundland was perceived as a financial liability. Nowhere was this more evident than in the response to the Commission of Government's reconstruction plan.

On the suggestion of the Dominions Office, the Commission of Government undertook an examination of Newfoundland's economy for the purpose of drawing up a long-range economic recovery program. This study continued into the summer of 1944. The result was a ninety-six-page report that called for a ten-year reconstruction plan for Newfoundland that was 'designed as the best means of promoting the economic and social development of the Island.' This program was designed to be financed by the United Kingdom, at an estimated cost of $100 million.[73]

The reconstruction plan included a wide variety of improvements and economic development projects. Almost $10 million was allocated to the fisheries for vessel construction, research, and experiments. Likewise, resettlement schemes, surveys, and other land developments were earmarked to receive almost $10 million. Other allotments included: $1 million for research and experiments in forestry; $6 million for industrial development; $2.5 million for tourism; $1 million for mineral exploration; $16 million for roads and bridges; $8.5 million for education; $7.4 million for health and welfare; $5 million for housing; $5 million for local government; and an additional $4.1 million for government buildings.[74]

The Newfoundland reconstruction plan met with decidedly mixed reactions in London. C.F. Cobbold of the Bank of England felt the whole idea to be ridiculous. Britain would have to borrow the required dollars from Canada, which under the present financial circumstances was a ludicrous proposal. 'However sympathetic' Britain was to Newfoundland's predicament, he wrote, 'it seems out of the question that we should prejudice our own prospects of meeting our great dollar difficulties by borrowing in any form from Canada for Newfoundland account.'[75]

In the Dominions Office, Clutterbuck took a more positive approach. He believed that the long-term reconstruction program held attractions for a wide spectrum of British opinion. Even for those convinced of the need for Confederation the plan was of value because it would make Newfoundland more enticing to the Canadians. Besides, he argued, without it, Newfoundland would collapse in the near future, which would in the long run cost the British treasury more. Confederation was unlikely at this time and the reconstruction plan was needed to tide Newfoundland over until the idea became more popular:

What the Canadians want is time, time to win over Newfoundland opinion and to bring home the advantages of the union of the two countries: what would suit them therefore would be something which was calculated to ensure reasonable stability in the Island until there had been opportunity for a policy of breaking down the barriers to take effect. This is exactly what our proposals are calculated to provide. If Newfoundland were to return to self-government, but without continued assistance from us, the result would almost certainly be chaos and a fresh crisis in a few years time; and the likelihood would be that this crisis would arrive before there had been any change of outlook towards Canada and while Newfoundlanders were still under the glamorous spell of the lavish American war-time expenditure in the Island ... Our proposals would relieve

Canadians of this anxiety; for ten years at least the financial and economic position of the Island would be reasonably assured, and this would give them time to get to work on laying fresh foundations for the future.[76]

Clutterbuck ruled out Canadian assistance either directly to Newfoundland or indirectly through the United Kingdom, seeing such assistance as political dynamite once it was discovered in Newfoundland. Hence, Britain would have to face the financial burden alone. Nevertheless, the Canadians should be kept in close contact on all developments. These contacts, however, must remain secret, 'since any suspicion in Newfoundland that we were in touch with the Canadians regarding our policy in the Island would have the most damaging results.'[77]

Clutterbuck's memo was incorporated into a joint Dominions Office–Treasury memo that circulated around Whitehall for comment. The verdict of the treasury was harsh. Lord Keynes, who had shortly before returned from tough financial negotiations in Ottawa, was astounded. 'When I first saw this,' he wrote of the reconstruction plan, 'I thought that $100 million must be a misprint for $10 million. I still think it is better so regarded.' Keynes agreed with many of Clutterbuck's conclusions but took exception to his reasoning: 'It is agreed that the right long-term solution is for Newfoundland to be taken over by Canada. The argument seems to be that the Newfoundlanders will overcome their reluctance to leave us and put themselves in the hands of Canada if we give them these great sums. It would have been natural to conclude the exact opposite, namely that, after this signal mark of our favour, the Newfoundlanders would be still more reluctant to part company with us.'

The bottom line for Keynes was that it would be too financially damaging to help Newfoundland. As an alternative, he suggested that Canada be approached to buy Labrador for the $100 million and the assumption of Newfoundland's debt. If this failed then 'some way should be found of making Newfoundland at the earliest possible date the responsibility of Canada.'[78]

A few days before Christmas, Sir John Anderson, the chancellor of the exchequer, discussed the Newfoundland problem with Cranborne. Anderson asked Cranborne to increase his contacts with the Canadians on the matter, to see if some arrangement could be worked out. In the meantime he requested that Cranborne refrain from making any promises of increased British aid, at least until Newfoundland's existing surplus had been used up. Cranborne replied that he could hold off only for a short period, and that, in his judgment, it was not a good time to press the Canadians too hard.[79]

The pressure from the treasury began to have its effect on Cranborne and the Dominions Office. The Commission of Government's original enthusiasm quickly evaporated as they began pruning the reconstruction plan down to more acceptable levels. Cranborne, meanwhile, was looking for any opportunity to bring the Canadians into closer contact on the Newfoundland question.

Cranborne got his wish in June 1945, but in unlikely surroundings. While he was attending the United Nations conference in San Francisco he was approached by Hume Wrong, who 'went out of his way to bring the talk round to Newfoundland.' Cranborne believed that Wrong was acting on specific instructions from Ottawa, and he reported the conversation to Machtig:

[Wrong] stressed the importance of the United Kingdom Government not finalizing measures for financial assistance to Newfoundland – or even going far in formulating them until things had been discussed with Canada who would in the ultimate event have to provide the dollars. I got the impression that the Canadian Government would not be very happy if we put Newfoundland in so stable a financial position that all incentive for her to join Canada was removed. The possibility of bringing about some close connexion between Canada and Newfoundland is from some further remarks that he made clearly in the mind of Canadian Ministers. For he said that they had been getting out some detailed figures as to what would be the annual cost of bringing the Newfoundland social services etc. up to date.[80]

This may have been wishful thinking on Cranborne's part because it got the Dominions Office off the hook by giving it a justification for backpeddling on the reconstruction plan. How could Britain proceed if the Canadians were so opposed to the idea? But there had been no Canadian cabinet decision on this question – Newfoundland had not really been discussed over the previous months and the Canadians were no closer to a 'Newfoundland policy' than they were in spring of 1944. Many in the government, such as Mackenzie King and C.D. Howe, no doubt favoured Confederation, but the political problems it presented precluded any overt efforts in that direction. Members of the DEA, such as Wrong, Robertson, and MacKay, were willing to go farther, but they too recognized that they were limited by political considerations.

Nevertheless, the Dominions Office believed that the Canadians were now more interested in Newfoundland's future. During the summer of 1945 planning was under way to establish a national convention, along the lines earlier suggested by A.P. Herbert. This would need cabinet approval, but the process had been held up by the election of a new Labour government under Clement Attlee. While things were being sorted out in London, Clutterbuck noted that it was 'clear that both from the financial and also from the political point of view, early discussions with the Canadians are called for.'[81]

Lord Addison, who at the end of July followed Cranborne as dominions secretary, was now saddled with the problem of Newfoundland. Addison wrote Hugh Dalton, the new chancellor of the exchequer, on 15 August, asking for his views on the reconstruction plan. He told Dalton that he wanted to make a statement on Newfoundland in the House of Commons in the autumn; Britain's obligation was clear and action could not be indefinitely postponed. This gave the Dominions Office approximately two months to get the views of the Canadians, to reach an agreement with the treasury, and to receive cabinet approval.[82]

Dalton replied to Addison that he agreed that action on Newfoundland's constitutional situation must be taken and that the Canadians should be consulted. But on the reconstruction plan he was opposed, seeing 'no prospect whatever of this country being able to provide the finance.' The difficulties this plan would produce were insurmountable: 'Quite apart from the effect on our own Exchequer,' he wrote, 'this presents us with an exchange problem which is quite insoluble. If the money is to be provided, it will have to come from Canada.'[83]

However sympathetic Addison may have been to the reconstruction plan, he recognized that it was doomed. Increasingly Addison came to feel that Newfoundland should be warned that the United Kingdom could not be expected to assist financially. With the option of financial aid vetoed by the chancellor of the exchequer and the treasury, he concluded that more emphasis must be placed on bringing the Canadians and Newfoundlanders together. The new interest of the Canadians in Newfoundland must be capitalized on, and to do so he decided to send Clutterbuck to Ottawa to open informal discussions.[84]

Clutterbuck arrived in Ottawa on 15 September and after comparing notes with Malcolm MacDonald, arranged a meeting with the Canadians for 18 September. Accompanied by Garner and Stephen Holmes, the deputy high commissioner, he met with Robertson, Wrong, MacKay, and J.S. Macdonald, the Canadian high commissioner in Newfoundland. Clutterbuck began the discussion with a review of the situation, explaining how hopes for the reconstruction plan had been 'dashed.' Britain's goal was financial stability for Newfoundland, but Britain's dollar position made long-term economic aid virtually impossible. Thus, Britain was forced to reconsider its whole Newfoundland policy and, before doing so, wanted to know the attitude of the Canadians.[85]

Clutterbuck was dismayed by the seemingly negative response he received. The Canadians pointed out that public interest in the Newfoundland question was at a minimum. It was pointed out that not one question had been raised about Newfoundland at the weekly DEA press conferences for more than two years. Nor, for that matter, had the Canadian government made any concerted effort to enhance Canada's image in Newfoundland. Moreover, union with Newfoundland would put an extra burden on the Canadian taxpayer, and the concept of 'special terms' for Newfoundland would be unacceptable to the other Canadian provinces. As they saw it, there was nothing Canada could do to help.

'I did not conceal my disappointment,' Clutterbuck reported. If neither Canada nor the United Kingdom could help, he asked, 'who could be surprised if [the] Newfoundlanders began to think seriously of turning to the United States?' Reference to the Americans elicited a more positive resonse: how, Clutterbuck was asked, would the British react if the Canadians indicated that they would welcome a call for Confederation? Clutterbuck answered that this would suit Britain fine – Confederation was considered by many in Britain to be Newfoundland's 'natural destiny.'[86]

During the course of his visit Clutterbuck also met separately with J.S. Macdonald and R.A. MacKay. From MacKay's calculations he learned that under the existing circumstances Newfoundland could exist as a Canadian province without the need for special treatment, providing the external debt was not taken into account. In a later private talk with Macdonald, he was heartened to discover that Macdonald believed that there was 'a substantial movement of opinion' in Newfoundland towards Confederation. Macdonald explained that the introduction of social-security measures in Canada, and particularly the children's allowance, was 'beginning to penetrate Newfoundland consciousness.'[87]

The Canadians stressed, however, that they were overstepping their authority by discussing possible solutions to the Newfoundland problem. It was clear that a decision would have to be made at the ministerial level before the officials could proceed much farther. This was pointed out to Mackenzie King by Norman Robertson in a memo dated 25 September 1945. The benefits of Confederation were reviewed and it was suggested that Canada could now offer Newfoundland better terms than previously possible, particularly if the financial arrangements discussed with the provinces a few weeks earlier were accepted. Now might be the best time to act – should the Canadians inform the United Kingdom that they would be willing to negotiate terms of union if Newfoundland sent a delegation to Ottawa?[88]

Mackenzie King was busy preparing for a trip to Washington and London, but on 27 September he found time to take tea with Malcolm MacDonald at Earnscliffe. The high commissioner brought the conversation around to Newfoundland. King repeated to MacDonald what he had told the House of Commons more than two years before: Canada would welcome a move on Newfoundland's part to join Confederation but it would be unthinkable to force the issue on the Newfoundlanders. However, King noted that the present was probably the best time to deal with the issue because it could be done without it becoming a matter of 'party politics' in Newfoundland. Clearly, King believed union was the natural and most desirable solution, but he was averse to 'crowding' the issue.[89]

MacDonald and Clutterbuck were extremely encouraged by Mackenzie King's remarks. They regarded King as a staunch Confederate whose caution was directed not at the end results, but rather at the methods used to achieve them. King had played his cards well. By showing just enough interest in union the British could read into his words precisely what they had already come to believe themselves: namely, that Confederation was the objective of the Canadians and although they were restricted in their action by political circumstances, they would welcome efforts on the part of the British to do what they could to push the idea along.

Clutterbuck reported these developments at a final meeting with the Canadian officials, and noted that the Canadians 'were delighted that they now had an objective to aim at.' He explained Addison's plan to make an announcement on Newfoundland in the near future and suggested holding additional meetings at that time 'to examine between us possible ways of influencing Newfoundland opinion behind the scenes.' As for the announcement itself:

It would, of course, be impossible to make any overt reference to union with

Canada in any such statement, but the Secretary of State would no doubt wish to consider how to deal in the statement with Newfoundland's reconstruction needs in such a way as not to impede the swing of opinion towards Canada. In this connection the Canadian officials expressed the view that it would be very desirable to make it clear in the statement that Newfoundland should not count on receiving further financial assistance from the United Kingdom. This would accord with the realities of the position and would, they thought, assist Newfoundlanders to turn their thoughts to Canada.[90]

Clutterbuck returned to London satisfied that his visit to Ottawa had been a success. A few weeks later, Addison capitalized on Mackenzie King's presence in London to discuss the Newfoundland question with him. They met in the Dominions Office on 18 October. Addison reviewed Britain's decision to establish a national convention in New-foundland. In light of the financial difficulties of both the United Kingdom and Newfoundland, he continued, the British government preferred Confederation as the ultimate solution. Mackenzie King referred to Newfoundland as a possible financial liability, but then noted that if the discussions then under way with the provinces proved to be successful Canada might be in a position to offer terms to Newfoundland. Of course, King wrote, 'we were simply thinking aloud and were committing no one to anything.' For King, 'All that was being said' was that Canada would not object to Britain 'lending such encouragement as it might find it possible to lend to the Island to make overtures to the Dominion if it so desired.'[91]

That was sufficient for Lord Addison, who was already in the process of completing a memorandum for the British cabinet. Two views dominated the memo: Britain's dollar shortage and Canada's changing attitude towards Newfoundland. Addison reviewed the rise and fall of the reconstruction plan, noting how the scheme had floundered because of Britain's inadequate supply of Canadian dollars. The Canadians, for their part, were reluctant to supply the dollars to either Newfoundland or Britain, but, Addison pointed out, they would not be averse to meeting Newfoundland half way if the Newfoundlanders expressed an opinion favourable to Confederation. Addison continued with a glowing tribute to the benefits of Confederation: union would increase the standard of living, provide jobs, enhance stability, and give the New-foundlanders a degree of financial security that they would be unable to provide for themselves. Under these circumstances, Addison wrote, we should 'adapt our policy to these changed conditions and to regard union with Canada as the objective to be aimed at. It would, of course, be fatal to take any overt steps to encourage Newfoundlanders in this direction, or even to let it become known that this is the solution we envisage. On the other hand, we must take care to say and do nothing which would be inconsistent with this objective or make it harder to achieve.'[92]

Newfoundland came up for cabinet discussion on 1 November 1945. Addison's memo and his outline for the creation of a national convention were discussed, and he repeated his belief in Confederation. There was general agreement on Addison's proposals, but two problems surfaced: Prime Minister Attlee questioned the system of election to the National Convention, suggesting that an alternative method, based more on a vocational basis, be looked at, and Aneurin Bevan, the minister of health, brought up the possibility of sending a report on the issue to an imperial conference to elicit the views of the other dominions. Addison agreed to consider these proposals, and until then a general decision was postponed.[93]

The reconstruction plan was now officially dead and on 8 November the Dominions Office sent the bad news to the Newfoundland government.[94] The best that Britain could offer was the remission of Newfoundland's sterling debt (estimated at £17 million), which would permit the Newfoundland government to take those funds directed to interest payments on this debt and channel them into development schemes of their own. This action would also have value as a gesture of good faith to the Newfoundlanders.

The British cabinet returned to the problem of Newfoundland on 27 November 1945. Addison said that he had considered the proposal to institute a vocational basis for the National Convention and had decided that it was 'impracticable.' As for bringing the matter up at an imperial conference he could not agree: it 'would be embarrassing, not only to Newfoundland, but also to the Dominions, particularly Canada.' Next, to meet the criticism that his statement was too Confederate when that was not necessarily Newfoundland's destiny, Addison agreed to soften the tone of his references to Britain's dollar shortage which might seem to encourage a movement towards union with Canada.[95] With these changes agreed to, the cabinet gave its approval.

A few days before the announcement of the National Convention was made to the House of Commons, Malcolm MacDonald informed Norman Robertson of Britain's decision. His report of Robertson's response is interesting in that it gives a clear example of Canadian policy regarding Newfoundland – a desire to expedite Confederation if possible while at the same time maintaining a non-committal stance at the government level. Robertson told MacDonald that the Canadian ministers had no formal suggestions to make, but on an informal level, the DEA would like to see a few alterations to the wording of the proposed terms of reference. Their concern stemmed from the belief that a rather limited interpretation could be placed on the present wording that might prejudice Confederation's chances.[96] The Dominions Office reassured the Canadians that there was no risk of this happening.[97] Besides, it was now too late to make any changes because the policy statement was scheduled for that very same day.

Prime Minister Attlee made the announcement in the House of Commons on 11 December 1945. He outlined the framework of the National Convention and the proposal to hold the elections in Newfoundland 'as early as climatic conditions permit.' The National Convention would provide the elected representatives of the Newfoundland people with the opportunity to

consider and discuss amongst themselves ... the changes that have taken place in the financial and economic situation of the Island since 1934, and bearing in mind the extent to which the high revenues of recent years have been due to wartime conditions, to examine the position of the country and to make recommendations to His Majesty's Government as to possible forms of future government to be put before the people at a national referendum.

But we must above all be careful not to promise what we may not be able to perform, and the special difficulties of our financial position over the next few years may well preclude us from undertaking fresh commitments.[98]

At long last the British government had acted on its obligation to Newfoundland. The announcement of the National Convention was widely welcomed in Newfoundland and sparked a revival of interest in political life. The return to open politics in Newfoundland was the beginning of a new chapter in Newfoundland's history; few at that time realized that it would also be the final chapter for the Dominion of Newfoundland.

IV

Joseph R. 'Joey' Smallwood was returning to Newfoundland from Toronto when he heard the news. He had registered at the Ford Hotel in

Montreal and bought the morning *Gazette* to read while he ate his breakfast. While waiting to be served he was astonished to learn of Attlee's announcement in London. He recalled his immediate reaction in his memoirs: 'I raced through the newspaper story and then read it more carefully, and then once again. I ate very little of that meal but soon went out into the streets of Montreal and walked for miles as I thought the matter over.'

For Smallwood, the path was clear: 'I was going to be in it. All the King's horses and all the King's men wouldn't stop me.' Within hours he had decided to embark on a thorough study of Confederation to see if union with Canada 'was the missing condition to successful responsible government in Newfoundland.'[99] Within weeks he had launched the Confederation campaign.

Like every Newfoundlander, Smallwood had been given the opportunity to participate in the debate to decide on Newfoundland's future. Equally, however, many of the decisions had already been made, or at least the choices facing the Newfoundlanders had been severely limited. Union with the United States or with the United Kingdom was out of the question, while financial stringency on Britain's part made the return of responsible government appear risky at best. More important, the British government had decided to help bring about Confederation if at all possible.

The war had almost severed the remains of the umbilical cord that had spanned the Atlantic between Newfoundland and the British Isles. The traditional lines of communications and transportation had been cut, physically isolating Newfoundland more than ever before. Moreover, the disruption of the pre-war trading patterns and the establishment of foreign bases on Newfoundland soil had introduced a fantastic degree of financial prosperity to the country, but had also virtually completed the integration of Newfoundland into the North American economy.[100] The problem caused by Britain's dollar shortage was merely a symptom of Newfoundland's entrenched economic dependence on Canada.

For many Newfoundlanders the dream to have responsible government and financial stability founded on the benefits gained from the international use of Newfoundland's airports and the country's strategic location was little more than a house of cards. The concessions desired never materialized and very quickly it was realized that the maintenance of only one international airport would produce a significant financial burden. Moreover, there was little hope that concessions would be freely given considering Newfoundland's weak bargaining position.

Conversely, the American interest in Newfoundland had declined from the early years of the war. There were two main reasons for this: first, as the war's centre of gravity shifted away from the Atlantic, Newfoundland's strategic value decreased; and second, the Americans had already received virtually everything they wanted from Newfoundland. American rights were locked in for ninety-nine years, and there was little need to even consider the bargaining of concessions for Newfoundland. Likewise, in civil-aviation matters, Newfoundland could be bypassed and an agreement reached with the British and Canadians.

In Ottawa the 'Problem of Newfoundland' was more carefully scrutinized, although only within a small group of officials did the matter attract much attention. On the one hand, the benefits of Confederation to Canada appeared greater than ever before; union would solve the lingering problems over defence and civil aviation, and provide the ultimate deterrent to American encroachments. On the other, the Canadians were inexorably drawn into Newfoundland's financial conundrum: if the United Kingdom decided to lend huge sums to Newfoundland, the Canadians would have to provide the dollars; if the British offered aid in the form of goods, this would most likely cut into Newfoundland's imports from the mainland and hurt Canadian exporters.

By 1945, this array of officials clustered around the Department of External Affairs had come to see Confederation as the best solution, but they acknowledged that they would have to wait for the politicians to catch up to their way of thinking. Until Confederation was politically acceptable in both Newfoundland and Canada, Canadian activity must be kept out of the public eye. To do otherwise would hurt the Canadian government at home and would likely damage the Confederate cause in Newfoundland. In a sense the war had brought Mackenzie King to the water, but in 1945 he remained hesitant to drink in public.

For the British government the problem was more complicated. British policy had been influenced by a number of factors: the sentimental ties to Britain's 'oldest colony' had been strengthened through Newfoundland's magnificent war effort and generous loans, Newfoundland continued to be seen in some quarters as a valuable asset for defence and civil-aviation purposes, and the Canadians appeared uninterested in stepping in to remove this burden from Britain. As the war progressed, however, sentimental ties and strategic value fell in the wake of Britain's financial predicament. And once the conclusion was reached that Newfoundland could not make it on its own, union with Canada became the inevitable outcome. Someone would have to pay to support Newfoundland – Canada was the logical choice. By late 1945, the British were willing to see any Canadian indication in this direction as a positive move.

The Canadians had not played a large role in the evolution of this policy, but it was an essential one. They opened the door on Confederation just enough to permit the British government to make union with Canada their goal. Without Canadian acquiescence, no action along this line would have been possible. Old beliefs in the 'natural destiny' of Newfoundland had converged with the harsh realities of the post-war world – and Confederation was the result. Now all that was left to do was to convince the people of Newfoundland.

8

The national convention

The announcement of the National Convention in December 1945 breathed new life into political discussion in Newfoundland. It was generally welcomed in the press, and most agreed that the time had come for Newfoundlanders to decide for themselves on their future course of government.[1] There was considerably less agreement on what that course should be; opinion ranged from the return to responsible government, to the maintenance of the Commission of Government, to commercial union with the United States, to Confederation with Canada.

At the same time, many Newfoundlanders continued to believe that the country was sitting on hidden treasure – either through the development of untapped sources of wealth such as Labrador, or through the negotiation of rental agreements or trade arrangements in return for making Newfoundland territory available to foreign powers. Moreover, there were those who considered that the United Kingdom had an obligation to continue helping Newfoundland. As the *Daily News* put it, with a bit of twisted logic: 'We should not seek financial aid at all but we have every right to ask for reasonable economic assistance.'[2]

The extent of Britain's obligation to Newfoundland was, of course, viewed differently in London. Britain's dollar shortage remained a severe problem for the treasury, and during 1946 huge sums were borrowed from North America. Not surprisingly, British policy towards Newfoundland continued to be shaped, as it had been in 1944–5, by this relentless financial crisis.

British policy-makers decided in 1945 that Confederation with Canada was the best future for Newfoundland. To force the Newfoundlanders into union would not do – after all, what had the war been fought for other than the right of nations to freely choose for themselves? But Confederation would at least be an alternative and the idea would be given the opportunity to flourish and succeed. The Canadians agreed with this line of thinking, and over the next two years Britain and Canada remained remarkably consistent in their efforts to implement this policy.

I

Once the war was over, much of the foreign military interest in Newfoundland quickly disappeared. The continuing importance of Newfoundland as a strategic area in the post-war period had been clearly recognized by the Advisory Committee on Post-Hostilities Problems, but once the wartime emergency had passed the Canadian military displayed little enthusiasm for maintaining a significant presence there.[3]

The Canadian Armed Services retreated from Newfoundland as rapidly as they had come in 1940. Within days of the Allied victory in Europe the Canadians began reducing their garrison in Newfoundland, and replacing commanding officers with officers of a lower rank. By the summer of 1945, these reductions left the Canadian garrison in Newfoundland at approximately 1,900. Over the following months and into 1946 the remains of the garrison were removed, leaving only a skeleton force for maintenance and adminstrative purposes.[4] Some of the Canadian-owned property was removed, but most of the surplus war assets were disposed of in Newfoundland.

The Canadian navy was equally keen to reduce its presence in Newfoundland. Over the summer of 1945, Botwood, Bay Bulls, and the smaller establishments at Wabana, Harbour Grace, and Corner Brook were closed down. By May 1946 only eighty-seven men and officers of the Canadian navy were left in Newfoundland. Likewise, the base in St John's harbour was handed over to the Admiralty. Interestingly, the British authorities were not eager to accept it, noting that the expenses for its upkeep would increase the strain on Britain's already weakened dollar supply. The suggestion was made that the Canadians take over the responsibility for this base, but Ottawa refused.[5]

The number of Americans in Newfoundland declined, beginning in 1943 and continuing through 1945. During the summer the U.S. army units at Fort Pepperell and Fort McAndrew were transferred out, leaving only those men needed for care and upkeep. The American air force maintained units at Goose Bay and Gander, claiming that they were required so long as there were American forces in occupation in Germany. In particular, Goose Bay maintained its strategic importance and the Americans were eager to extend their stay. This desire to stay in Goose Bay caused a degree of tension between the Canadian and American governments, until late 1946 when the Americans officially asked for permission to maintain units at the airport for training and surveillance purposes. The Canadians, who were firmly in control of the base, were willing to go along on an interim basis, providing that the emphasis was on the training aspects of the agreement.[6]

There still remained, however, all those problems that had been postponed until the end of the war. The Canadians had been promised fifty-year leases for their installations at Gander and Botwood under the 1941 agreement. Similarly, promises had been made with regards to Bay Bulls and Torbay, but the necessary confirming acts had never been passed by the Commission of Government. Moreover, Canadian military rights at the Newfoundland bases (with the exception of Goose Bay) had been left to be decided in the post-war period.

Talks were held in Ottawa between representatives of the Commission of Government and the Canadian government in April and May 1945. The Newfoundlanders agreed that the appropriate confirming acts should be passed but felt it unwise to do so until the Canadians and the Newfoundlanders had thoroughly discussed mutual defence needs. Canadian post-war needs might not be sufficiently provided for in the projected acts and, conversely, the Commission of Government might act on property for which the Canadians had no further use.[7] The use of these properties for civil aviation was also still in question. The Newfoundlanders argued that these questions should be settled first, before they would move on the confirming acts. The Canadians accepted the Newfoundland proposal, providing a conference to iron out these problems be held within twelve months.[8]

A preliminary and unofficial talk was held on 20 December 1945, during the Bermuda conference on civil aviation. None of the participants had the authority to discuss military questions, but the conference did furnish the opportunity to establish a framework for future talks. MacKay outlined the wishes of the Canadian government: the continued military use of Gander and Torbay; storage facilities for equipment; and, although no plans had been made to station military forces at these two airports, special powers were considered necessary during an emergency situation. For the most part the Newfoundlanders were agreeable, although some concern was expressed over the continuing military use of Torbay.[9]

It was agreed during this meeting that a full conference would be held in Newfoundland by 1 February 1946. The conference was scheduled to open in St John's on 29 January and a little more than a week before the Canadians outlined for the Newfoundland and British governments their position regarding the Newfoundland bases. A Newfoundland-Canada defence understanding was considered necessary because of the interdependence of Canada and Newfoundland in defence and security matters. Military action was not at that time contemplated, but it was essential to maintain a degree of preparedness in case an emergency arose.

On a more specific level, the Canadians were willing to forfeit any claims for a lease at Gander providing the Newfoundlanders agreed to give them powers during a crisis. This arrangement would permit the Newfoundlanders to fulfil their promise to operate Gander as their designated international airport. Emergency rights were also requested for St John's harbour. The Canadian claim to Torbay was stronger and they asked that the title for this airport be confirmed for the Canadians, giving them similar military rights to those at Gander. As for Botwood and the marine railway at Bay Bulls, the Canadians were willing to return them to the Newfoundland government. To do so was no great sacrifice on the part of the Canadians – Botwood had been declared surplus by the RCAF the previous summer.[10]

The Canadian proposals became the basis for discussion for the St John's conference, which lasted from 29 January to 5 February 1946. The Newfoundland delegation consisted of commissioners J.S. Neill and H.A. Winter, and the UK delegation included St John Chadwick and M.W. Low from the Air Ministry. The Canadians were represented by Frank Bridges (the minister of fisheries), J.S. Macdonald, and R.A. MacKay. All three delegations included a number of technical advisers.

The meetings were friendly and informal, and there were few significant obstacles preventing all sides from reaching a satisfactory agreement. The major problem was that the announcement of the National Convention a few weeks earlier had, in a sense, put the Commission of Government on notice, and they were reluctant to do anything that might upset public opinion in Newfoundland. Increasingly they saw themselves as a 'caretaker administration' that should not make long-term commitments for the people of Newfoundland. The best they could offer was a three-year agreement, and this was accepted by the Canadians.[11]

Nevertheless, a fairly broad agreement emerged. The Canadians re-transferred Gander, Botwood, and Gleneagles to Newfoundland in return for emergency military powers there and $1 million for the surplus RCAF buildings, hangars, and equipment at Gander. If hostilities broke out the Canadians could request and resume control and responsibility for Gander. The Canadian position at Torbay was secured and they were given fee simple title to the land.

The three governments agreed to hold periodic talks to review and co-ordinate Newfoundland's defence needs. In addition, there were several more points of agreement concerning military reserves, rights of patrol, and other small transfers of land. Moreover, the United Kingdom was granted the use of Goose Bay and Torbay on notification of the Canadians. The use of St John's harbour was discussed but agreement was left for further discussions between the British and the Canadians. The agreement was to come into effect as of 31 March 1946, but the RCAF was permitted to stay at Gander until the end of May to help smooth the transfer. Lasting three years, the agreement could be terminated after twelve months' notice from any of the participants.[12]

With the signing of this agreement in St John's and London, a complex chapter in Canadian-Newfoundland relations had been brought to a close. Wartime negotiations had produced a wide spectrum of agreements, ranging from ninety-nine-year leases, to tripartite arrangements, to outright grants – all of which remained to be solidified once the war was over. Moreover, it was recognized that Canada and Newfoundland would continue to share common defence needs in the post-war world. With the return of peace these problems could be dealt with in a calmer and more reasoned fashion, and at the same time, a sharp eye could be kept on future defence needs.

II

The elections for the National Convention were not scheduled to be held until June 1946, after the spring break-up. The task of the National Convention was to investigate Newfoundland's economy as well as debate future forms of government. To help them in their efforts, the United Kingdom supplied Professor K.C. Wheare, an 'expert adviser' on constitutional matters, and sent two officials to prepare an economic survey of Newfoundland.[13] The first few months of the National Convention were centred on the preparation of a number of reports on the Newfoundland economy. But the investigative powers of the National Convention were restricted; for instance, the commissioners were not to be held accountable for their past actions, nor were they obligated to appear before the public meetings of the convention or make available their private papers or files of the government.[14]

Also included within the National Convention's frame of reference was the power to end a delegation to Canada to discuss Confederation. This was cleared through Ottawa before it became official. Sir Eric Machtig, the permanent under secretary, informed Norman Robertson of the Dominions Office plan and Robertson passed the information along to Prime Minister King. Robertson later told Machtig that King found the proposal quite acceptable.[15]

The Dominions Office was also on the move in other areas in the months before the opening of the National Convention. Early in the spring, Sir Humphrey Walwyn was replaced as governor by Sir Gordon Macdonald, who more closely reflected the wishes of the new British Labour government. Only a few days after his inauguration the new governor met with J.S. Macdonald, the Canadian high commissioner. Macdonald told the high commissioner that he had been briefed by both Attlee and Lord Addison, the dominions secretary, before he had left London, and explained that the British government favoured the idea of Confederation and hoped that the people of Newfoundland would come to support it as well. As for himself, the new governor believed that the rounding out of Confederation would be a good thing for Newfoundland, Canada, and the British Commonwealth as a whole.[16]

Some preliminary preparations were also being made in Ottawa. J.S. Macdonald was eager to ensure that the Canadians were not caught flatfooted, without concrete proposals to offer the Newfoundlanders should they decide to seek union with Canada. With the likelihood of a delegation's being sent to Ottawa to discuss terms, Macdonald showered the Department of External Affairs with telegrams advocating action by Ottawa. Many unanswered questions remained, including those dealing with the constitutional propriety of a government negotiating directly with an appointed delegation rather than with government representatives.

Others, such as R.A. MacKay, shared these concerns, and in an effort to be more prepared to deal with them, a small interdepartmental committee was brought together in the spring of 1946. This committee was chaired by MacKay and included representatives from External Affairs, National Defence, Transport, Finance, Trade and Commerce, Fisheries, Reconstruction and Supply, the Bank of Canada, and the Privy Council Office. Its purpose was to put together a cabinet memorandum on the likely effects that union with Newfoundland would have on

Canada.[17] Only a few meetings were held, but by the end of the summer considerable work had been accomplished.

The National Convention was elected on 21 June 1946, and after a lengthy waiting period met for the first time on 11 September. It consisted of forty-five men elected in thirty-seven electoral districts. There were no property qualifications for voting in the election, although a residency requirement was included in an effort to ensure representation by a greater variety of occupation and opinion. The desired result failed to materialize; although thirteen merchants were elected, together with a sprinkling of journalists, trade unionists, civil servants, and various professionals, the National Convention included no fishermen.[18]

In his book *Politics in Newfoundland*, S.J. Noel rightly separates the members of the convention into three groups. The first and largest section was dominated by the group of merchants who advocated the return to responsible government and unleased blistering attacks on the Commission of Government for its past sins. The second was a small group of members who remained undecided on what was best for Newfoundland. Finally, there was an even smaller number of Confederates, mainly from outport constituencies and led by J.R. Smallwood.[19]

The National Convention established a number of committees to investigate various aspects of Newfoundland's economy and to report back to the main body. Reports were presented dealing with public health and welfare, finance, tourism, forestry, the fishery, mining, local industries, transportation and communications, education, and agriculture. The plenary sessions tended to be less productive, often deteriorating into endless attacks on the Commission of Government and bitter debates between the major factions.

With the proceedings of the National Convention well under way it became necessary to step up efforts in Ottawa to prepare the Canadian government to deal better with any overtures from St John's. High Commissioner Macdonald travelled to Ottawa, and on 16 October he attended an interdepartmental meeting on the economic implications of union with Newfoundland, chaired by MacKay. Macdonald was in the process of putting together a detailed memorandum for Louis St Laurent, the new minister for external affairs, covering the whole Newfoundland question. The Department of Finance submitted a report of its investigations which pointed to what would become the primary difficulty for the Canadian government; despite the difficulties in economic forecasting of this nature, it was clear that as a province a gap would remain between Newfoundland's revenues and expenditures. The difference would have to be made up by Ottawa.[20]

It was left up to Macdonald to pass the bad news along. These findings were incorporated into Macdonald's seventeen-page memorandum which was given to Lester Pearson, the new under secretary of state for external affairs. Macdonald reviewed the opening of the National Convention and gauged the state of opinion for and against Confederation. In a straightforward and intelligent manner Macdonald noted that pro-Confederate feelings in Newfoundland were essentially negative in nature and rooted in 'the feeling that Newfoundland's economic position is rather precarious and that Newfoundlanders would enjoy greater prosperity and a more assured future in a turbulent world if they were part of the Dominion.' While family allowances and old-age pensions held some attractions, more support for Confederation would likely spring from the more general dislike for the present state of affairs in Newfoundland and the apprehension among thousands of Newfoundlanders over returning to the old system of responsible government. Macdonald also shared the view common in Ottawa that Confederation would have a much better chance of succeeding as a question on a referendum, rather than as a 'party question' under responsible government. Very early on Macdonald recognized that Confederation would likely come second on a ballot with three choices, and in a second referendum could possibly win.

Macdonald turned next to the advantages and disadvantages of union. For one thing, he noted, it would put an end to the problems of civil and military aviation rights in Newfoundland, which had sparked so much debate over the previous years. Likewise, Confederation would make Canada a larger and more populous nation, enhancing its influence and standing in the world.

On the negative side he pointed out that an independent Newfoundland could well be an aggressive competitor in the fish markets of the United States, the West Indies, South America, and several Mediterranean countries. Furthermore, the negotiation of trade agreements between Newfoundland and other powers might include an opening of its market to the products of these powers – directly harming Canada's strong position in Newfoundland's economy. The logical extension of this scenario, Macdonald concluded, could involve the sale of Labrador to another country or the political alliance of Newfoundland with a foreign power – obviously, the United States.

Weighed against these factors, of course, was the financial outlay that the Canadians would have to make. For this reason Macdonald argued that the time had come to decide if Canada should take the necessary steps to ensure Newfoundland's early entry into the dominion. If the answer was no, then the Confederates in the National Convention should be told informally, to prevent them from raising what would then be embarrassing questions. If, however, the answer was yes, then the Canadians should let these same people know so they could act accordingly, and the United Kingdom should be asked to publicly state that Newfoundland should not expect to receive further economic aid from the United Kingdom. Finally, he argued that an interdepartmental committee should be established to undertake an exhaustive study of the numerous aspects involved in the preparation of terms of union.[21]

In addition to St Laurent and Pearson, Mackenzie King, J.L. Ilsley, the minister of finance, and Frank Bridges, the minister of fisheries, received Macdonald's memo, and it was discussed at the cabinet meeting of October 30. After reviewing the situation, the cabinet agreed that Canada would welcome a delegation from Newfoundland to discuss terms, should the National Convention decide to send one. In addition, the cabinet agreed to formally establish two working groups: first, an interdepartmental committee to prepare reports on possible terms to be offered a Newfoundland delegation, as well as the legal procedure and the tactics involved in such discussions. In addition, more factual information was required, especially on the economic and financial obligations of union. Second, a cabinet committee was created to supervise the interdepartmental committee and to advise the government on the best course of action.[22]

Naturally, the decision-making power rested with the cabinet and the cabinet committee. The increasing importance with which the Canadian government viewed the problem of Newfoundland was revealed in the composition of the cabinet committee, which consisted of St Laurent as chairman, Brooke Claxton, Ilsley, Bridges, C.D. Howe, Douglas Abbott, J.J. McCann, and Senator W.M. Robertson. St Laurent was not expected to be able to attend all the meetings, and in his absence Claxton would act as chairman. J.R. Baldwin of the Privy Council Office was appointed secretary to this committee, and, as a member of the interdepartmental committee as well, he was given the extra task of liaison between the two.

The cabinet decisions of 30 October were soon put into action. On 12 November 1946 Pearson informed Norman Robertson, Canada's new high commissioner in London, of these developments and instructed him to unofficially advise the British government that the Canadians would welcome a delegation from Newfoundland.[23] No mention was made of how the Canadians wanted the British to handle the situation, but the feeling was growing that the United Kingdom should be asked to hold back from any promises of generous long-term support for Newfoundland.

Meanwhile in Ottawa, the Interdepartmental Committee on Canada-Newfoundland Relations (ICCNR) held its first meeting on 9 November. Attendance fluctuated, depending on the agenda, but there was a core group present at most of the meetings. This group included R.A. MacKay, who chaired the meetings, Baldwin, Paul Bridle of External Affairs, Mitchell Sharp and A.B. Hockin from the finance department, James Coyne and G.S. Watts from the Bank of Canada, and Stewart Bates from the Department of Reconstruction and Supply.

During the first few meetings a number of ideas were introduced to deal with the problem of Newfoundland's finances. One suggestion was to permit Newfoundland to maintain a 'provincial customs tax' to offset revenue lost when import duties were taken over by Ottawa. Another was to turn Newfoundland into a federal territory which would permit the Canadians to give it special subsidies not given to the provinces. As for Newfoundland's existing debt and surplus, it was felt that the former should be borne by Canada, Newfoundland, and the United Kingdom, while the latter should be left to Newfoundland for domestic development. There was also a good deal of talk concerning the proposal to include representatives from the United Kingdom in the upcoming discussions, which would, they hoped, have the effect of making the Canadians appear less 'anxious' to lure the Newfoundlanders in.[24] These issues could not be settled immediately, and in the meantime, a number of subcommittees were formed to prepare reports on a variety of topics.

The Canadians also took steps to explain their attitude towards Newfoundland to the United Kingdom. On 19 November Pearson invited Sir Alexander Clutterbuck, the new British high commissioner, and Joe Garner, his deputy, to the East Block for an informal discussion on Newfoundland. Clutterbuck told Pearson what he wanted to hear, namely that the British government had previously informed the Newfoundlanders that generous financial assistance from the United Kingdom could not be expected in the future. Pearson realized that Confederation had a much better chance of beating responsible government in a referendum if the Newfoundlanders knew that they would otherwise be on their own financially.

Regarding Newfoundland's national debt Clutterbuck could not be so forthright. Personally he felt that the United Kingdom should shoulder this burden and he believed that the Dominions Office would agree. Unfortunately, however, the rest of the government would probably oppose the idea. The matter was not pursued further, and the discussion ended with an exchange of generalities between Clutterbuck and Pearson on the need for the benefits of union.[25]

The Canadians expected the decision over sending a delegation to Canada to be made early in 1947. Efforts were therefore stepped up to complete as much groundwork as possible before the new year. On 2 December the cabinet committee met to discuss the preliminary report of the ICCNR. It was too early to make any clear-cut decisions, but there was general agreement that the first discussions with the Newfoundlanders should not be too detailed or binding. During the early stages, exploratory talks, with representatives of the United Kingdom in attendance, were all that was considered necessary.[26]

The ICCNR also scheduled a number of meetings during the last few weeks of the year to discuss a number of subcommittee reports. High Commissioner Macdonald agreed to come to Ottawa a few days before Christmas to participate in the discussions. On 16 December, he brought the other members of the committee up to date on recent events in Newfoundland. He noted that the movement for Confederation was 'as yet rather undeveloped,' and pointed out that Confederate support was probably stronger among the general public than it was in the National Convention. As for the leading Confederates, Macdonald pointed to two men – Gordon Bradley and J.R. Smallwood – as being 'ideal ... to stump the country in favour of Confederation.' Bradley was a prominent politician from the pre-commission days and an eloquent and intelligent man with a wider vision of Newfoundland's destiny. Smallwood, for his part, was unpopular in St John's because of his 'tactless and egotistical actions,' but he had considerable support in the outports.[27]

Smallwood's problem at first was to be taken seriously by the Canadians. He had written the prime minister for information on Canada shortly after the National Convention had been announced, but received little more than perfunctory acknowledgment. During the summer he had visited Ottawa and spoke with St Laurent for a few minutes, and, more important, began a friendship with J.W. Pickersgill in the Prime Minister's Office. But Smallwood did not seem to be the man for the job. In Macdonald's view he was 'a good propagandist,' but 'not a very substantial man.' These feelings were intensified in November by the defeat of Smallwood's premature motion to send a delegation to Canada.[28]

The ICCNR met again on 17 and 18 December. Considerable attention was given to the question of what to do with Newfoundland's national debt. There was some doubt over how much should be left to Newfoundland and to what extent the Canadians should step in. Macdonald was sympathetic to Newfoundland's position, and he argued that the country should not be expected to meet this debt – how could the Canadians ask the Newfoundlanders to contribute to Canada's national debt as Canadians if the rest of the country refused to include Newfoundland's burden? Moreover, removing this debt (which had been such a sticking point in the negotiations over the past seventy-five years) would give the Confederation movement a considerable psychological boost.[29] This issue would have to await cabinet decision, but there was agreement that the United Kingdom should be expected to shoulder some of the burden.

Another problem emerged in the ICCNR meetings over the procedure to be followed in dealing with the Newfoundland delegation. The split erupted over whether or not the Newfoundland delegation should be offered concrete terms, and whether it was possible to offer Newfoundland terms that would in any way be acceptable. Again, further action had to be postponed 'until guidance had been received from higher authority.'[30]

The ICCNR submitted its findings to the cabinet, along with a memorandum written by Pearson. These documents were brought up in the cabinet meeting held on Christmas Eve 1946. St Laurent reviewed the report of the ICCNR, noting that the committee estimated that the cost to Canada to incorporate Newfoundland would be $10 to $15 million per year above the additional new revenues received. As Pearson pointed out in his memo, it now became necessary to decide whether Confederation should be welcomed at any cost, or whether a limit should be made, beyond which the Canadian government would not go.

Mackenzie King told the ministers that all were agreed that Newfoundland should be brought into the dominion, but at the moment it was difficult to be precise, particularly with the touchy taxation negotiations with the provinces that had begun the previous autumn. The two sides had draw back to evaluate and study their respective positions, leaving the tax arrangements unsettled. The cabinet concurred with King's statement and it was agreed that the British be informed that the Canadians wanted to bring Newfoundland in, but could not give concrete terms, at least until the federal-provincial negotiations were finished.[31]

Pearson informed the British government of these decisions early in the new year. Apart from this, however, little action could be taken; the members of the ICCNR continued their investigations but formal meetings were postponed in the absence of policy directions from the cabinet. The Canadians, of course, could keep a keen eye on the developments in St John's. This was made easier by the steady stream of telegrams from the High Commissioner's Office. Because of his influential position in St John's, Macdonald was able to keep on top of the changing, and often volatile happenings in the city and across the country. For instance, through his dinner engagements with St John's merchants he was early made aware of the major opponents to Confederation.[32]

The National Convention picked up in January 1947 right where it had left off in 1946 – bitter debates over Newfoundland's future continued, with regular attacks on the Commission of Government. Smallwood had emerged as the unquestioned champion of Confederation, and in the National Convention he wisely directed his efforts to building up Confederation rather than tearing down the Commission of Government. The convention debates were broadcast nightly on the radio, and while the supporters of responsible government were hammering away at the existing government, Smallwood was busy scoring political points for Confederation by speaking directly to the people of Newfoundland. Because of his vast energy, intelligence, and determination, Smallwood had fashioned a firm grip on the Confederation movement. The Canadians would have to deal with him, whether they wanted to or not.

Smallwood exhibited his skill as a strategist early in February 1947, by getting a resolution that included a call for an investigation into Confederation passed by the National Convention. By allying himself with Robert Job and his scheme to send a delegation to Washington for trade talks, Smallwood was able to draw off enough support for his own motion in return for his supporting Job's. The result was that, on 4 February, Job's resolution was carried 30 to 8. The resolution stated that the Commission of Government be approached for information concerning:

1. What steps if any can be taken for establishing improved economic or fiscal relationships between the United States of America and Newfoundland,

particularly bearing in mind the present occupation of certain Newfoundland territory and the fact that free entry is given to the United States for its importations into Newfoundland.

2. What financial or fiscal relationships could be expected between the Government of the United Kingdom and Newfoundland:
   1. Under continuation of Commission Government in its present form;
   2. Under a revised form with elected representatives thereon;
   3. Under Responsible Government in approximately its previous form;
   4. Under any other suitable form of Government.

3. What could be a fair and equitable basis for Federal Union of The Dominion of Canada and Newfoundland, or what other fiscal, political or economic arrangements may be possible.[33]

As Smallwood anticipated, the Commission of Government rejected any suggestion of opening talks with the Americans. In a meeting with the commissioners on 8 February, several members of the National Convention (including Smallwood, Bradley, and Job) were informed that such a proposal was outside the terms of reference of the National Convention and therefore impossible to grant. The other proposals – talks with the Canadians and the British – were more acceptable, and on 1 March the National Convention passed two resolutions – to send delegations to London and Ottawa.[34]

On the surface the resolutions were fairly straightforward: a delegation would visit London and then return to St John's to submit a report to the National Convention before the second delegation left for Ottawa. Before this agenda was accepted, however, there was a flurry of activity between the Canadian and British governments over the best way to deal with the situation. The Canadians believed that, with the federal-provincial tax arrangements still in limbo, it would be best to have the Newfoundlanders visit London first, to give the Canadians more time to prepare themselves.[35] It was also felt that by going to London first, the Newfoundlanders would learn the bad news from the British, leaving them to look on Confederation in a more favourable light.

For the British it was a little more complicated: there was some doubt over the wisdom of allowing a delegation to come to London at all. While they were willing to do as the Canadians wished – by not making any generous offer to the Newfoundlanders – they were not keen on delivering such a harsh measure in public. It is interesting, moreover, that the concern of the British policy-makers was directed more at recalcitrant Labour backbenchers than at the Opposition. Attlee, Dalton, and Addison and other Labour leaders had accepted Confederation as British policy, but they could not rely too heavily on the Labour MPs as a whole. As Machtig told Robertson on 4 March, the British felt that a delegation to London would be open to persuasion from those on both sides of the House who felt that responsible government was the best solution to Newfoundland's difficulties. For this reason, the Dominions Office suggested that the Newfoundlanders address written questions to London and then visit Ottawa, the hope being that the Newfoundlanders would find Confederation so attractive that it would preclude the need for anything more than written answers from London.[36]

These thoughts were echoed by Clutterbuck during a 5 March meeting with Escott Reid and Paul Bridle. Clutterbuck reminded the Canadians that many Labour MPs did not view Confederation as Newfoundland's destiny, and thus the Newfoundlanders would 'be subject to rather strong persuasion' from many of these MPs to strive for responsible government. But the British realized, however, that they would have to receive a delegation if pressed to do so – and the Newfoundlanders had made it fairly clear in their resolution that this is what they wanted.

Clutterbuck also brought up two other significant points. First, he noted that the Dominion Office disagreed with the Canadian plan to keep the talks with the Newfoundland delegation at the 'exploratory' level. In Britain's view, the more precise the Canadians could be with regards to the terms of union, the better chance Confederation had of winning in the referendum. Second, Clutterbuck informed the Canadians that the British would be willing to assume Newfoundland's sterling debt, but only after Newfoundland had become part of Canada. The reasoning here was simple: to publicly announce that the United Kingdom would assume Newfoundland's debt beforehand would lead the advocates of responsible government to demand equal treatment. This the British wished to prevent because the interest on Newfoundland's debt provided the United Kingdom with more than $3 million Canadian each year – a source of dollars they would prefer to maintain.[37] It is indicative of the strength of Confederate feelings in the Dominions Office and British government in general that for a fledgling but independent Newfoundland, the British could offer little in the way of financial help; but with Newfoundland as a province of Canada the British were willing to forgo a steady source of much-needed foreign currency. In effect it was the price the British were willing to pay to have the Canadians take Newfoundland (and its potential future deficits) off their hands.

Both the Canadian government and the National Convention had made it clear that they preferred that the Newfoundland delegation visit London first. The British government acquiesced but stipulated that this event could not take place until after the Easter recess, which meant April 1947 at the earliest. Moreover, the delegation was to submit written questions to the Dominions Office beforehand, and these would be the framework for the discussions.[38]

In Ottawa the official request from the governor of Newfoundland to receive a delegation was discussed in the cabinet on 26 and 28 March. It was agreed that a delegation would be welcomed, although there was still some disagreement over how far the Canadians should be prepared to go. Mackenzie King advised caution, warning that 'careful consideration' should be given to the reactions of the Opposition parties and the provincial governments.[39] This was agreed to as well, and before answering Newfoundland's request St Laurent showed the leaders of the Opposition parties a copy of his reply and received their concurrence.[40]

The questions posed by the National Convention for the British government covered a wide range of topics, including the cancellation of the public debt, development loans, readjustment of the 1940–1 bases deal, the possibility of the British paying interest on Newfoundland's wartime interest-free loans, potential trading arrangements with the United Kingdom, and the financial responsibility for Newfoundland's airports. The British government's replies were prepared in the Dominions Office, most likely with the assistance from the Newfoundland governor and commissioners.[41] Next, they were circulated to other government departments, the treasury in particular, for their views. Lord Addison, the dominions secretary, wrote Hugh Dalton, the chancellor of the exchequer, that he felt it necessary to make a general statement concerning Britain's continuing dollar shortage. This, he felt, would 'counteract the Convention's rather optimistic hopes.'[42] Dalton, who had the previous year strongly opposed the Newfoundland reconstruction scheme, could not agree more. He wrote Addison: 'I agree with the line you propose to take. Newfoundland should join Canada, and the sooner this can be brought about the better. We ought to avoid any suggestion of willingness to offer counter-attractions, and in any case we simply cannot afford generous gestures in the dollar area.'[43]

Not surprisingly, when the Newfoundland delegation arrived in

London in April there was no chance that they could alter the British position in any significant manner. Nevertheless, four meetings were held with Lord Addison and a number of officials from the Dominions Office and the treasury between 29 April and 7 May. Governor Macdonald and Commissioner A.J.Walsh had also made the journey to Britain and were present at the meetings.

For the most part the discussions revolved around aspects of the Dominions Office responses to the Newfoundland questions. The British case was clear and straightforward: little hope or comfort could be offered the Newfoundlanders – then or in the foreseeable future. Newfoundland's sterling debt could not be taken over by the United Kingdom, and, although the interest-free loans were greatly appreciated, the British could not now begin to pay interest. Development loans were ruled out as being an 'unusual' gesture to be made to a country with responsible government. As for the u.s. bases, the United Kingdom argued that there was no way that the United States would permit the renegotiation or revision of the 1941 Leased Bases Agreement. If, however, the Newfoundlanders chose responsible government, nothing would prevent them from trying to reopen the issue. On the broad question of trade and tariffs the British were necessarily vague, but no less discouraging. There was no telling what kind of future arrangements could be made, but for the present the United Kingdom was doing all that it could.[44]

The tone for the discussions was set by Lord Addison at the first meeting,when he told Peter Cashin: 'This country is burdened with terrific debts and we have had ... to sacrifice all or the greater part of our overseas assets; we have 40 per cent. of our shipping at the bottom of the sea, and therefore with the best of goodwill in the world we are not in a position, however kindly may be our disposition, to be generous in these matters.'[45] The Newfoundlanders responded in kind, in their own memorandum, putting forward Newfoundland's case for economic assistance from Great Britain.[45] Addison was unmoved by these arguments and he stood by his original statements.

The meetings themselves were equally unproductive. One British civil servant reported that the visit of the London delegation had run 'true to expected form: the peddling of wares, the attempt to belittle the work of the Commission of Government; to claim as a right u.k. financial responsibility for Newfoundland; to air personal grievances and political opinions. Nothing constructive emerged.'[47] Addison made it clear to the Newfoundlanders that it was he who decided what questions would be put on the ballot in the referendum, and this naturally included putting Confederation on, even if it was not recommended by a majority of the National Convention. This possibility disturbed a few of the Newfoundlanders, as did Addison's refusal to answer hypothetical questions. As a result, ill feelings surfaced and the conversations soured, often deterioraing into pointless circles of petty arguments, caustic jabs, and unanswered questions.

Yet the bottom line had been drawn by the end of the delegation's stay in London. Addison told the Newfoundlanders that should they choose to maintain the Commission of Government, they could expect continued assistance from Great Britain; if they chose responsible government, then they would be on their own completely. As if to remove any remaining doubt, Addison made a formal announcement in the House of Lords on 13 May 1947.

The beleaguered London delegation returned to St John's with the wind in the sails of responsible government considerably diminished. Responsible government supporters were, in general, disheartened by the results of the London delegation; for instance it was argued that Governor Macdonald and A.J. Walsh were in London to 'sabotage' the meetings.[48] Peter Cashin was particularly outraged and made strong statements against the Dominions Office and the treatment given the delegation. Editorial opinion ran along fairly predictable lines. Those papers that were open to Confederation, such as the *Evening Telegram*, showed no surprise at the cool reception received by the London delegation. Papers in favour of responsible government castigated the Dominions Office and the Commission of Government for again betraying Newfoundland.[49] On more common ground there was a realization that it was wishful thinking to expect the British to come through with generous support. As one reporter for *The Fishermen's Advocate* wrote: 'Of course they brought back nothing. In the old days of dole England did very little for us – and she had plenty of money then. What can we expect her to do for us now when she is broken by war?'[50]

On the Confederate side there was little more enthusiasm. While in London, Gordon Bradley for the first time publicly spoke in favour of Confederation: 'My impression has been that the United Kingdom is in an economic jam herself,' he said, adding that, 'I can't see how she can do much for us.' Consequently, he predicted a swing towards Confederation – providing the terms were good.[51] Otherwise Bradley and Smallwood were disappointed by Britain's apparent willingness to support Newfoundland for a further period under Commission of Government.

Aware of the latent support for Commission of Government among the people of Newfoundland, they considered this gesture on Britain's part as a serious threat to the chances of Confederation. On 15 May, Bradley and Smallwood met with High Commissioner Macdonald, who shared their concerns, to warn him of the need for the Canadians to offer generous terms in order to win the day for Confederation.[52]

The London delegation had returned to Newfoundland empty-handed, and in retrospect, the mission appears to have been little more than an exercise in public relations. Indeed, while the Dominions Office had intimated that Britain might be generous towards Newfoundland under Confederation this magnanimity was not extended to Newfoundland under responsible government or government by commission. And with this policy firmly entrenched in Whitehall, the delegation to London was doomed to failure before it began. The eyes of the National Convention and the people of Newfoundland now turned to Ottawa to see if the Canadians had anything better to offer.

III

Preparations in Ottawa to receive a delegation from the National Convention continued unabated throughout the spring and early summer of 1947. Although the ICCNR rarely met officially, the subcommittees put the finishing touches on their particular reports. Schedules were drawn up dealing with the comings and goings of the delegation, and a rough agenda was put together. Timing was important – was it wise to delay the visit until late summer (when the federal-provincial tax arrangements would, they hoped, be settled), leaving the Newfoundlanders to cool their heels in St John's? The growing impatience in Ottawa and St John's overruled this possibility, and it was agreed that June would be the most suitable time to hold the talks. Finally, the end of June was selected, in order to prevent the paths of the Newfoundlanders from crossing that of President Truman, who would be visiting Ottawa earlier in the month.

The financial questions surrounding the potential union of Canada and Newfoundland, not surprisingly, dominated the investigations. Newfoundland's ability to function as an economically viable province was questionable at best. Likewise, how would Canada's trade position be affected by union? After all, Newfoundland was Canada's eighth largest trading partner, and the dependence of Newfoundland on Canada was far greater.

Much of the concern was focused on the Newfoundland tariff. Under Confederation Newfoundland's tariff would be replaced by the Canadian one and the revenues would be directed to Ottawa rather than to St John's. With lower Canadian rates in place, the people of Newfoundland would immediately benefit from reduced prices, and, moreover, Canadian goods would enter Newfoundland duty-free. The removal of the Newfoundland tariff would, however, produce a serious revenue loss to any Newfoundland government, which had previously relied on the tariff for its main source of income. By looking back over the previous years and comparing what the Newfoundland government collected from import duties with what would have been collected had Newfoundland been a province at that time revealed a deficit of approximately $10 million.[53]

Conversely, Confederation offered some real benefits to Canada. Newfoundland goods would now enter Canada free of duty, but since Canada imported so little from Newfoundland this loss of revenue was considered negligible. But the removal of the tariff on Canadian products (which already played a dominant role in Newfoundland) could confer a significant competitive advantage. Lists were drawn of Newfoundland's imports from sources other than Canada and it was argued that Canada could supply a major portion of these products. It was estimated that 54 per cent of Newfoundland's imports outside of Canada could be filled by Canadian suppliers. Taking into consideration established trading patterns and consumers preferences, the potential value would be increased, but could still bring in an estimated $4 million each year for Canadian exporters.[54]

These benefits were sufficient in themselves to make Confederation more attractive, but there was a darker side as well. An independent Newfoundland would remain a competitor, and if the talks between the two countries soured, there was no telling what the Newfoundlanders would do. Clearly there was strong support across the country for closer economic ties with the United States, and union with the Americans was a distant but potent threat. Moreover, closer economic ties alone could prove disastrous to those Canadians who exported to Newfoundland. Should the Americans be given a competitive edge through lower tariffs into Newfoundland (in exchange for the free entry of Newfoundland fish into the United States, for example) Canada would be effectively excluded from a large portion of the Newfoundland market. Although impossible to estimate, by removing from an export list to Newfoundland those products which were not at present imported by the United States, Canada (and the Maritimes in particular) would be hard pressed to maintain its exports in such basic products as flour, potatoes, beer, dairy products, paint, textiles, and automobiles. Similarly, Newfoundland fish would receive a competitive advantage in the American market, which would likely result in a drop in Canadian fish exports.[55]

From the point of view of trade and tariffs, it was clearly to Canada's advantage to bring Newfoundland into Confederation. The problem remained, however, to bridge the gap between Newfoundland's revenue and expenditures as a province. Under the assumption that Newfoundland would enter into a tax-rental agreement with Ottawa, it was estimated that Newfoundland would receive at least $4 million from the federal government, in addition to per-capita subsidies of approximately $440,000. Furthermore, a case could be made for an extra 'special statutory subsidy' of nearly $1.5 million, resulting from Newfoundland's extra difficulties in communications and transportation. Unfortunately, even with these grants and subsidies, a Newfoundland provincial government would suffer severe budget deficits (around $3.5 million annually). On top of this, Ottawa would have to supply the funds to bring Newfoundland's services up to the level of the other provinces and to institute some kind of development program. There was also the problem of Newfoundland's national debt and the obligation of the Canadians to take over the debt-ridden Newfoundland railway. These variables were unknown factors in 1947, but it was estimated that Confederation would cost Ottawa between $10 million and $20 million annually.[56]

A number of proposals were suggested to bridge this gap without enraging the other provinces, ranging from a 'Confederation grant' to Newfoundland, to the rental and development of Labrador by Canada, to the establishment of a Newfoundland customs duty or sales tax to bolster provincial revenue.[57] These ideas were debated within the ICCNR, but it was up to the cabinet to decide. The question still remained for the cabinet, moreover, of how to deal with the upcoming talks with the Newfoundland delegation – either as exploratory discussions or as full-scale negotiations for union.

To ease the burden of decision somewhat, the Department of External Affairs prepared a memorandum (at the request of the cabinet committee) on the 'Advantages of Incorporating Newfoundland into the Dominion.' The benefits for trade and development were reviewed, as were the less tangible (but not less potent) factors of increased population, land, and new untapped natural resources. Interestingly, the security advantages of Confederation were presented more with the United States in mind than any of Canada's potential 'enemies.' The likelihood of Newfoundland's falling under American domination was clearly viewed as a distinct possibility. The repercussions of a Canadian withdrawal from Newfoundland would be felt across the country and might produce 'a sense of national frustration,' leading to the further 'absorption of Canada within the United States orbit.' In conclusion the DEA argued that the present was a 'unique opportunity for completion of confederation as conceived by the fathers.' And failure at this point might 'close the door' for all time.[58]

During the two weeks before the arrival of the delegation from St John's, the Newfoundland question was discussed on several occasions in both cabinet and cabinet committee meetings. Gradually Louis St Laurent, the minister of external affairs, had emerged as the strongest pro-Confederate in the cabinet. He stressed to the less enthusiastic ministers the benefits of Confederation and the need to act before the Americans did. Of the ministers who showed a continuing interest in this subject, St Laurent could count on the support of C.D. Howe and Brooke Claxton. On the other side of the fence was J.L. Ilsley, the former finance minister and now the minister of justice. Ilsley argued that extreme caution should be used in the upcoming talks. The Nova Scotian's resistance was essentially political, stemming from the fear that Newfoundland would be offered better terms than those available to the other provinces, especially the Maritimes. Mackenzie King, one of the earliest and strongest supporters of maintaining close relations with Newfoundland, increasingly began to weigh the political questions surrounding Confederation. Concerned with a political backlash from the other 'have not' provinces if a special deal was made with Newfoundland, King was reluctant to make any pledge of this sort. The root of the problem was that King was unsure of the support from the Maritimes on this issue and he hesitated to move without it. He noted the 'eagerness' of Pearson and St Laurent on this issue and wrote in his diary that 'External Affairs will want to have Newfoundland brought in at once.'[59] Moreover, King was uncomfortable with the thought of negotiating terms with a delegation that had no real authorization to do so, and he increasingly came to feel that union would be best brought about after responsible government had been restored in Newfoundland.

In light of these varying outlooks, the cabinet made two interesting decisions. First, the Newfoundland delegation would be informed that Newfoundland would be welcomed as a province and would receive treatment equal to that of other Canadian provinces. Presumably, therefore, the discussions would essentially be an opportunity to exchange information on the nature of Confederation. Second, after a referendum victory for Confederation, the Canadian government would then be willing to negotiate terms of union with Newfoundlanders 'authorized to negotiate federal union.'[60]

The Newfoundland delegation arrived in Ottawa on 24 June. In addition to Bradley as chairman and Smallwood as secretary, it included Gordon Higgins, Thomas Ashbourne, the Reverend Lester Burry, Charles Ballam, and P.W. Crummey. They were welcomed at the Ottawa railway station by St Laurent and one of the hottest summers the capital had seen in many years. The delegation was checked into the Château Laurier and later that evening the Newfoundlanders were entertained at a reception and dinner hosted by the prime minister at the Ottawa Country Club.

The first official meeting between the two sides was held the following day (25 June) in the Railway Committee Room of the House of Commons (the rest of the meetings were held in Room 258). The Canadian team was basically made up of the members of the cabinet committee – St Laurent, Ilsley, Abbott, McCann, and Bridges. In addition, an array of Canadian officials were also on hand to help with any specific questions. Mackenzie King attended the first meeting and made a welcoming speech. Bradley responded for the Newfoundlanders and then the meeting was adjourned until later the same day. King was quite pleased with the occasion and enjoyed himself, except when St Laurent suggested that he and Bradley have themselves photographed in front of the large painting of the Fathers of Confederation. In King's mind this 'was going a little too far.'[61]

At the second meeting the two sides exchanged reports containing information on the two countries, and then adjourned for a week of study. The Newfoundlanders returned a week later with a list of questions on various aspects of the constitution and workings of the federal system. Their inquiries covered a wide range of interests, such as marriage and divorce, education, public lands, national parks, the appointment of judges, and representation in the House of Commons and senate. The Canadians took the list, promising written statements within a week.[62]

Before too long it became apparent that plenary sessions were not the most suitable vehicle for carrying on the in-depth investigation of the various subjects that was needed. Thus, eleven subcommittees were formed over the following weeks to look at a number of topics in a more detailed fashion.[63]

With the creation of the subcommittees, and given the nature of the discussions themselves, it is not surprising that the visit of the Ottawa delegation lasted far longer than that of the London delegation. This well suited the Newfoundlanders, particularly the Confederates, who were in no hurry to return to St John's. It was believed that a referendum held that summer would go against Confederation, and therefore it was in their interests to delay their return until it was too late to schedule a vote for that year.[64]

What the Newfoundlanders were really concerned with was terms. The time factor was not seen as essential, providing the delegation could bring an 'offer' back to St John's with them. And as the negotiations progressed, more and more attention was focused on the tough questions of finance. The 'budget gap' was there for all to see – would the Canadians commit themselves to bridge it? Moreover, to prolong the discussions needlessly while having no intention of giving concrete terms could have significant repercussions, particularly in Newfoundland. Bradley informed the Canadians that if the terms were good enough he would come out as a strong advocate for Confederation; if not, he would retire to his home in Bonavista and watch from the sidelines. At this point the Canadians were putting their hopes on Bradley to lead the Confederate campaign in the referendum and they believed that, without him out front, Confederation would never get off the ground. Thus, there was further pressure on the Canadians to come up with a concrete offer.[65]

On 11 July, a number of officials, including Pearson, J.S. Macdonald, MacKay, Baldwin, and Paul Bridle, met with St Laurent to discuss this problem. St Laurent was told that the negotiations could not hope to avoid the difficult questions very much longer. It was recognized that the solution at this point was essentially political; to make an offer that included special subsidies would stir up trouble at home. Furthermore, if they were rejected in Newfoundland, the Canadians' only accomplishment would have been to have supplied ammunition to other covetous provinces. Nevertheless, the time had come to decide.[66] St Laurent met with the prime minister the same day and informed him of this problem. King noted that he had earlier warned the cabinet of the potential backlash, but did not suggest putting an end to the negotiations.[67]

St Laurent brought this issue up at the 18 July cabinet meeting. He described the situation for the other members and listed four probable commitments that the Canadians would have to make: Canada would have to assume Newfoundland's national debt, financially support the Newfoundland Railway, negotiate a tax-rental agreement similar to that offered the other provinces, and proffer a special subsidy to meet Newfoundland's anticipated budget deficit. All this would end up costing the Canadians a considerable amount – total federal revenues gained from Newfoundland would amount to approximately $20 million; the Canadian expenditures could grow to $35 million.

Mackenzie King followed St Laurent with the hope that if the Canadians made an offer they could count on the Newfoundlanders accepting. He suggested that perhaps the best way of dealing with the situation would be to introduce a resolution on the issue in Parliament, ostensibly to remove it from the realm of 'party politics.'

The cabinet meeting proved to be a pivotal one; the cabinet reversed its June decision and agreed to move ahead on the negotiations and to make a 'serious effort' to bring Newfoundland in. This meant that a more complete offer would be made. If it became necessary to offset any political backlash, the cabinet also agreed to seek parliamentary approval of the terms. This discussion was a signal to continue negotiations and to bring them to a successful conclusion. Smallwood, who had been waiting anxiously outside the Parliament Buildings, was flashed the good news by J.S. Macdonald at the conclusion of the meeting.[68] Later the same day, St Laurent met with the prime minister. King recorded in his diary that St Laurent 'stressed the value it would be to my name and to the future to have Newfoundland come into Confederation while I am still Prime Minister.'[69]

With the air cleared in this way the subcommittees put the final touches on their reports. A number of lesser problems remained – the sale of oleomargarine (which was at that time prohibited in Canada), the ferry services connecting the island with the mainland, compensation for workers, and the need for an economic survey. These were worked out, either in subcommittee or private meetings between Bradley and Smallwood and one or two Canadian officials.[70]

Matter were further complicated with the death of Frank Bridges on 10 August. Not only was Bridges an important participant in the talks, he was also the New Brunswick representative in the cabinet, and the only direct link to Premier McNair. Bridge's death threw a wrench into the whole negotiations with Newfoundland as far as Mackenzie King was concerned. The one thing that King did not want was to make Confederation a party issue, and he feared that it might develop that way in the by-election he would have to call in New Brunswick.

King and St Laurent disagreed on this point during the cabinet meeting on 14 August. St Laurent believed that the terms of union should be left to stand on their own merits, noting that probably 80 percent of the country would support the bringing of Newfoundland into Confederation. King agreed but argued that this would be true only 'until they know the terms. Once the terms were known, the different provinces would begin to take exception to them.' Newfoundland would have to be given special terms, King said, and as a result: 'We would be asked why we were treating strangers better than our own people and supporters.' King saw even darker and more dangerous implications: 'They all would question the terms. We would have utter chaos in Canada, and the Government would be beaten, and we would be further away from federation with Newfoundland than ever.'[71]

The matter was again discussed in the cabinet on 25 August. King got his way and the cabinet agreed not to finalize the terms until after New Brunswick had a cabinet representative. A by-election would be held as soon as possible, but until then what Canada had to offer must be kept secret. On the same day, Premier McNair met with King and the two discussed the upcoming by-election. McNair agreed with King's desire to keep the Newfoundland issue out of the by-election, and he believed that if this could be done the Liberals would win the seat easily. A few days later Milton Gregg was chosen as the Liberal candidate.[72]

This new development was an unfortunate one for the Newfoundlanders. Apart from Bradley and Smallwood (who was a member of all the subcommittees), the members of the delegation longed to return home to Newfoundland since there was a decreasing number of things to do. In addition, the National Convention, which had adjourned in the absence of the Ottawa delegation, was growing restive over the long delay. Early in September, angry telegrams were sent to Ottawa demanding the immediate return of the delegation. Bradley refused to leave until the work of the delegation was completed, but clearly he could not hold off indefinitely.[73]

If the Canadians would not release the terms until after the by-election, the question remained of what to do with the Newfoundlanders until then. One suggestion was to pack the delegation up and send them on a fact-finding mission to the Pacific, but the idea was quietly dropped.[74] Bradley was increasingly eager to finish the negotiations. Given the desire of the delegation to return home and the possible adverse effects a long delay could have on public opinion in Newfoundland, it was decided that it would be best to permit the delegation to leave without the terms. After the by-election, the Canadian government could then reach a final decision and send the terms to the National Convention.[75]

This line of thinking was agreeable to both sides, enabling the negotiations to be brought to a swift conclusion. The final meeting took place on 29 September. For the most part it was an occasion for the exchange of formalities, including warm words of appreciation from St Laurent and Bradley. On being questioned by the Newfoundlanders, St Laurent said that the financial aspects discussed should be considered 'the limit to which the government would go.' As for the other terms, however, the Canadians would be more flexible. But, warned St Laurent, should the terms be rejected, completely new terms would have to be negotiated if the question of union rose again in the future.[76]

With the summer gone, the Ottawa delegation returned to St John's to face a truculent National Convention. In Ottawa, the work on the terms continued. A memorandum containing the proposed terms, written largely by MacKay, was ready by the end of September. King's first reaction was negative; he felt that 'we were giving Newfoundland pretty much everything that she wanted without adequately weighing what Canada would be getting in return.'[77] Moreover, with the York-Sunbury by-election still three weeks away, discussion of the terms in cabinet was postponed until late October.

On 20 October, Milton Gregg was elected in York-Sunbury with a solid majority, which was 'a source of great relief and joy' for Mackenzie King.[78] More important, with this hurdle surmounted, the path was cleared for the cabinet to decide on the terms. To this end, after three cabinet committee meetings to discuss the terms, on 28 October, St Laurent submitted the 'Proposed Arrangements' for cabinet approval.

St Laurent gave the ministers a brief review of the salient points. First, Newfoundland and Labrador would become a province like all the others and receive similar public services. Second, the federal government would take over the Newfoundland Railway, Gander airport, the public broadcasting system, the publicly owned telegraph services, and other services that normally fell under federal control. Third, the federal government would assume the responsibility for Newfoundland's sterling debt on the grounds that it represented 'a fair estimate of the amount of Newfoundland debt incurred for purposes which would presumably have been the responsibility of the government of Canada had Newfoundland been a Province.' Newfoundland's accumulated surplus would be left with the province for development purposes.

On the financial side, Newfoundland would be given the normal statutory subsidies under the BNA Act, a 'special annual subsidy' of $1.1 million, the right to enter a tax-rental agreement (based on those given to other provinces), and an additional transitional grant of $3.5 million, diminishing after three years by 10 per cent per year for a total of twelve years. Also, as a kind of safety catch, a royal commission would be appointed eight years after union to prepare a report on the financial position of the new province. This was a proposal that Smallwood had backed strongly. There were a number of other provisions listed by St Laurent, including the maintenance of a Newfoundland-mainland steamship service, transitional unemployment benefits (for those dislocated by union), the application of the Maritime Freight Rates Act to Newfoundland, and the manufacture and sale of oleomargarine.

St Laurent finished with a statement that these terms were the least that could be offered in order for Newfoundland to function normally, while at the same time, given the sympathies of the other provinces, the most that Canada could afford to give. The cabinet discussed the terms and gave its approval.[79] In his diary, King wrote that the discussion 'passed off very pleasantly and with complete unanimity.' He also noted that an 'understanding' was reached concerning the resolution for Parliament: the issue would not be introduced until after the people of Newfoundland had had a chance to vote on the terms.[80]

Newfoundlanders got their first opportunity to see the terms on 6 November 1947, when they were presented to the National Convention. For the next few months, attention was focused on St John's as the National Convention debated the 'proposed arrangements.' Because responsible government was a known quantity it received little treatment; Confederation, however, was examined and discussed again and again, under Smallwood's careful direction. In his memoirs, Smallwood estimates that while only four days were given to discussing responsible government, Confederation received thirty-four days of attention.[81]

For weeks on end the advantages of Confederation were heard by thousands of Newfoundlanders across the country who listened in on the radio. In a sense the campaign had already begun, and Smallwood wisely understood where the final decision would come from. If it had been left up to the National Convention, however, Confederation would not have stood a chance: on 29 January 1948 the National

Convention voted 29 to 16 against including Confederation in the referendum. Regardless of Smallwood's relentless efforts, only two choices were recommended: 1 / responsible government as it existed prior to 1934; and 2 / Commission of Government.

Smallwood and the Confederates immediately went on the attack against the 'twenty-nine dictators' who wanted to keep Confederation off the ballot. Bradley spoke on the radio and a petition was circulated, eventually gathering almost 50,000 names. A small group of Confederates presented it to the governor who promised to send the petition along to London. Smallwood was shocked to find a week later that it never actually left St John's, only a telegram indicating the reason for the petition and the number of signatures. Smallwood now 'had to live through an interminable, intolerable, maddening wait for word from London!'[82]

In retrospect, it is clear that there was no reason for Smallwood to be apprehensive. The Commonwealth Relations Office, as the Dominions Office was now called, had reserved for itself the final judgment as to what was going on the ballot, and given Britain and Canada's feelings on the issue, there could be only one decision. The strong support for Confederation revealed by the petition could legitimize the actions of the CRO, but Confederation was put on the ballot because it was the policy favoured by Canada and Britain.

The only uncertainty for the British was whether the Canadians would want Confederation on the ballot under these circumstances. Several days before the vote was taken in the National Convention, Norman Robertson met with Sir Eric Machtig and Governor Macdonald, who was in London for a visit. What the British wanted to know was whether the Canadians would approve the inclusion of Confederation if the National Convention voted against it.[83] As far as the British were concerned, the course was fairly straightforward. Lord Addison, who was filling in for Philip Noel-Baker, the secretary of state for Commonwealth affairs, while the latter was in New York, wrote to Attlee on 3 February: 'There is no doubt that Confederation with Canada at the right time presents the best hope for Newfoundland, and that the sooner it comes the better. But the question is one for Newfoundland people to determine. We ought so to handle the matter as not to risk Confederation being relegated to the background for many years to come.'

Attlee concurred with Addison and he contacted Noel-Baker in New York for his opinion. Meanwhile, Governor Macdonald decided to fly to

New York to discuss the question directly with Noel-Baker. The latter had planned a trip to Ottawa on his return home, but he was cautioned against this, because, Machtig wrote, Macdonald felt 'that Newfoundland public opinion would regard visit by you to Mr Mackenzie King at this stage as an attempt by United Kingdom to force Confederation with Canada on Newfoundland.' Noel-Baker cancelled his trip to Ottawa and wired his approval home to Machtig.[84]

At this stage the Canadians were asked for the go-ahead to put Confederation on the ballot. On the ministerial level the Canadians backed off quickly; during the 5 February cabinet meeting it was decided that the government did not wish to be consulted on this issue at all. As Pearson put it to Clutterbuck, this approach was taken in order to permit the government to tell the House that it was entirely a UK decision.[85] It was on the unofficial level that the Canadians let their feelings be known. It was not considered necessary to press the United Kingdom to include Confederation – they knew they did not have to. It was sufficient to state that if the British government felt that the apparent support for Confederation in Newfoundland warranted its inclusion on the ballot, the Canadians would not object.

Robertson was instructed to bring the question up in London, and in particular stress that the Canadians hoped the British would make a clear statement of the extent to which they would be able to continue supporting Newfoundland. The Canadians had found the statement made to the London delegation in 1947 a little vague, and, moreover: 'It may be that in view of the serious deterioration in the United Kingdom's exchange position since the statement was made, the government might be prepared to be more explicit on this point.'[86]

Robertson reported to Ottawa that Addison strongly favoured putting Confederation on the ballot. Machtig agreed as well, but he was concerned that the United Kingdom not appear to the Newfoundlanders to be forcing it on them. 'This was an impression they wished to avoid,' Robertson informed Ottawa.[87]

Discussions carried on in this fashion throughout February. Only a few minor problems emerged. For instance, the Canadians believed that the retention of Commission of Government should be for ten years as opposed to the five years suggested by the British. There was also some disagreement over the statement that an affirmative vote would lead to the negotiation of 'full terms.' This appeared to some Canadians as an invitation to the Newfoundlanders to reopen the whole negotiations – something the Canadians did not want to do.[88] These were relatively minor points that in no way sidetracked Britain's decision to include Confederation on the ballot.

Britain's decision was made known on 11 March 1948. The governor announced that there would be three choices on the ballot paper: 1 / Commission of Government for a further period of five years; 2 / responsible government as it existed in 1933 prior to the establishment of Commission of Government; 3 / Confederation with Canada. The United Kingdom had decided that 'it would not be right that the people of Newfoundland should be deprived of an opportunity of considering the issue at the referendum.' If no clear majority was won on the first ballot, the most unpopular choice would be dropped and a second referendum held. And if a majority voted for Confederation, then 'means would be provided to enable the full terms and arrangements for the constitution of Newfoundland as a Province of Canada to be discussed and settled between authorized representatives of Newfoundland and Canada.'[89]

*The National Convention had been a curious exercise. Despite its espousal of democracy and the excitement and interest that it provoked, it had, in the final analysis, proved itself to be virtually totally ineffective. Granted, the United Kingdom had valid reasons for including Confederation on the ballot over the decision of the National Convention, but, as S.J. Noel wrote: 'For all the effect of its decision, the National Convention might just as well never have met.' Indeed, the National Convention served only to further the interests of the Confederates, by providing them 'with a unique platform from which to launch their campaign.'[90]

From the inception of the National Convention British policy towards Newfoundland focused on bringing the country into Confederation. At every turn steps were taken to help realize this goal. The greatest concern for Whitehall, it appears, was that the Canadians – not the Newfoundlanders – would back out. If the Canadians could be persuaded to be generous enough and if the affair was engineered effectively, it was believed that there was sufficient latent support for Confederation to carry the day.

For the British there was a fine line to tread between promoting Confederation as much as possible and not appearing to force the issue and thereby damage their own cause. As a result, it was considered wise to paint a dark picture of their precarious financial position and to make few promises of aid to an independent Newfoundland. Yet, at the same time, it was also important to offer continued support at the existing levels; to do otherwise would play into the hands of those who claimed to see a 'conspiracy' in the actions of the British and Canadians. As one official in the treasury put it: 'It is in our interest and Newfoundland's that she should accept the very reasonable offers from Canada. Newfoundland is linked with Canada financially and economically and the intensity of our financial difficulties with Canada is a measure of the difficulties we should find in continuing help to Newfoundland. This is recognized by the c.r.o., and u.k. policy is to try to get Newfoundland to join Canada. On the other hand it was not considered possible, for general reasons, to drive Newfoundland into doing so, by saying that the uk. would otherwise not contemplate further liabilities.'[91]

With its inclusion on the ballot, Confederation was put on an equal footing with responsible government. In addition, the idea had been well aired and debated across the country for more than a year, and considerable support had emerged. Perhaps most important, the movement had found in J.R. Smallwood a leader who would champion the cause with a fierce determination unmatched by any rival supporters of responsible government.

9

'We are all Canadians now'

The Canadian and British governments had largely engineered the inclusion of Confederation in the referendum. Since the end of the war it had been their aim to at least give the Newfoundlanders the option to choose union with Canada. The co-operation between the two governments had proved significant, if unofficial and ill defined, and in 1948–9, this policy finally came to fruition.

It is one thing to give people a choice; it is quite another to make them choose. The final decision was, of course, for the Newfoundlanders to make, and the influence wielded by the Canadians and the British was necessarily secondary. In fact, if the Canadians had any clear policy during the referendum campaigns, it was to be seen to be doing absolutely nothing to affect the decision. This seeming neutrality was demonstrated in replacing J.S. Macdonald with Paul Bridle as acting high commissioner in Newfoundland. Bridle was a junior official in the Department of External Affairs and it was felt that he could better maintain a low profile in St John's while allowing the Canadians to exercise a degree of influence, both politically and financially, to help secure a successful outcome.

Once the decision to join Confederation was made, moreover, great pains were taken by the Canadians to ensure a satisfactory conclusion to the final negotiations. Changing circumstances forced a renegotiation of several key elements of the agreement, and its acceptance was not always a sure thing. But, by autumn 1948 the Canadians had come too far and devoted too much energy to the problem of Newfoundland to let the solution slip through their fingers.

I

Noel-Baker's announcement that Confederation would indeed be on the ballot paper was like a pistol shot signalling the start of the referendum campaign. For the rest of the spring and early summer, Newfoundland was divided into opposing camps, while a fierce battle was waged to determine the country's future.

Gordon Bradley was nominated president of the Confederate Association, founded on 26 March, but it was 'campaign director' Smallwood who ran the show. Harold Horwood, who was also a member, recalled the rudimentary beginnings of the Confederate campaign: 'We started with no organization whatsoever. There were Smallwood and half a dozen of us here in St John's, including a few delegates to the convention who launched the organization. We had no organization outside. We met in Smallwood's living room one night and decided we would launch the confederate organization as such.'[1] To help fill in the gaps outside St John's, Smallwood wrote 101 prominent men in outport communities and invited them to become vice-presidents in the Confederate Association, a move designed as much to boost morale in St John's as to garner support in the outports.

The Confederate campaign was directed from a cramped room on Water Street in St John's. Smallwood gathered around him a diligent and extraordinary crew of converts to Confederation, including Gregory Power, Irving Fogwill, Ray Petten, Phillip Forsey, and Harold Horwood. But the lion's share of the work was taken on by Smallwood himself; in addition to speech writer and chief organizer, he was also the strategist and prime campaigner. Every move or speech of importance had Smallwood's indelible stamp of approval on it.

Smallwood's campaign methods were equally unorthodox. Where there were roads he campaigned by car; where there were none he took to the air and campaigned from an old seaplane fitted with loudspeakers. In this way Smallwood gained access to even the remotest Newfoundland communities. Yet Smallwood's zeal in campaigning did not lead to recklessness; most of his efforts were directed by an overall plan. 'There just was not enough time,' he wrote in his memoirs, 'and the Island was too big and the money too scarce, to allow us to hold a large series of public meetings. In any case, I saw that one public meeting that ended in disorder would do terrible damage to our cause throughout the country. This I had to avoid at all costs. I never held a single meeting in either campaign in any place where I was not sure of getting a great reception; and I held meetings in such places purely for the publicity that they would generate, in order to help create a bandwagon psychology throughout the Island.'[2]

The other arm of the Confederate campaign was the weekly newspaper The Confederate. It was written and edited mainly by Smallwood, with the help of Gregory Power, the assistant campaign director, whose biting wit had the ability to infuriate all opponents. The creed of Confederate journalism was simple: hammer away at the weakness of responsible government and push hard the benefits most Newfoundlanders would receive from services such as family allowances and old-age pensions. Smallwood was aided greatly in this task by a Toronto cartoonist whom he had hired while in Canada with the Ottawa delegation. *The Confederate* never aspired to journalistic heights, but through the constant repetition of a handful of facts it served well enough to drive the Confederate point of view across.

Running an island-wide campaign, along with a weekly newspaper, naturally took a lot of money. Donations were accepted from all across the country, but unfortunately for the Confederates, most of Newfoundland's wealthy citizens supported the return to responsible government. The pool of Newfoundlanders living in Canada was also tapped: Smallwood sent Charles Penney on a trip to Canada to elicit support and cash from these ex-Newfoundlanders. The Confederate cause found greater success from the more lucrative but less documented practice of selling senatorships to eager Newfoundlanders willing to risk their money on a Confederate victory.[3]

An even more important source of funds for the Confederate campaign was found in Ottawa. Early in the campaign High Commissioner Macdonald reported to Ottawa of the severe money troubles of the Confederates, and he argued that in order to improve the chances of the Confederates, the necessary dollars should be found for them.[4] It was, of course, impossible for the Canadian government to publicly fund the Confederate campaign, but this was not the case for the Liberal party.

Going out to collect the money, one Confederate remembered, was 'hard stuff.' The first contacts Smallwood made were with C.D. Howe and Senator Neil McLean, who was the party treasurer for the Liberals in New Brunswick. Senator McLean, who had an interest in a large fish cannery in Newfoundland and was a staunch Confederate, gave a reported $50,000.[5] From Howe and McLean Smallwood was sent to Senator Gordon Fogo, the national director of the Liberal party. At this point Ray Petten, the treasurer for the Confederate Association, took over from Smallwood. Fogo was reluctant to give directly from the party fund, but he gave Petten a list of potential private donors. 'Most of these,' recalled Horwood, 'were brewers and distillers and vintners — people who were in a rather sensitive position, and who, if the word were dropped from the Liberal Party that they should do a favour for somebody else, would be very apt to do the favour.'[6]

Although there are no cheque stubs to provide documentation, estimates of the total amount collected (from both Newfoundland and Canadian sources) run anywhere from $150,000 to a quarter of a million dollars.[7] In any event, the Confederate campaign did not grind to a halt because of a lack of funds. It was almost to the contrary, as Gwyn notes: 'Smallwood frequently amazed his more cautious colleagues by flashing thick wads of bills and, with the panache of a cod culler, parcelling out payments to almost any comer, including several who were never seen again.'[8]

There is no evidence that it was ever discussed, but the Liberals had reason to believe that Smallwood would lead a Liberal party in Newfoundland after Confederation. After all, Smallwood had been a Liberal before the fall of responsible government in 1933 and his contacts with Ottawa were almost exclusively Liberal ones. A victory for Smallwood and Confederation, therefore, would also likely produce five or more Liberal seats in the House of Commons – an added bonus.

The opponents of Confederation were not so lucky. United more in their opposition to Confederation than in support of a particular cause, the wide spectrum of those who favoured responsible government (for any reason: full independence, union with the United States, or even to better negotiate Confederation) lacked a leader of Smallwood's calibre to champion their cause. Moreover, the Water Street merchants and most of the business class across the country who gave their support to responsible government were less generous on the financial side.[9]

The nucleus of the Responsible Government League contained a number of St John's businessmen and ex-members of the National Convention. The fiery Peter Cashin emerged as the leader, and although he could enthral an audience with his oratory, he never controlled the league in the way Smallwood did the Confederate Association. Consequently the Responsible Government League lacked the organization and direction of the Confederates.

The Responsible Government League published its own paper, *The Independent*, and it was the equal of *The Confederate* in sensationalism, virulence, and venom. Cartoons showed Mackenzie King holding a Newfoundlander upside down to shake out his money while a Quebec lumberjack stood by with arms crossed, no doubt eyeing Labrador.[10] In addition to the Confederate cause, particular anger was vented on

Mackenzie King, French Canada, the British government, and the way Confederation was put on the ballot.

Evidence of the disunity within the ranks of the responsible government forces was the formation of the Economic Union party. The new party was founded on a rather ill defined and totally unexplored goal of economic union with the United States, and the reasoning was simple: 'Canada can give us family allowances but she cannot give us markets. America can give us the markets out of which we can pay for our family allowances and other social services as well. The path of reason is the restoration of self-government and the dispatch of a delegation to Washington to talk things over and see what kind of advantageous agreement we can make. This is Newfoundland's great chance if we have the wisdom and vision to see and take it.'[11]

Led by Chesley Crosbie, a wealthy businessman, and with Don Jamieson and Geoffrey Stirling directing the campaign, the party became a potent threat. Through the pages of Stirling's newspaper, the *Sunday Herald*, economic union was touted as a panacea for Newfoundland's economic woes – and this message found many sympathetic ears across the country. Relations with the United States were close; thousands of Newfoundlanders had emigrated there, and thousands more had directly benefited from the jobs and dollars that had come with the u.s. servicemen.

An indication of the seriousness with which the possibility of economic union was taken was Smallwood's offer of the premiership to Crosbie if the leader of the Economic Union party would desert his party for the Confederates. Smallwood expressed his 'alarm' over the increase in support for economic union to L.O. Sanderhoff, an official in the American Consolate in St John's. Interestingly, Sanderhoff asked Smallwood which he would prefer, all things being equal, union with Canada or the United States. Smallwood told him that 'theoretically he would prefer the United States; but he doubted that certain problems could be solved, and stated that in any event no proposals had ever been made.' Smallwood later added 'somewhat facetiously' that 'if it were not for the Canadian family allowances, he would "throw up the sponge" and quit sponsoring Confederation. He agreed that family allowances constituted the biggest "talking point" of the Confederationists.'[12]

On the other side Crosbie, Stirling, and others made trips to Washington and Ottawa to push their new cause. In Ottawa, Stirling told T.B. Sanders, the second secretary in the American embassy, that

Crosbie had 'enough "dirt" on Smallwood thoroughly to discredit the latter near the end of the present campaign.'[13] Part of this 'dirt' came out a few weeks later when Stirling was in Washington. Speaking with two State Department officials, Stirling 'referred to an alleged association of 25 years ago between Smallwood and Trotsky, and allowed us to believe that was all we would need to know about Smallwood.'[14]

There were a number of major flaws, however, that precluded any possibility of success for the Economic Union party. The first and obvious problem was that economic union was not on the ballot, and to achieve it, responsible government would first have to be restored since only then could negotiations begin. The second, and more important drawback was the attitude of the United States. Although a number of American senators were sympathetic to the concept, the idea was never given serious consideration in Washington. For those who did look at it, there were significant drawbacks; for one thing, the New England fishermen were adamantly opposed to any proposal that might improve the competitive position of Newfoundland fish in American markets. Moreover, such action would undoubtedly lead other countries, such as Norway and Iceland, to demand similar privileges in the U.S. market. Finally, as one State Department official put it, 'Canada was obviously more important to the United States than was Newfoundland,' and the Americans were not likely to move, given the known sensitive feelings of the Canadians regarding Newfoundland.[15]

Consequently, the Americans adopted a policy of total silence on this question. After a visit to Washington by Geoffrey Stirling, Andrew Foster of the State Department wrote that 'any manifestation of interest by officials of the United States Government would obviously be received with considerable misgivings in Canada and the United Kingdom and might be considered as undue interference in the domestic political affairs of a foreign country.'[16] Unfortunately, the silence of the American consulate in St John's was taken in some quarters as tacit acceptance of the idea of economic union – if the Americans were opposed, why didn't they say so?

The Economic Union party was a direct challenge to the Confederates, but Smallwood retaliated with a brilliant move. By playing up the fact that economic union meant closer relations with a non-British nation, Smallwood was able 'to steal their patriotic clothes' and ride on the campaign slogan 'Confederation – British Union.'[17]

The referendum campaign was a fiercely debated contest that divided neighbourhoods and families, and at times turned violent. For weeks on end it dominated life in Newfoundland as nothing else had done before. The results were : 69,400 (44.55 per cent) for responsible government; 64,066 (41.13 per cent) for Confederation; and 22,311 (14.32 per cent) for Commission of Government.[18]

A second vote was scheduled for 22 July and the campaign began again, this time between Confederation and responsible government only. A new twist was added to the second campaign: old sectarian divisions resurfaced in the opposing camps and old battles were fought once more. The antipathy of the Roman Catholic hierarchy to Confederation stemmed from the fear that in union Newfoundland might lose its system of denominational schools and that a hard-pressed provincial government might cut back financial support for these schools. There were other concerns as well, ranging from a distaste for divorce to a fear of being swallowed up in a largely Protestant Canada. While acknowledging that Confederation might produce material benefits for the people, the church considered the loss of the traditional Newfoundland way of life too high a price to pay.[19]

The results of the first referendum had shown that Catholic districts had tended to vote for responsible government while Protestant districts had leaned towards Confederation. And once one side used religious terms as an explanation for the first outcome, the other side naturally followed suit. Through the pages of the Catholic monthly, *The Monitor*, the Catholic church extolled the virtues of independence and the evils of Confederation. Unable to let this pass, the Orange Lodge (of which Bradley was a former grand master) attacked the church for bringing the sectarian issue into the campaign. To neither side's credit, the two opposing camps exchanged accusations, slanders, and counter-charges that gave a sharper and more bitter edge to the already severe divisions within Newfoundland society.

Different accounts of the second campaign place varying degrees of emphasis on the influence of the sectarian issue. No doubt some Newfoundlanders voted on sectarian lines, and since Newfoundland was two-thirds Protestant this could only help the Confederates. Years later, after the smoke had cleared, the Confederate Gregory Power continued to believe that it was the sectarian influence that put Confederation over the top.[20] But this interpretation is valid only in isolation: there were numerous other factors involved (mainly economic ones) on which the vote was decided.[21]

The key to the second ballot was, of course, the large body of Newfoundlanders who voted for the retention of Commission of

Government on the first ballot and would now have to choose one of the other alternatives. The Confederates had envisioned such a scenario and had refrained from antagonizing those people through attacks on the Commission of Government during the first campaign.[22] The Confederates received a tremendous boost in this direction soon after the first vote, when two of the Newfoundland commissioners – Herbert Pottle and Herman Quinton – came out in support of Confederation. As a result of their public speeches and radio broadcasts many undecided voters undoubtedly swung their votes to Confederation. No attempt was made to stop them – there was little that the governor could have done even if he had wanted to. On the contrary, the governor regarded 'with alarm the prospect of Newfoundland being restored to [the] unfettered ministrations of local politicians,' and, after the defeat of Commission of Government, he did what he could to further the Confederate cause.[23]

Likewise, a number of other prominent Newfoundlanders threw their support behind Confederation, including such businessmen as Sir Leonard Outerbridge, Eric Bowring, and Arthur Monroe; John McEvoy and Leslie Curtis (both lawyers); and Walter Monroe, the former prime minister of Newfoundland. Most of these individuals contributed to the Confederate coffers, and, as has been frequently pointed out, were eventually rewarded for their efforts: Outerbridge became lieutenant-governor, Pottle became a minister in Smallwood's government, and Quinton was made a senator.[24] Others, like McEvoy who harboured ambitions of his own to lead the Confederates, likely saw the opportunity for personal advancement in hopping on the Confederation bandwagon. It was certainly not done as a vote of confidence in Smallwood's leadership. Wainwright Abbott, the new American consul-general in St John's, met with one of these new converts to Confederation a few days before the second vote. This unnamed gentleman 'gave me to understand ... that when the Confederates won, they (meaning chaps like himself) would give Joe Smallwood the gate. Other people had the same idea about Hitler, if you remember.'[25]

At any rate, the swing of these people to Confederation undoubtedly lent an air of respectability to the Confederates that was badly needed. Late in June, Smallwood and Bradley wrote C.D. Howe the good news. With the addition of the 'respectable element,' they wrote, the chances of a Confederate victory 'now look[ed] excellent.' The introduction of the sectarian issue, they informed Howe, had 'provoked an underground reaction. The population is two-thirds Protestant. The consequence may be that the Catholic Church will throw its influence our way, or at least drop its pressure the other way. In any case, even without Catholic support, it looks like a comfortable majority for Confederation.' But, Smallwood and Bradley continued, they were not out of the woods yet. With another month of campaigning ahead of them, the Confederate money was running dangerously short: 'We need money desperately. Taking into account what we will raise locally, we must have at least another $20,000 ... We need it *quickly*.'[26]

The second campaign went right down to the wire. Early voting from the Avalon Peninsula favoured responsible government, as it had on the first ballot, but as the outport votes poured in there was a clear swing towards Confederation. It took several days to get all the returns in, but when all the smoke had cleared, 84.9 per cent of eligible Newfoundlanders had voted and the final result was: 78,323 (52.34 per cent) for Confederation and 71,344 (47.66 per cent) for responsible government.[27]

With the campaign finished and the voting over, the two sides drew back, waiting for a decision from the Canadians. Confederation had won, but only with a slim majority – was it enough to satisfy Mackenzie King's statement that the verdict must be clear and 'beyond all possibility of misunderstanding'?

Although the final decision had not yet been made, the Canadians had in fact been preparing for such an eventuality for more than two months. The deputy ministers of the concerned departments had been put on notice to be prepared to act once a favourable vote for Confederation had been obtained.[28] Moreover, a number of meetings with British officials were held in London and Ottawa to make the necessary procedural arrangements in the event of a Confederate victory.

Sir Eric Machtig and Patrick Gordon-Walker, the under secretary at the CRO, made it clear to Norman Robertson that the British government would regard 50 per cent plus one as an acceptable majority to go ahead with Confederation. Naturally, the final decision was for the Canadians to make, but, as Noel-Baker put it in a cabinet paper, 'we should regard any majority, no matter how small, as conclusive.' If the Canadians said no, then responsible government would immediately be restored. Contingency plans for this eventuality were also being made in London.[29]

On the procedural side the British had two goals: 1 / to bring in Confederation as quickly as practicable; and 2 / to play as small a role as possible in implementing it. Regarding the first goal, Machtig expressed to Robertson some unease at the Canadian cabinet decision that the end of March or early April 1949 would be the earliest possible date for union. This date was chosen largely to coincide with the beginning of the fiscal year on 1 April. It was believed that such a long delay would play into the hands of the anti-Confederates and might lead to 'serious political unrest' in Newfoundland. On the second point, Machtig told Robertson that the United Kingdom had no desire to debate the terms of union in the British House of Commons. Instead, they suggested amending section 146 of the BNA Act which provided for the entrance of Newfoundland into Confederation after the United Kingdom had received addresses from the 'Legislatures' of Canada and Newfoundland. The proposed amendment would permit the Commission of Government to act in place of the non-existent Newfoundland legislature, thereby allowing the union to take place under an order-in-council from the United Kingdom.[30]

The British were eager to get these matters settled at once. A tentative timetable was drawn up, and Governor Macdonald told the Canadians confidentially that he had already decided on the delegation to be sent to Ottawa for the final negotiations – with five of the seven representatives being Confederates.[31] But the Canadians had some reservations over the British scheme. St Laurent believed it would be sufficient to have Newfoundland and Canada address the king and to have the UK government either issue an order-in-council or introduce an act in Parliament embodying the terms to remove any doubt of the legality of the union. This procedure could lead to a debate on the terms in London, which was exactly what the British did not want.[32]

While these negotiations were under way the Canadian ministers were wrestling with the problem of responding to the results of the referendum. Mackenzie King's anxiety was growing daily, and he became increasingly reluctant to move ahead on the issue. King had remained fairly consistent in his belief that responsible government should be restored in Newfoundland first, before union was brought about. If it were not, then he hoped a very substantial majority of Newfoundlanders would vote for Confederation. In his view, a slim majority for Confederation was fraught with danger, and in such a case the Canadians should hold off from bringing Newfoundland in.[33]

Even St Laurent had his moment of doubt. As the date of the second referendum approached, he too wondered if it was advisable to act if the vote was very close. [34] The difference between St Laurent and King, however, was that St Laurent viewed the problem less from a political standpoint than King did. St Laurent often put the question into a larger international context, and he was clear in his own mind on the necessity of bringing Newfoundland into Confederation. In the House of Commons on 19 June St Laurent was pressed by John Diefenbaker and others to inform the House what the Canadian government would do if only a slim majority voted for Confederation. St Laurent said he could not answer hypothetical questions, but later gave his own view:

I may be an optimist, but I do believe that the Canadian nation is destined to occupy an important place in world affairs. I do believe, further, that the place in world affairs would be better preserved by a territory which extended right out to the broad ocean and if access thereto was not closed to Canada by another sovereignty over the territories of Newfoundland and Labrador.

Because of that attitude, we made offers which would involve quite costly requirements from the Canadian people at the present time. But I think we would have been remiss in our duty to future generations of Canadians not to have done so. That offer having been made, if there is a desire on the part of the people of Newfoundland to accept it, I think the government will be disposed to recommend to Parliament that it be implemented.[35]

Diefenbaker had received a number of entreaties from concerned Newfoundlanders. One, from James Halley, a St John's lawyer, asked Diefenbaker: 'Is no voice to be raised in the Canadian Parliament in behalf of justice for Newfoundland?' Halley sent similar telegrams to a British MP and an American senator. Interestingly, Halley was given Diefenbaker's name by Eugene Griffin, the Ottawa correspondent for the *Chicago Tribune*. Halley told an American official in St John's 'that Diefenbaker had been selected because he is strongly under the influence of Griffin who ... does most of Diefenbaker's thinking for him.'[36]

As the results of the second referendum became known in Ottawa, the spirits of Sir Alexander Clutterbuck in the British High Commission began to lift. He predicted a victory of from 5,000 to 10,000 votes for Confederation, and if this proved true, there was 'no doubt' that 'all concerned here on official level, from Pearson downwards, will regard majority as fully adequate for proceeding with Confederation, and will make recommendation to Ministers accordingly.'[37]

This prediction was, for the most part, very true. The most notable illustration was that of J.W. Pickersgill, who, in anticipation of

Mackenzie King's continued misgivings, compiled a list of Liberal party percentages during King's tenure as leader, none of which exceeded the Confederate vote of 52 per cent. Therefore, when King telephoned 'and asked my opinion of the vote, I was able to tell him how favourably the vote for Confederation compared with the support he had received in successive elections which he had regarded as clear expressions of the will of the Canadian people.'[38] King no doubt got the point.

The influence of civil servants like Pickersgill unquestionably was a factor in the decision to accept the Newfoundland results, but it was probably not the determining one. After all, the majority was almost 7,000 votes and the Canadian government had already gone too far to back out at this late date. Such a move could backfire and indefinitely postpone Confederation and make the Canadians look foolish in the process. Besides, there had been relatively little backlash from the provinces when the terms had been announced the previous autumn. More important, there was history to be considered, and for Mackenzie King, on the verge of retirement, this was crucial. Confederation 'was the logical end to it, and probably in the course of time it will be among the accomplishments of the administration of which I am the head. It will be that of the rounding out of Confederation by the addition of a tenth province. This will be completing the nation in its physical boundaries as it has already been completed in its complete autonomy and its position as a nation within the British Commonwealth of Nations.'[39]

Given the strong feelings of the UK authorities, the Canadian civil servants, and most of the cabinet, the final decision was surprisingly easy to make. On 27 July, King told the cabinet that the Canadian government 'could hardly do other than accept the result as the verdict of the people of Newfoundland and make the necessary arrangements to give effect thereto.'[40] There appears to have been no opposition in the cabinet, and it was agreed to accept Newfoundland as a Canadian province. Later, Mackenzie King reflected on the whole affair: 'I had never dreamt that my name would probably be linked through years to come with the bringing into Confederation of what will be the 10th province and quite clearly the last. Having relation to my grandfather's part in laying the foundations of responsible government, it is interesting that it should be left to me as practically the last of the completed tasks before giving up the Leadership of the Party.'[41]

The announcement of the Canadian decision was made public on 30 July. The reason for the three-day delay was ostensibly to be sure that the totals were accurate, but it is possible that the decision was withheld until after the 28 July provincial election in Quebec. In the meantime, R.A. MacKay had been dispatched to St John's to assess the post-referendum state of opinion in Newfoundland.[42] His reports largely reinforced the government decision on the need to act swiftly and in a positive manner.

In his official statement, Mackenzie King suggested that the entrance of Newfoundland into Confederation would be welcomed all across Canada, and he invited 'authorized representatives' to come to Ottawa to negotiate final terms of union.[43] Not all Newfoundlanders responded favourably to this announcement, but most resigned themselves to their fate. Many Newfoundlanders, however, continued to oppose Confederation and the way it was being implemented. For instance, a columnist in *The Monitor* was particularly bitter: 'I do not mean to insinuate that the Confederate leaders are Communists. Perhaps they are not. But I do say that they used communistic tactics to obtain the small majority they secured in the second referendum. By pitting the poor against the rich, the outports against St. John's, the Protestants against the Catholics, they succeeded in accomplishing the communistic aim of "Divide and Conquer". Divide, they did, perhaps for all time. Whether they have finally conquered remains to be seen.'[44] But J.R Smallwood could not contain his joy. He telegraphed his appreciation to Mackenzie King, and suggested that King 'will go down in history as the greatest Newfoundlander since John Cabot.'[45]

II

Everyone agreed that now that the decision had been made, the process of union should be started immediately. To this end, both the cabinet committee and the Interdepartmental Committee on Canada-Newfoundland Relations were reconvened to make the necessary preparations to receive the Newfoundland delegation.

The reconstituted ICCNR contained at least one member from every department that would play any part in bringing Newfoundland into Confederation. Pearson was appointed chairman, but in the under secretary's expected absence, this role was filled by R.A. MacKay, the vice-chairman. Because of its rather unruly size, a much smaller steering committee was established, also under MacKay's chairmanship, to co-ordinate the work of the main committee and the various subcommittees, and to act as the main channel of communication with the Newfoundland delegation. The steering committee was the key working group, and in addition to MacKay, it consisted of J.R. Baldwin of the Privy Council Office, Alex Skelton from Trade and Commerce, J.E. Coyne from the Bank of Canada, Mitchell Sharp from the Finance department, and Paul Pelletier, also from the Privy Council Office, who acted as secretary. Late in September, Walter Harris, the parliamentary assistant to the secretary of state for external affairs, was added to the group to act as liaison with the cabinet committee.

The work of the ICCNR generally fell into two categories: 1 / preparing for the upcoming negotiations with the Newfoundlanders; and 2 / preparing for the administrative change-over when Newfoundland actually became a province. To reach these targets, five subcommittees were established. The first was the Legal and Procedure subcommittee, which, as its name suggests, was to examine the constitutional procedure and legal questions surrounding union. The second was the subcommittee on Fisheries. During the referendum campaigns considerable attention was given to the fate of the Newfoundland Fisheries Board under Confederation and it was believed that the Newfoundlanders would want to maintain the established system after union. Third, a Finance and Economic Policy Committee subcommittee was established to deal with the crucial financial questions, ranging from transitional grants to the national debt. The fourth was the Transportation and Communications subcommittee, which dealt with those topics falling under this broad heading, such as the railways, steamships, radio, postal service, and civil aviation. Finally, an Organization of Administrative Services subcommittee was set up to oversee the integration of Newfoundland and Canadian services.

More on the logistical side, a central office was established in Ottawa and permission was asked to expand the High Commissioner's Office in St John's. Numerous officials were eager to travel to Newfoundland to gauge opinion, collect information and statistics, and make a start on the eventual Canadian takeover. For instance, a number of officials were sent on an investigative trip to determine the effect of union on Newfoundland's secondary industry. Moreover, on 1 September C.J. Burchell was returned to St John's as high commissioner to help smooth out any difficulties during the transition period. Eventually the High Commission was moved to larger quarters in St John's and other offices were established in the same building.

MacKay was quick to recognize a potential problem, so it was decided that official visits should be co-ordinated through the steering committee so as not to give the impression of an 'invasion' or that Newfoundland was being annexed. MacKay was appreciative of the sensibilities of the Newfoundlanders, and was eager that nothing should be done to upset their feelings. He cautioned the other members of the ICCNR not to ride roughshod over the Newfoundlanders in their zeal to implement Confederation. Rather, the Canadian officials should 'exercise great care against giving offence or being in any way patronizing towards Newfoundlanders or about Newfoundland conditions.'[46]

The cabinet committee was similar in its makeup to the previous one; it included St Laurent as chairman, Claxton (who acted as chairman when St Laurent was absent), Howe, Douglas Abbott, the minister of finance, and J.J. McCann, the minister of national revenue. Later R.W. Mayhew, the minister of fisheries, and Pearson, who had just donned political clothes as the external affairs minister, were added. On 25 September, Milton Gregg was also appointed to the group, on the suggestion of Stewart Bates, the chairman of the Fisheries subcommittee, that it was important to have a Maritime minister on the cabinet committee.[47]

Over the next few weeks the subcommittees put together their reports for the cabinet committee, presenting them to the ICCNR at its 29 September meeting. MacKay included an informal report of his own and all were submitted and discussed at the cabinet committee meeting on 1 October. St Laurent discussed the procedural steps to be taken to bring Newfoundland in and also reviewed the status of the negotiations. MacKay's memo had brought up the apparent contradiction between the 'Proposed Arrangements' of 1947 and King's 30 July 1948 statement: namely, that the Newfoundlanders might get the idea that the financial terms could be renegotiated. St Laurent suggested that the Newfoundlanders be told at an early date that the 1947 terms were to be used as the framework for the new talks. This procedure did not preclude 'internal adjustment' of the terms, but did set limits to prevent the discussions from becoming unmanageable.[48]

The Canadians were basically prepared to meet the Newfoundland delegation by the first week of October. In St John's, preparations were also well under way to meet the Canadians. Days after the second referendum, Governor Macdonald announced the composition of the delegation and to one's surprise it included Smallwood and Bradley. A.J. Walsh, the Newfoundland commissioner for justice and defence, was picked to lead the group. Others included John McEvoy, a lawyer, a Confederate (although not a Smallwood supporter), and a former chairman of the National Convention; Philip Gruchy, the vice-president of the Anglo-Newfoundland pulp and paper plant at Grand Falls; Gordon Winter, a St John's merchant and former president of the Newfoundland Board of Trade; and Chesley Crosbie, the prominent businessman and leader of the Economic Union party. Crosbie and Winter were included as the two anti-Confederates, although Winter was not considered as vehemently opposed as Crosbie. Crosbie had immediately published a statement accepting the decision of the Newfoundland people but reserved the right not to sign the final terms if he did not think they were sufficiently beneficial for Newfoundland.[49]

The announcement of the delegation was met with little enthusiasm and considerable disappointment in Newfoundland. For the Responsible Government League it was particularly hard to swallow because the delegation contained none of their members. Once more there were widespread cries of 'conspiracy.' As the secretary of the league, W.L. Collins, wrote Mackenzie King: 'These deliberate attempts to stifle [sic] any expression of opinion from the Responsible Government movement forces the League to the conclusion that the three governments concerned are proceeding with a prearranged plan to force this country into Confederation.'[50]

In the meantime, the Newfoundland delegation held a preliminary meeting on 9 August. Smallwood and Bradley were not in attendance, having travelled to Ottawa to attend the Liberal national convention. While the fate of Confederation had been decided, their political futures had not, and here was an opportunity to make political contacts and solidify their positions. Both gave speeches and Smallwood received a standing ovation following his reference to 'We Canadians.' Mackenzie King missed Bradley's speech and half of Smallwood's, which he found 'humorous.' He was not sure however, that it was a good idea having them appear on the stage, but later, after sitting with the two Newfoundlanders, he couldn't help feeling that 'there was something quite significant about this little feature of the evening.'[51]

The Newfoundland delegation arrived at Uplands airport in Ottawa on 5 October 1948, and, as in 1947, checked into the Château Laurier. The first meeting with the cabinet committee was held the next day. Opening speeches were made for the press by St Laurent and Walsh, and shortly afterwards the two sides adjourned. Over the next two months more than twenty formal meetings were convened, with many more informal ones held to deal with specific problems. As well, the cabinet committee continued to meet on its own, as did the Newfoundland delegation and, on occasion, the ICCNR.

On the ministerial level, St Laurent and Claxton dominated the talks. St Laurent in particular had taken on as his own the union of Canada and Newfoundland. Moreover, during the course of the negotiations St Laurent replaced King as prime minister, which further enhanced his prestige. King played no role in the talks. On the odd occasion, if neither St Laurent nor Claxton were present, the joint meetings would be chaired by C.D. Howe. Lacking St Laurent's charm, Howe was somewhat less courteous in his dealings with the Newfoundlanders. Elmer Driedger, who attended many of the meetings (including, unofficially, some of the Newfoundlanders' private meetings) as the representative of the Justice department, later recalled the shocked reaction of Walsh and the other Newfoundlanders when their particular questions or problems were gruffly dismissed by the less diplomatic Howe.[52] As for Lester Pearson, who had in one way or another been dealing with the 'Problem of Newfoundland' since being an observer to the negotiations for the 1941 Leased Bases Agreement, he was deeply involved in the creation of NATO, and consequently had little time to devote to the talks with the Newfoundlanders.

During the plenary sessions, A.J. Walsh did almost all the talking for the Newfoundlanders. Smallwood, and to a lesser degree Bradley, continued to participate more fully in the unofficial meetings, but there was less actual 'negotiating' done in 1948 than in 1947. Moreover, as in 1947, it was more a question of the Canadians deciding among themselves to meet the needs of the Newfoundlanders than it was actual bargaining between the two sides. Nevertheless, the threat that the talks would break down completely if demands were not met was a tactic used effectively by the Newfoundlanders.

For the most part the negotiations were smooth and straightforward. The Newfoundlanders regularly brought up suggestions or problems, and if the Canadians could meet their wishes then the terms would be adjusted accordingly. If not, the Newfoundlanders usually accepted the decision of the Canadians, normally because what the Newfoundlanders wanted would not fall under federal jurisdiction and therefore had to be dealt with by the Newfoundland authorities. For instance, the Newfoundlanders asked the Canadians if they would take over the full pensions of those civil servants who started their careers in the Newfoundland civil service. The Canadians refused, leaving the Newfoundland government with the responsibility for its portion of the pensions for the years prior to 1949.[53] In other instances, dealing with such questions as passport renewals, free time on the CBC, and the division of public buildings between the federal and provincial governments, the talks became little more than a forum for the exchange of information. Furthermore, many of the potentially troublesome subjects, such as education, divorce, and the sale of oleomargarine, had already been decided in 1947, and needed only fine-tuning in 1948. This is not to suggest that there were no serious obstacles; on the contrary, there were a number of difficult problems to be overcome, dealing mainly with the financial question and, to a lesser degree, with the fisheries.

The fisheries problem gives a good example of the willingness of the Canadians to be flexible. Over a period of years the Newfoundlanders had established a marketing system that proved itself extremely effective. At the root of this was the Newfoundland Fisheries Board, which was established in 1936 to oversee the inspection, licensing, grading, and exporting of the yearly catch. In the Canadian federal system, the control of the fisheries fell under federal jurisdiction, but, as mentioned above, this became a referendum issue (especially for the Responsible Government League), and most of the Newfoundlanders called for its preservation. Hence the normal practice was sidestepped and the Newfoundland Fisheries Board was permitted to continue functioning for five years after union.[54]

The financial problem was a little more complicated, dealing with the transitional grants, the sterling debt, and Newfoundland's surplus (part of which was in a blocked sterling account). The Economic and Finance subcommittee re-examined the 1947 proposals and checked its own figures, taking into account the changing circumstances over the previous year. No matter how it was looked at, there was one inescapable conclusion: Newfoundland's financial hole would be larger than earlier anticipated.

Mitchell Sharp, who chaired the subcommittee, wrote that even with federal assistance along the 1947 lines, 'a large prospective deficit will still remain.' For Sharp the solution was not necessarily to increase the transitional grants since this kind of relief would postpone the required provincial action to remedy the situation; he argued for the immediate implementation of new provincial taxes and the development of other sources of provincial revenue. Unfortunately, it would take time for these new sources to be developed, and until then the Canadians would most likely have to bear the burden.[55]

In a lengthy memo for C.D Howe, Alex Skelton largely agreed with Sharp. The Newfoundlanders estimated that the provincial deficit would run around $10 million per year – and this included the transitional payments at the 1947 level. Skelton whittled down these estimates (for instance, the Newfoundlanders had underestimated their share of the tax agreement by $1 million), but still came up with a figure of between $4.5 million and $6 million. This figure was roughly the same as that presented by Sharp to the cabinet committee on 20 October.

How this difference was to be made up developed into the major sticking point in the negotiations. The idea of stipulating the introduction of a sales tax or property tax in the terms was anathema to the whole Newfoundland delegation. Indeed, Walsh adamantly refused and threatened to resign from the commission if this was forced on Newfoundland.[57] While the Newfoundlanders recognized that these taxes would have to be brought in as soon as possible, they were extremely reluctant to publicly make such an unpleasant announcement. Instead, the Canadians should rely on 'the good faith and good judgement' of the Newfoundlanders to do the right thing; to publicize it 'would merely throw ammunition to the opposition.'[58]

The Canadian officials were willing to come more than half way to meet the Newfoundlanders. The proposal was made to increase the transitional grants to $7 million the first year, diminishing over ten years. This would bring the total grant up to $50.4 million (the 1947 total was $26.25 million). Skelton believed that he had the support of MacKay on this point, but Sharp and Coyne argued that this was too generous, although they too recognized that the Canadian contribution would have to be raised.[59]

Some action had to be taken. While the Newfoundlanders appeared to be eager to reach an agreement, this could not be counted on. Crosbie was really just along for the ride, and the Canadians believed him to be merely looking for an excuse to reject the terms. While Walsh, Smallwood, Bradley, and McEvoy were considered very pro-Confederate, the Canadians were apprehensive that Gruchy and Winter would follow Crosbie's lead and refuse to sign the terms. If one opted out he wouldn't be missed, but if the delegation was split nearly in half this would fuel opposition in Newfoundland and could seriously damage the possibility of successfully concluding an agreement.[60]

This predicament was discussed in the cabinet on 3 November. St Laurent informed the ministers of the extent of the financial problem, and warned that if the Canadians did not come up with the money, the negotiations would probably break down.[61] St Laurent's mind was probably made up, but he nevertheless received encouragement from two different quarters. J.W. Pickersgill played on his sense of history and told him that the bringing of Newfoundland into Confederation would be his greatest achievement as prime minister.[62] The other came in a letter from Pearson who was away in Paris. More assistance for the Newfoundlanders was the only way that Pearson saw around the problem: 'I still feel that the national interest requires that Newfoundland should be brought into federation if at all possible and that the present may be our last opportunity to do so. I think, therefore, that we should be prepared to improve our financial proposals to the extent necessary on assumption that the Newfoundland delegation do not make impossible demands, and if this can be done without raising difficulties with existing provinces.'[63]

One suggestion made by the Newfoundlanders to bypass this logjam was to have the United Kingdom assume at least part of the Newfoundland debt, and then have the Canadians raise their contribution to Newfoundland an equivalent amount. But this was not acted upon for several reasons. For one thing, the British government would not likely be willing to assume this debt. Although Clutterbuck had mentioned the possibility in 1947, it had never been seriously examined in the United Kingdom, and Clutterbuck spoke for the CRO – not for the treasury. Moreover, it was argued that it made little real difference whether the Canadians or the British assumed the debt. As Claxton had written to Pearson more than a year before:

From the point of view of dollars and cents, I do not see that it matters very much whether we take over the debt and offset either the principal or carrying charges against what the U.K. owes us or whether the U.K. waives payment. Politically, however, I don't see that the U.K. would find it easy to waive the debt today, and our appearing to add to its burdens at the same time as the U.K. was appearing to be 'liquidating the Empire' would not be popular in the U.K., U.S., Newfoundland or in some sections of Canada. Consequently, while our taking over the debt would not be politically popular in some sections of Canada, I believe that there is more to be said for it than against and conceivably it might impress the people of Newfoundland.[64]

Besides, as St Laurent pointed out to the cabinet on 9 November, any such undertaking would take some time to negotiate and the Canadians had to have a decision soon to prevent the talks from breaking down. He felt it was impossible for the Canadians to promise additional aid only on condition that at some future date a deal with the United Kingdom be negotiated, and he argued that the cabinet should move ahead on its own. St Laurent presented new figures, representing a compromise, suggesting that the Canadian grants be raised by $16.5 million, spread over eight years. There was no disagreement and the cabinet authorized the cabinet committee to proceed on these grounds.[65]

The Canadians made this proposal to the Newfoundlanders at the meeting on 10 November. Before finally agreeing to it the Newfoundlanders attempted to up the total amount by $2 million and to shuffle the payment schedule, but these suggestions were vetoed by the Canadians. One concession was offered: the Newfoundlanders were not obligated to take all the grant for a particular year and they could, if they chose, hold it over until next year.

To calm any fears of future financial disaster, the promise to appoint a royal commission to review Newfoundland's financial standing within eight years of Confederation was enshrined as Term 29. The final wording was worked out by St Laurent, with the help of R.A. MacKay and Mitchell Sharp.[66] Likewise, the Newfoundlanders got to keep their surplus (with some restrictions on how they could spend it), along with a promise from the Canadians to convert the savings in the blocked sterling account into dollars.

Once this hurdle was overcome the negotiations could be brought to a successful conclusion. Many of the terms – such as those dealing with the sale of oleomargarine, education, public welfare and pensions, veterans' benefits, and transportation services – were similar to those in the 1947 'Proposed Arrangements,' but there were also a few new terms. In addition to those changes discussed above (on the financial question and the maintenance of the Fisheries Board) it was agreed that Newfoundland patents and trademarks would be recognized under Canadian law, and the new provincial government would not be forced to impose any new taxes if they contradicted any government arrangement already in existence.

By early in December the final touches were being put on the new draft terms and a signing date was set for 11 December. Crosbie announced that he would sign, but the rest of the Newfoundland delegation was satisfied that the terms offered the most that could be hoped for. The Terms of Union received cabinet approval on 10 December and they were accepted by the Commission of Government the following day. The signing ceremony was held in the Senate chamber and was fairly simple, with St Laurent and Claxton representing Canada. Both St Laurent and Walsh spoke, expressing their warm appreciation and gratitude, together with their hopes for the future.[67]

Several shortcomings of the terms have become apparent since 1949 – from the *débâcle* over Term 29 to the failure to provide for extensive highway contruction – but from the vantage-point of 1949, the terms were generous ones. Through the removal of the debt load, the preservation of the surplus, the larger transitional grants, and the implementation of Canadian social services, Newfoundland was able to achieve a degree of development and rise in the standard of living that any government in an independent Newfoundland would have been extremely hard pressed to match. And, furthermore, there were relatively few restrictions placed upon the new province to direct or restrain the functions of the provincial government.[68]

III

The Terms of Union covered a wide spectrum of financial, constitutional, and technical arrangements, but there remained a number of other problems that bear mentioning, such as the fate of St John's harbour and the other Admiralty property in Newfoundland, the settlement of Newfoundland's treaty obligations, and the American bases. These topics had not been thoroughly discussed during the Confederation negotiations because there was really nothing that the Canadians and the Newfoundlanders could do between themselves to settle them. Nevertheless, it was left to the Canadians to deal with these questions, not only during the negotiations but also well into the post-Confederation period.

The problem of the Admiralty properties was relatively easy to solve. The United Kingdom had extensive property in Newfoundland (mainly in the vicinity of St John's) including dockyards, garages, wharves, a repair depot, and other odd bits of land. The Canadians believed that once Newfoundland became a part of Canada these properties should come under Canadian control. On 1 December 1948, the Canadian cabinet agreed that the British should be approached with the request to transfer all its rights in Newfoundland to the Canadians without charge. Within a week Claxton had written Clutterbuck with a formal request.[69]

The Admiralty was not opposed to the ideas of transferring these properties to the Canadians, providing the Canadians take over the liability and give assurances that the facilities could be used by the United Kingdom in any future hostilities. After all, the u.k. government had accepted the responsibility for the St John's naval base only reluctantly in 1945. But there was a disagreement over the price. The Admiralty had spent in the neighbourhood of $30 million on the base and facilities, and they considered that in 1949 they were still worth $22 million. Their argument was that the facilities were considerable and the buildings were still in good condition.[70]

Discussions continued through the spring and summer and on 2 September 1949 a meeting was held in Ottawa to thrash the problem out. Unfortunately nothing was settled: the two sides squabbled over the value of the property and the Canadians argued that it would infringe on Canadian sovereignty to give the United Kingdom any guarantee for use of the base. Finally, a week before Christmas 1949, the Canadians offered $7 million for the property and gave some assurances for its emergency use by the United Kingdom. The Admiralty found these terms acceptable and in January 1950 an agreement was reached.[71]

On the problem of Newfoundland's treaty obligations the Canadians did not have the luxury of time; to avoid unnecessary misunderstandings a solution had to be found by the date of union. The question was to what extent Canada should be responsible for treaties dealing with Newfoundland made prior to union. To no one's surprise, the Canadians and the British came up with differing answers.

The British had no interest in maintaining any treaty obligations on behalf of Newfoundland and it was considered important to have the Canadians either terminate the existing treaties or take on their obligations. On 19 November 1948, a meeting was held in the Foreign Office, with officials from the cro in attendance, to examine this question. The treaties relating to Newfoundland were divided into three categories: 1 / those extended specifically to include Newfoundland; 2 / those applying directly to Newfoundland in a territorial sense; and 3 / those applying to Newfoundland only as a part of British territory.[72]

A second informal discussion took place one week later in Ottawa, this time between Canadian and British officials. The British case was reviewed and was generally well received by the Canadians. But it was pointed out that a problem might arise if Newfoundland was committed to give most-favoured-nation treatment to a particular country that Canada was not – surely the Canadians would not have to honour an agreement like that? After union, Newfoundland would automatically fall within the Canadian tariff and laws and, consequently, it was argued that any obligations on Newfoundland's part would naturally lapse on the date of union.[73]

In the meantime the Justice department and legal advisers on both sides of the Atlantic delved into their law books, in search of any treaty obligation applying to Newfoundland and for precedents of this kind of union. Was Confederation to be regarded as the union of two countries, or the cession of part of one territory to another, or the annexation of a territory by a larger state? In each case different rules would apply. If Confederation was viewed as the union of two countries, then Canada might be expected to shoulder all of Newfoundland's obligations – as had happened when Madagascar was brought into the French Empire. Cession of territory, however, brought with it only those treaties considered 'local' in nature. The precedent for this was the cession of East Africa to Germany in 1888. Interestingly, conquest, based on the 1912 capture of Tripoli by the Italians, was the most effective way of acquiring territory – the conquered area brought absolutely no treaty obligations along with it. The Canadians decided that Confederation was an example of one nation ceding a bit of territory to another.[74]

Lists were drawn up covering all the treaties that affected Newfoundland either directly or indirectly. The lists were quite extensive, ranging from the 1849 Treaty of Friendship, Commerce and Navigation with Costa Rica, to the 1875 Seaman Deserters Agreement with Greece, to the treaty of Peace and Commerce with Denmark, dating back to 1660–1. The British tended to feel that each case should be dealt with on its own merits. Their concern was rooted in the fear that a cavalier denunciation of particular treaties by the Canadians might lead to retaliation against Britain by some of the offended states.[75]

The Canadians circumvented this jumbled set of circumstances by, in a sense, disregarding it altogether. They adopted the position that after Confederation all Canadian treaties would apply to Newfoundland and consequently all of the treaties applying to Newfoundland would lapse, except those of a local nature. Of this latter group, the Canadians found two: first, the Leased Bases Agreement, and second, Article i of the 1818 Commercial Convention with the United States.[76] Because Newfoundland's treaties would lapse automatically, the Canadians believed that no action was necessary. Out of courtesy, however, the various nations concerned in agreements were informed on the date of union.

An interesting application of this policy was exhibited in the civil-aviation agreements, especially those which appeared to deal specifically with Newfoundland territory. The Canadians did not want to take over Britain's agreements, which included some fifth-freedom rights in Newfoundland; this was a right that the Canadians had always been reluctant to grant. It was decided that the air agreements were 'in essence commercial'; the fact that they included landing rights in Newfoundland was considered ancillary. As a result, they would not be considered 'local' in nature and would lapse after Confederation. In any event, as noted in chapter 6, British-American rights would lapse automatically after Confederation and new agreements would have to be reached. The other countries who were concerned would then be approached individually to abandon their fifth-freedom rights.[77]

The British had little choice but to acquiesce in the Canadian decision. Fortunately, most of the concerns and fears expressed in 1948–9 were never realized. The incorporation of Newfoundland into the Canadian trade and tariff system was undertaken with relative ease. There was little negative reaction from the international community, and after the Canadian position was explained it was generally accepted.

The problem of the American bases did not work itself out as neatly as did the problem over Newfoundland's treaty obligations. During the referendum campaigns the question over the fate of the American bases in Newfoundland was raised on a number of occasions. Although it did not turn into a major issue at the time, there were many Newfoundlanders, mostly in the vicinity of the bases, who feared that union with Canada would lead to the withdrawal of the Americans and the jobs they provided.

The American presence in Newfoundland was still substantial. On 30 September 1948, there were a reported 1,802 military personnel stationed at the bases. In addition, there were 1,600 permanent civilian employees at work at the sites, and most of these were Newfoundlanders. The total operating cost ran at a little over $9 million per year – not including naval expenditures at Argentia. Not surprisingly, this was a source of jobs and dollars most Newfoundlanders preferred not to lose.

For many Canadians, the problem of the U.S. bases posed an extraordinary dilemma. The presence of the American bases on Canadian soil ran contrary to the idea of Canadian sovereignty, and had been resisted by the Canadian government for many years. But there were other considerations as well. First, no one questioned that the United States had a legal right to these bases, and the thought that Canada should try unilaterally to take them over was never seriously considered. Second, the Canadian government believed that these bases continued to play a significant role in hemisphere defence, and there was little desire to have them closed down. Third, the Canadians realized that they were physically and financially ill-equipped to assume the responsibility for the bases – this would have to be left with the Americans.

The crux of the problem was the extraterritorial rights held by the Americans under the Leased Bases Agreement. In addition to customs privileges and the right to establish their own postal facilities, the Americans had almost total civil and military jurisdiction in the base areas and the right to take action outside the leased areas in time of emergency. While these rights were perhaps justifiable during a war-time crisis, they were no longer so in 1948.

Shortly after the 22 July refcrendum the Canadians quietly took steps to initiate discussions with the Americans. In August, James Forrestal, the American secretary of defence, sat in on a Cabinet Defence Committee meeting and the issue was briefly discussed. Over the following weeks both Claxton and Pearson brought the issue up with American officials in Ottawa to see what kind of importance the United States still placed on the bases.[78]

Claxton reviewed the problem at the cabinet meeting held on 3 November 1948, while the Confederation negotiations were still under way. He realized that the Canadians could do little to remove the Americans even if they wanted to, but argued that an effort could be made to modify some of the terms of the lease. The cabinet agreed and decided that informal conversations with the Americans be started immediately.[79]

Hume Wrong, the Canadian ambassador in Washington, was sounded out on the matter over the telephone by Claxton. Wrong in turn spoke to J.D. Hickerson of the State Department on the best way to handle the problem. Hickerson was not overly optimistic on the prospects for changing the terms, using 'the analogy of a mortgage, the terms of which are not modified on the sale of the mortgaged property except by agreement between the owner of the property and the holder of the mortgage.'

Wrong and Hickerson agreed that any initiatives should be taken through the State Department, rather than the defence establishment, which would likely be most resistant to change. As for the style, they urged a formal written note to the secretary or under secretary of state. But this note should be general in nature, suggesting that the two sides may wish to renegotiate certain aspects of the agreement, leaving all specifics until a later date. Wrong expected difficulties even then and wrote Claxton: 'I think that we have to start from scratch, and it is likely to be an obstacle race.'[80]

Claxton was less willing to keep the specifics out of the Canadian note. The negotiations with the Newfoundlanders were quickly coming to an end and the Canadians were increasingly eager to resolve the matter. He informed Wrong that the question was now considered to have top priority, and would be taken to the prime minister–president level if necessary. He included a statement to be given to the under secretary which incorporated the changes in the agreement that Ottawa wanted over the issues of jurisdiction, customs privileges, postal facilities, and rights outside the leased areas. He left it to Wrong's discretion to decide how much to leave in writing and how much to deliver orally.[81]

Wrong stuck to his original plan, and in the note presented to Under Secretary Robert Lovett on 19 November, no mention was made of the specific changes desired by the Canadians. He did, however, give an indication of the Canadian concerns orally. Wrong argued with Claxton that a too detailed statement 'would prejudice the chances of a successful outcome,' and then went on to note that he was unclear just why this was such an urgent matter. As he saw it, the Canadians were in for a long and difficult period of negotiation.[82]

Claxton replied to Wrong the same day, noting that with the Canada-Newfoundland negotiations coming to a close, the Terms of Union soon would have to be introduced into Parliament. To avoid embarrassing questions concerning the bases, the government wished to have some kind of affirmative reaction from the Americans. It was also desirable to get an early reply because the Canadian case would be weaker if Canada 'had already agreed to union before receiving any indication of the attitude of the United States.'[83]

The early reaction of the Americans was not good. Wrong reported that neither Congress nor the Pentagon would be enthusiastic about reopening the negotiations. In any event, it would probably be a lengthy process. In the meantime, Hickerson had been feeling out the opinion of the three services. This was no easy task, because he had 'to shake them' from their belief that some definite concession should be given in return.[84]

The matter remained stalled at this level until early in the new year. Late in January the Canadians tried a new tack; Wrong was informed that a 'legal view' was prepared and it seemed that before Canada could accept the obligations of the base deal, 'it would be necessary for the Canadian Government to pass implementing legislation so that the provisions of the Bases Agreement would be applicable under Canadian law.' This would open the whole affair to debate in the House of Commons – perhaps to avoid what would certainly 'prejudice present defence relationships,' the Americans would be willing to relinquish their non-military and extraterritorial rights?[85]

This new approach bore little fruit and in February 1949, Prime Minister St Laurent brought the matter up while visiting President Truman in Washington. Truman was co-operative but there was little he could do on the spot. As a result, he asked St Laurent to have prepared a full statement of the Canadian demands. This was done and presented to the American ambassador in Ottawa by Claxton and Pearson on 19 March 1949.[86] Wrong later recorded that Truman said that 'he and Acheson ought to be able to cope with these so as to give us at any rate some satisfaction.'[87]

The position the Canadians presented to the Americans was based on two earlier statements: the PJBD recommendation of 29 November 1946, and the joint defence statement by Truman and Mackenzie King in February 1947. The former said that 'defence co-operation projects in either country should be agreed to by both Governments, should confer no permanent rights or status upon either country and should be without prejudice to the sovereignty of either country.' The latter stipulated that mutual co-operation between the two countries would be 'without impairment of the control of either country over all activities in its territory.'[88]

Efforts between Ottawa and the State Department dragged on well into 1949, and little progress was made in solving the problem. Eventually the issue was handed over to the PJBD and General Mc-Naughton, the chairman of the Canadian section. McNaughton had already discussed the question with his American counterpart and reported that he believed there was a degree of softening of the American position.[89]

The PJBD discussed this problem early in 1950, and in its recommendation of 30 March it largely met the Canadian demands. Exemptions for the Americans in customs duties and income taxes were reduced, and American rights of jurisdiction were to be eliminated on the approval of the two governments. The American postal privileges were not removed totally, only restricted to non-civilian post offices for mail directed to the United States or its possessions. Although the recommendations did not give the Canadians everything they wanted, they would remove the most objectionable aspects of the Leased Bases Agreement.[90]

It took more than a year to secure Canadian and American approval for these recommendations. They were studied and approved by the Cabinet Defence Committee in April 1950, and on 1 August President Truman gave his consent. Canadian cabinet approval was given on 21 March 1951, and, after another year of waiting, the decision was formalized in an exchange of notes between Canada and the United States in February and March 1952.[91]

IV

The Terms of Union were signed on 11 December 1948 and the date of union was set for 31 March, 1949. The original plan called for union on 1 April, to coincide with the start of the fiscal year, but was changed after protests by Smallwood and others. As Smallwood put it: 'I didn't want to spend the rest of my life listening to taunts that Confederation had come on All Fools' Day,' and the Canadians agreed.[92]

Term 50 laid down the procedure to be followed: the terms would be approved by the Canadian Parliament and the government of New-foundland, and then the whole affair would be confirmed by the Parliament of the United Kingdom. This was basically the procedure advocated by St Laurent the previous summer. It was argued that this course would limit the debate in Canada to one stage (by preventing an additional debate on amending section 146 of the BNA Act), and limit the role of the United Kingdom to deciding whether or not to pass the agreement and not to debating the terms. This course was agreed to during conversations in Ottawa held in the autumn of 1948.[93]

The passage of a confirming statute by the British Parliament would, in effect, be an amendment to the BNA Act. St Laurent defended this by arguing that this method was chosen because action could not be taken under section 146 as it now stood. Moreover, because the United Kingdom was still responsible for Newfoundland, the Canadians could not act unilaterally and 'gather in a territory that was subject to the legislative and administrative jurisdiction of another autonomous nation.'[94] As a precedent for this course of action he pointed to the 1930 agreement that transferred the natural resources of Saskatchewan and Alberta to the respective provincial governments. The two provinces had been created under the BNA Act and therefore the transfer of natural resources was in fact an amendment to that act. The transfer was approved by Ottawa and the two provincial governments and then confirmed by the United Kingdom – precisely what the government advocated doing with respect to Newfoundland.[95]

The Terms of Union were introduced in the House of Commons on 7 February 1949. St Laurent spoke at some length on the recent history of the referendum and negotiations, and reviewed the terms and the procedure to be followed. He then turned to the matter at hand:

We are here now considering a matter of great moment. In the last two wars we realized how close we were to each other and how close we had to be in order to survive. In this troubled world I think we, both in Newfoundland and in Canada, feel that in this way our risks are more apt to be successfully met and any dangers overcome than was possible even with the non-constitutional union of spirits and hearts that united us during the last two wars. I earnestly hope it will be the view of this house that this union of Canada and Newfoundland is desirable in the interests of the people of these two lands, and as a lesson to the whole world of what can be accomplished by men of goodwill.[96]

Over the following days the terms were exhaustively examined, but no serious opposition emerged, and on 11 February the terms were passed with the support of all the parties. The only major flap was sparked by George Drew, the new leader of the Conservative party, in an attack launched against the Address to the King which was introduced on 14 February.

Drew attacked the government for apparently circumventing the need to involve the provincial governments, merely for 'convenience' sake. As Drew's lieutenant, John Diefenbaker, put it, the government 'has endeavoured to get around the constitution, because it believed it could not bring about confederation within the terms of the constitution.' This could set a dangerous precedent, Diefenbaker continued, and be used as a justification for further changes. 'Surely,' he added, 'we have not come to the position that, whenever a section of the British North America Act becomes inconvenient if carried into effect, all parliament has to do is, by a majority of parliament, to pass an address whereby the inconvenience is removed, regardless of what may be the result to the constitution.'[97]

Drew moved an amendment to St Laurent's address, claiming that it was necessary to discuss the issue with the provincial governments. In his view the address should be passed only on the 'satisfactory conclusion of the consultation' with the provinces. Drew's move was foiled by Wilfred LaCroix (a Liberal MP) who added a sub-amendment that called for the *consent* of the provinces. This was more than what Drew had in mind and he, along with the rest of the Conservatives and Liberals, voted against it. With this rather curious turn of events, Drew was, as one another put it, 'neatly hoist with his own petard.'[98]

The only other highlight of the debate was the speech by Mackenzie King. This was special not so much for what King said, but because it proved to be his last speech in the House of Commons. King was warmly received by both sides of the House, but the divisions remained and the unanimity that St Laurent had hoped for was not to be. In the end the Address to the King passed by a vote of 170 to 74, with the CCF backing the government and the Conservatives and Social Credit members voting against it.[99]

The next few days were devoted to amending the Statute Law of Canada to make provisions for the inclusion of specific reference to Newfoundland in Canadian laws. On 14 February, the bill was introduced in the senate and it was duly passed on 17 February. Four days later, on 21 February, the Commission of Government also gave its approval to the Terms of Union. All that remained was to have the United Kingdom confirm what the Canadians and Newfoundlanders had agreed to.

Time was running out if the union was to take place as scheduled, and the British government would have to move quickly. Early in February, Noel-Baker had prepared a memorandum on the question for the cabinet, and this was discussed on two occasions during that month. It was agreed that the Canadians and themselves had acted fairly, and that 'to depart from the policy hitherto followed would cause grave difficulties in Newfoundland and with the Canadian Parliament.'[100]

The bill to confirm the terms, or the BNA (Amendment) Bill, was introduced to the British House of Commons on 22 February, but its easy passage was not assured. St John Chadwick, who gives a full account of the bill's passage in his book *Newfoundland: Island into Province* (1967), wrote that while the bill 'should by tradition have been taken as a formality and as a measure on which the House would not divide or inject a note of controversy, political feelings on this occasion still pulsed strongly, giving the debate a far more controversial character than would normally be the case.'[101]

Most of the controversy was introduced by the independent MP Sir A.P. Herbert, a former member of the Goodwill Mission, and his ally in the House of Lords, Lord Sempill. Considerable opposition to Confederation remained in Newfoundland after the second referendum, mainly among staunch supporters of the Responsible Government League. These Newfoundlanders circulated a petition of their own (which gathered approximately 50,000 signatures), took the Commission of Government to court to prevent it from approving the Terms of Union, and appealed to Herbert to take up the cause for them in London. Herbert couldn't resist – after all, the rules of cricket could not be changed without a two-thirds majority, why should a dominion be permitted to disappear on only 52 per cent of the vote?[102]

Herbert had championed the cause of the Responsible Government League the previous autumn and over the winter (including an attempt to introduce his own Newfoundland bill), and he took up the banner again in March 1949. On 2 March, he moved an amendment to the bill calling for its suspension until it was approved by a Newfoundland legislature. In his memoirs (in a chapter entitled 'Dominion Murder'), Herbert reviews at length his speech and the debate in the House of Commons, but it was clear from the start that he had little support. His amendment was defeated 217 to 15, and on 9 March the bill was passed.[103]

In the House of Lords, Lord Sempill moved a similar amendment to that introduced by Herbert in the Lower House. This motion met with equally little success and on 22 March the bill passed. Royal Assent was given the next day, 23 March – little more than a week before the union was to take place.[104]

While the bills were working their way through Parliament, the wheels of union were being put in motion in Ottawa and Newfoundland. Under the Terms of Union, the Newfoundland constitution would be reinstated as it had existed in 1933 and Newfoundland laws would remain valid until replaced by Canadian ones. Now the long and arduous task of reviewing all the Canadian statutes began. In other areas as well preparations were being made to implement the federal system in Newfoundland. To get ready to distribute the family allowances an office was established in St John's and, as Richard Gwyn notes, letters were mailed to eligible parents bearing the inscription 'Dear Mum and Dad.'[105]

Brief mention should be made of the selection of the first Newfoundland cabinet and provincial government. In J.R. Smallwood's mind there was no question at all that he should be made premier and Bradley appointed to the Canadian cabinet; in fact, the ink of the Terms of Union was barely dry when he 'announced' the makeup of his cabinet.

On 5 January, almost three months before the union took place, Smallwood told those gathered at a Confederate Association dinner held in his and Bradley's honour that the latter would become a federal cabinet minister and that an anti-Confederate would not be asked to form a government. As Wainwright Abbott, the American consul-general, recalled, Smallwood 'thus indicated that he, himself, expected to form the cabinet. While that Mr. Smallwood had to say was not new, it confirms predictions.'[106]

For those in Ottawa, the decisions were not so easy to make. Bradley was well liked and it was an easy task for St Laurent to ask him to join the cabinet. After a brief period of misunderstanding the matter was settled. The problem was to find a suitable and available post. Thanks largely to J.W. Pickersgill, J.A. MacKinnon, the minister of mines and resources, was persuaded to resign his portfolio, enabling Colin Gibson to move over from the position of secretary of state. This freed the job for Bradley. Pickersgill made sure everything went off smoothly – and this included writing both MacKinnon's resignation and St Laurent's reply.[107]

St Laurent was not, at first, over-eager to have Smallwood appointed premier because he would appear to be giving political advantage to a known Liberal. But Smallwood was the obvious choice. As leader of the victorious Confederate Association (that was quickly transforming itself into the Newfoundland Liberal party), Smallwood's position was untouchable, and he could logically claim the prize as his own. Although St Laurent toyed with the idea of keeping the Commission of Government, or at most appointing a caretaker government, it was generally agreed that it would be unacceptable to maintain the Commission of Government both because it was appointed by the United Kingdom and because it had shown itself to be relatively unpopular in the first referendum.[108] It therefore became necessary to appoint a lieutenant-governor who would in turn choose a premier.

Sir Leonard Outerbridge was the early front-runner. Interestingly, although he was Smallwood's and Bradley's favourite, Outerbridge was not at all comfortable with the idea of appointing Smallwood as premier. When rumours to this effect reached Ottawa, the focus turned to A.J. Walsh who was more amenable to Smallwood, believing him to be 'the inevitable leader.'[109] Walsh was also a Roman Catholic and his appointment would balance those of Bradley and Smallwood, both of whom were Protestants.

Eventually it was decided that Walsh would be appointed lieutenant-governor and then he would appoint Smallwood premier. Some time after the first election Walsh would step down and Outerbridge would take his place. This idea was put to Walsh in a letter from St Laurent on 8 March and a few days later Walter Harris was sent to St John's to smooth things out.[110] By the end of the month the situation was arranged to everyone's satisfaction.

There were few celebrations to welcome the new province. In St John's, Colin Gibson was present as Walsh was sworn in as lieutenant-governor and the Canadian presented him with a certificate of Canadian citizenship. Later that day, Walsh swore in Smallwood as Newfoundland's provincial premier. Outside in the cold grey day it was strangely quiet. As Richard Gwyn wrote: 'There were no demonstrations or parades. Plans for St Laurent and the federal cabinet to come to St John's were cancelled. The anti-Confederates called off a march to Gibbet Hill, which was to be headed by an open truck bearing a coffin. Above dozens of houses in St John's and in nearby settlements hung black flags, many made from dyed flour sacks. Here and there the unofficial flag of Newfoundland, the pink, white and green, flew at half mast. At the base of one pole was the placard, "We let the old flag fall." A few people wore black ties and armbands.'[111]

In Ottawa, Bradley was officially brought into the cabinet and both he and St Laurent delivered speeches. Bradley, well known for his eloquence, did not let his listeners down. In an often-quoted passage he said: 'In fancy I can see them now – Macdonald, Brown, Cartier in Canada and Carter and Shea in Newfoundland – bending over this scene in silent and profound approval. We are all Canadians now.'[112] Next, St Laurent and Bradley carved the first strokes of the Newfoundland coat of arms on the tenth plaque on the Peace Tower – left empty for just such an occasion when the Parliament Buildings were rebuilt after the fire of 1916. With this simple ceremony, a new era in the history of Newfoundland had begun.

10

Conclusion

For something that was 'inevitable,' the union of Canada and New-foundland was a long time coming. Since 1867, most Canadians, if they gave it any thought at all, considered Newfoundland's natural destiny lay in union with Canada. But, despite increasing contact between the two countries, mutual suspicion and a narrow self-interest tended to sidetrack the few attempts at union that were made. Confederation only came about when the conditions were right – and this did not happen until the Second World War.

The Second World War revolutionized the importance of Newfound-land. In 1939 Newfoundland lay virtually undefended, but in a matter of a few years a series of agreements were negotiated that transformed it into an island fortress. Over the course of the war Newfoundland made a significant contribution to the Allied effort, first as a bastion in the defence of the western hemisphere, then as a base for convoy defence, and finally as a stepping-stone for the ferrying of aircraft overseas for the invasion of Europe.

The need to defend Newfoundland sparked a re-examination of Canada's 'Newfoundland policy.' The weakness of Newfoundland's defences underlined the weakness of Canada's own east coast, and it was recognized that to adequately defend the latter, the former must necessarily be included in defence plans. As a result members of the Department of National Defence were some of the first to become aware of Newfoundland's new importance. But as the military planners got what they felt they needed in Newfoundland, in terms of defence arrangements and the use of Newfoundland territory, their interest tended to wane.

This shift of focus away from Newfoundland was not emulated by sections of the Canadian government and the Department of External Affairs. The fall of France and the establishment of American bases in Newfoundland sent shock waves through Ottawa that did not dissipate over the following years. Because of Newfoundland's important strategical position, its precarious constitutional status, and the fear that the growing American presence there would lead to 'another Alaska,' Canada's relations with Newfoundland suddenly became the 'Problem of Newfoundland.' No longer could Canada take Newfoundland for granted, or assume that the rest of the world would give way in deference to Canada's 'natural interest' there.

Inevitably, the constant need to shore up Canada's position led many Canadians to search for a permanent solution to the problem of Newfoundland. An interesting illustration of this attitude was revealed by J.E. Read, legal adviser in the Department of External Affairs, who wrote in the wake of the Goose Bay controversy: 'I am unable to see how any practical solution can be worked out for the Newfoundland problem without Confederation. We have been going along for three-quarters of a century upon the assumption that only financial and economic matters are important. I should have thought that the last five and a half years would have taught us that finance and economics are not the only important aspects of life.' Read continued by asking if 'it is worthwhile for us to go on trying to suck and whistle at the same time. We know we need Newfoundland and Labrador as much as we need Nova Scotia.'[1]

The realization that Canada 'needed' Newfoundland struck a responsive chord in the Department of External Affairs. Clearly Newfoundland's new importance would not vanish with the coming of peace; on the contrary, the country would continue to play a significant role in the Canadian scheme of things – strategically, economically, and in matters of civil aviation. For these reasons Canada's role in Newfoundland had to be put on a more permanent basis.

The influx of new men with new ideas into the DEA produced a shift to a more active foreign policy that paralleled the expansion of Canada's economic and military strength. Within this framework, relations with Newfoundland occupied a significant, if less than central position. When Norman Robertson addressed a meeting of five officials in 1946 with the words: 'There are here ... just about everyone in Ottawa who is interested in Newfoundland,' he was not far off the mark.[2] Canada's relations with Newfoundland never caught the Canadian public's imagination; news from Newfoundland was given little more than perfunctory treatment by Canadian newspapers, rarely were questions dealing with Newfoundland raised at press conferences, and opinion polls revealed a public attitude that bordered on indifference.

In any event, there was little domestic public pressure put on Ottawa to act with regard to Newfoundland, and the Canadian government was given a relatively free hand in executing its policies. Conversely, while relations with Newfoundland were an exercise in diplomacy and an important political issue, little effort was made to involve the Canadian public in any significant manner. Public opinion was, of course, a factor to be considered, but even the Opposition parties were left in the dark most of the time. In this respect the bringing of Newfoundland into Confederation was largely a one-party, rather than a bipartisan political issue in Ottawa.

On the political level, two men, Mackenzie King and Louis St Laurent, were responsible for the major decisions that led to Confederation. From 1940 onwards King displayed a keen desire to keep Newfoundland within the Canadian 'orbit,' and he appeared constantly aware of the long-term implications of Canadian policy. King's well-known penchant for caution did not surface until near the end, long after the war was over. Only when relations with Newfoundland posed a threat to domestic political tranquillity did King get cold feet. Fortunately for the Confederates, St Laurent stepped in for King when the latter appeared to be faltering. Although St Laurent differed somewhat from King in his approach, he never doubted the wisdom of bringing Newfoundland in. St Laurent shared Pearson's internationalist approach to world affairs, and, if nothing else, the addition of Newfoundland would enhance Canada's security in an increasingly dangerous world.

The influence of the United States in all this was extraordinary. The presence of American bases on Newfoundland soil was a constant reminder to the Canadians that their own position there was indeed tenuous. Furthermore, the force of American power and the fear of what the United States *might* do were also genuine concerns for the Canadians. These concerns were prevalent even as late as 1948 when it was feared that the United States might come out in favour of economic union with Newfoundland. The Canadian anxiety over the intentions of the United States may have appeared needless and even ridiculous in some American eyes, but it was very real none the less. Time and again Canadian actions in Newfoundland were justified on the basis that if Canada didn't move, then the Americans would.

The other factor of note was the United Kingdom. Over the years the British government displayed a fairly consistent attitude towards the problem of Newfoundland – a strong pro-Confederate undercurrent mixed with a good dose of self-interest. Confederation was viewed as the best long-term solution and any offers from the Canadians to assume some of the burdens were welcomed in Whitehall. But this was not a unanimous position, as shown by Lord Beaverbrook and Sir A.P. Herbert, nor did it prevent clashes with the Canadians, for example, over Goose Bay or the control of Gander and Botwood.

Britain's economic plight at the end of the war strengthened the pro-Confederate feelings in London, but there was little that the British could do until the Canadians and the Newfoundlanders came around. Thus, when the Canadians began to show interest after the war, the British jumped at the opportunity to finally settle the Newfoundland problem. And once it became known that the Canadians would welcome a move on Newfoundland's part to join Canada, Confederation became the goal of British policy.

Together the Canadians and the British did all they could to bring about union while at the same time trying to appear to be letting the Newfoundlanders decide for themselves. In this sense there was an Anglo-Canadian 'conspiracy' at work behind the scenes. Yet there was little that could be labelled sinister in this collaboration; it was more a genuine belief that the national interest of all three countries would be better served through Confederation.

Confederation was given every break along the way, but ultimately the collaborators could do no more than present the option of union with Canada – the final decision was for the Newfoundlanders to make. And, despite all the efforts of the previous years, the vote was surprisingly close. Had it not been for the contribution of J.R. Smallwood and his small group of Confederates, the work of the Canadians and the British might well have been in vain.

Once the vote was taken and the decision made, however, there could be no turning back. The Canadians had committed themselves to act, and the wheels were put in motion to bring Newfoundland in. In the end the only serious problem that remained was the high cost that accompanied union; but by then the Canadians had already reached the conclusion that it was a price worth paying.

Notes

CHAPTER ONE Introduction

1 For a good description of the geography and economy of Newfoundland, see R.A. Mackay, ed., *Newfoundland: Economic, Diplomatic, and Strategic Studies*, chapter 1.
2 Newfoundland, *Census of Newfoundland and Labrador, 1935, Interim Report*
3 MacKay, table 4, 512
4 Newfoundland, *Census 1935, Interim Report*
5 On the development of the fishing economy in Newfoundland, see David Alexander, 'Newfoundland's Traditional Economy and Development to 1934,' 17–39.
6 Great Britain, *Newfoundland Royal Commission 1933 Report*, 8
7 Royal Commission Report, 8–9; MacKay, 107–11
8 MacKay, table 4, 512
9 Ibid, table 6, 514
10 Ibid, table 13, 522
11 Ibid, 203–4
12 Ibid, 204–5
13 S.J.R. Noel, *Politics in Newfoundland*, chapter 2
14 James Hiller, 'Confederation Defeated: The Newfoundland Election of 1869,' 70–1
15 For a brief discussion of the French shore question, see Peter Neary, 'The French and American Shore Questions as Factors in Newfoundland History,' 95–122.
16 Hiller, 'Confederation Defeated'; H.B. Mayo, 'Newfoundland and Confederation in the Eighteen-Sixties,' 125–42

17 G.F.G. Stanley, 'Further Documents Relating to the Union of Newfoundland and Canada, 1886–1895,' 370–86
18 Ibid; A.M. Fraser, 'The Nineteenth-Century Negotiations for Confederation of Newfoundland with Canada,' 14–21
19 For a general discussion see Peter Neary, 'The Issue of Confederation in Newfoundland, 1864–1949'
20 Noel, 82–148
21 Richard Gwyn, *Smallwood, the Unlikely Revolutionary*, 41
22 MacKay, 74; see also Noel, 189–90
23 Noel, 189; MacKay, 71
24 I would like to thank the Honourable J.W. Pickersgill for the correspondence between R.B. Bennett and the Newfoundland government, October 1931.
25 J.R.S. Smallwood, *I Chose Canada: The Memoirs of the Honourable Joseph R. 'Joey' Smallwood*, 183–5
26 Noel, 209
27 Royal Commission Report, 72
28 Ibid, 178; Chadwick, *Newfoundland: Island into Province*, 159
29 Royal Commission *Report*, 223
30 Ibid, 224
31 Great Britain, *Papers Relating to the Report of the Royal Commission, 1933*, 2
32 W.J. Browne, 'The Last Sitting of the House of Assembly,' 30
33 Great Britain, House of Commons *Debates*, 12 December 1933
34 Canada, House of Commons *Debates*, 1 February 1934
35 *Winnipeg Free Press*, 24 November 1933
36 24 November 1933
37 Noel, 226
38 Newfoundland, *Report by the Commission of Government on the Economic Situation, December 1934*
39 Noel, 231
40 See A.W. Currie, *Canadian Economic Development*, 421
41 Frederick W. Rowe, *A History of Newfoundland and Labrador*, 416
42 Thomas Lodge, *Dictatorship in Newfoundland*, 248
43 Thomas Lodge, 'The Present Position of Newfoundland'
44 Lodge, *Dictorship in Newfoundland*, 192
45 See Richard. Clark, 'Newfoundland 1934–1949 – A Study of the Commission Government and Confederation with Canada,' and H.A. Cuff, 'The Commission of Government in Newfoundland: A Preliminary Survey.'
46 Susan McCorquodale, 'Public Administration in Newfoundland during

the Period of the Commission of Government: A Question of Political Development,' 26
47 Lodge, *Dictatorship in Newfoundland*, 265
48 Magrath to Bennett, 13 April 1933, PAC RG25 D-1 vol 731, file: 94
49 Skelton to Herridge, 24 November 1933, ibid, file: 93
50 High Commissioner to Dominions Office, n. 109, 19 June 1931, PRO T160 / 716 / F10646/1
51 Canada, House of Commons *Debates*, 26 March 1934
52 Ibid, 7 February 1933

CHAPTER TWO Who defends Newfoundland?

1 On the Newfoundland Defence Scheme, see *DRCN* doc. 2.
2 Commander H.A.C. Lane, RN, memo, 15 March 1938, *DRCN* doc. 7
3 JSC memo, 22 March 1937, PAC RG24 vol 2787, file: HQS 7410 vol. 1.
4 C.P. Stacey, *Arms Men and Governments: The War Policies of Canada, 1939–1945*, 87. See also Norman Hillmer, 'The Pursuit of Peace: Mackenzie King and the 1937 Imperial Conference,' 149–72.
5 For several comments and reactions, see Lane to Chief of Naval Staff, 15 March 1938, and Wing Commander G.V. Walsh memo, 20 March 1938, PAC RG24 A vol 2787, file: HQS 7410 vol 1.
6 JSC memo, 5 April 1938, ibid
7 Ibid
8 Skelton to LaFlèche, 11 April 1938, ibid
9 JSC memo, 21 April 1938, PAC Howe Papers, vol 30, file: x-30
10 Chairman of Defence Committee, J.A. Winter memo, *DRCN* doc. 15
11 JSC memo, 21 April 1938, PAC Howe Papers, vol 30, file: x-30
12 LaFlèche to Skelton, 13 June 1938, PAC RG24 A vol 2787, file: HQS 7410 vol 1
13 Skelton to LaFlèche, 14 June 1938, ibid
14 Ashton memo, 16 June 1938, ibid
15 Prime Minister to Dominions Secretary, n. 185, 27 July 1938, NPA GN 1/3A, file: 320/35
16 Devonshire to King, 21 October 1938, ibid
17 Ibid
18 Batterbee to Campbell, 21 October 1938, ibid
19 Campbell to Batterbee, 22 November 1938, *DRCN* doc. 21
20 Batterbee to Campbell, 21 October 1938, NPA GN 1/3/A, file: 320/35
21 Campbell to Batterbee, 22 November 1938, *DRCN* doc. 21
22 JSC memo, 27 December 1938, PAC RG24 A vol 2787, file: HQS 7410 vol 1
23 Campbell to Batterbee, 22 November 1938, *DRCN* doc. 21

24 On Canadian foreign policy see R. Bothwell and J.L. Granatstein, '"A Self-Evident National Duty": Canadian Foreign Policy, 1935–1939,' 212–33.

25 Canada, House of Commons *Debates*, 8 September 1939

26 Secretary of State for External Affairs to Governor, 5 September 1939, NPA GN 1/3/A file: 694/38; Governor to Secretary of State for External Affairs, 6 September 1939, DRCN doc. 39

27 Governor to Dominions Secretary, 27 September 1938, ibid, doc. 16

28 L.E. Emerson memo, 30 September 1939, ibid, doc. 45. One major exception was the request for three hundred revolvers, which the Canadians could not provide.

29 See G.W.L. Nicholson, *More Fighting Newfoundlanders: A History of Newfoundland's Fighting Forces in the Second World War*, 521–31.

30 Government of Newfoundland to Dominions Office, n. 288, 15 September 1939, PRO AVIA 2/2285

31 Herbertson to C.W. Dixon, 30 October 1939, ibid

32 DO to Newfoundland Government, n. 408, 5 November 1939, ibid

33 Minutes of meeting of Commission of Government, 27 October 1939, NPA s4 2-3, file: Iron Ore – Bell Island

34 Governor Walwyn to Campbell, 14 November 1939, ibid

35 Commission of Government memo, no date (given to Skelton 22 November 1939), PAC RG24 A vol 2787, file: HQS 7410 vol 1

36 Ibid

37 25 November 1939, ibid

38 This correspondence is reprinted in DRCN doc. 58–62.

39 Ibid, doc. 62

40 Read memo for Under Secretary of State for External Affairs, 29 February 1940, PAC King Papers J4 vol 367, file: 3878

41 A.D.P. Heeney to Read, 14 March 1940, DRCN doc. 64

42 Campbell to Walwyn, n. 4, 17 March 1940, NPA s4 2-3, file: Iron Ore – Bell Island

43 Ibid

44 Walwyn to Campbell, n. 138, 25 March 1940, ibid

45 L. E. Emerson memo, 23 March 1940, DRCN doc. 67

46 Governor to Dominions Secretary, n. 168, 8 April 1940, ibid, doc. 69

47 Governor to Dominions Secretary, n. 229, 30 April 1940, PRO AVIA 2/2285. See also DRCN doc. 72.

48 Ibid

49 Dominions Secretary to Governor, 10 May 1940, PRO DO35 / 745 / N265/8; also, DRCN doc. 73

50 Governor to Domionions Secretary, n. 298, 26 May 1940, DRCN doc. 78
51 Street to Dixon, 30 May 1940, PRO AVIA 2/2285
52 Ibid. See also Dominions Secretary to Governor, n. 1143, 5 June 1940, ibid.

CHAPTER THREE Bases, boards, and bureaucrats

1 J.W. Pickersgill, ed., *The Mackenzie King Record*, vol 1, 93
2 C.P. Stacey, *The Military Problems of Canada: A Survey of Defence Policies and Strategic Conditions Past and Present*, 16
3 Toronto *Globe and Mail*, 15 August 1940
4 Canada, House of Commons *Debates*, 18 June 1940
5 Secretary of State for External Affairs to Governor of Newfoundland, n. 13, 14 June 1940, NPA GN 1/3/A file: 320/35
6 C.P. Stacey, *Arms, Men and Governments*, 369; Pickersgill, *Mackenzie King Record*, vol 1, 111–14; this reasoning would later be repeated during the St Pierre and Miquelon affair.
7 See David G. Haglund, '"Plain Grand Imperialism on a Miniature Scale": Canadian-American Rivalry over Greenland in 1940,' 15–36; Stetson Conn, Rose C. Engelman, and Byron Fairchild, *Guarding the United States and Its Outposts*, chapter 17; William L. Langer, *The Challenge to Isolation, 1937–40*, 683–8; Stacey, *Arms, Men and Governments*, 367–70.
8 Pickersgill, *Mackenzie King Record*, vol 1, 112
9 CWC *Minutes*, 14 June 1940
10 CSC, 'First Draft of a Plan for the Defence of Canada,' 9 July 1940, DRCN doc. 85
11 Nancy H. Hooker, ed., *The Moffat Papers: Selections from the Diplomatic Journals of Jay Pierrepont Moffat, 1919–1943*, 315
12 Ibid, 317
13 Pickersgill, *Mackenzie King Record*, vol 1, 125
14 Stacey, *Arms, Men and Governments*, 333–6; 'Report of a Meeting at Washington to Discuss the Defence of the Atlantic Coast,' 15 July 1940, DRCN doc. 86
15 'Report of a Meeting at Washington,' ibid
16 See Norman Ward, ed., *A Party Politician: The Memoirs of Chubby Power*, 195.
17 Minutes of a Meeting Held at Government House, 20 August 1940, NPA S4 2-1 file: Commission of Government 1934–48, Justice and Defence
18 Ibid
19 Ibid

20 Ibid
21 Ibid
22 St John's *Evening Telegram*, 22 August 1940, See 28 August for the paper's reaction to the talks.
23 Stacey, *Arms, Men and Governments*, 339
24 On the workings of the PJBD see H.L. Keenleyside, 'The Canada–United States Permanent Joint Board on Defence, 1940–1945,' 50–77; C.P. Stacey, 'The Canadian-American Joint Board on Defence, 107–24; Maurice Pope, *Soldiers and Politicians*, 161–7; Stanley W. Dziuban, *Military Relations between the United States and Canada: 1939–1945*, 36–9. For the PJBD recommendations concerning Newfoundland, see DRCN Appendix A.
25 Mackenzie King and Roosevelt had agreed on the telephone that the defence of Newfoundland should be the first area for discussion. Mackenzie King memo, 22 August 1940, PAC RG25 D-1 vol 780 file: 393 (IV-250)
26 PJBD, Journal of Discussions and Decisions, 26 August 1940, DRCN doc. 210
27 Ibid
28 CWC *Minutes*, 5 September 1940
29 Churchill to Roosevelt, 15 May 1940, Francis L. Loewenheim et al., eds., *Roosevelt and Churchill: Their Secret Wartime Correspondence*, doc. 8
30 W.S. Churchill, *Their Finest Hour*, 342–56
31 Langer, 745; R.A. Divine, *The Reluctant Belligerent: American Entry into World War II*, 89
32 Divine, ibid; Dziuban, *Military Relations*, 164–6
33 Pickersgill, *Mackenzie King Record*, vol 1, 125
34 Ibid, 129
35 War Cabinet *Minutes*, 14 August 1940, PRO CAB 65 vol 8
36 Churchill, *Their Finest Hour*, 349; Pickersgill, *Mackenzie King Record*, vol 1, 130
37 Pickersgill, ibid, 132
38 Ibid, 134–5
39 Minutes of a meeting of the CSC, 21 August 1940, DRCN doc. 209; General Crerar 'had assumed that this new arrangement between the United Kingdom and the United States would mean that Canada would retire from Newfoundland defence arrangements in favour of the United States.' Skelton memo, 22 August 1940, PAC King Papers, J4 vol 401, file: 77. See also DRCN doc. 135.
40 Skelton memo, 22 August 1940, PAC King Papers, ibid
41 CWC *Minutes*, 27 August 1940

42 Campbell to Skelton, 4 September 1940, PAC RG25 D-1 vol 781 file: 395

43 Dominions Secretary to Governor, n. 715, 6 September 1940, NPA s4 2-1 file: 'Naval and Air Bases for U.S.A.'

44 Why this was so was not stated; see also Governor to Dominions Secretary, no. 59, 12 September 1940, ibid; W.C. Hankinson to Skelton, 24 September 1940, DRCN doc. 254.

45 Quarton to State Department, n. 993, 19 August 1940, NAW RG 59 811.34544/3

46 30 August 1940

47 21 August 1940

48 Governor to Dominions Secretary, 23 August 1940, NPA s4 2-1

49 Governor to Dominions Secretary, n. 591, 12 September 1940, PRO FO 371 / 24260 A4167; for the reply of the Dominions Office see Dominions Secretary to Governor, n. 763, 22 September 1940, NPA s4 2-1 file: 'United States Bases.'

50 On 10 October 1940 the CWC discussed and gave its approval to the proposal. See DRCN doc. 218 / 219 / 220.

51 Conn, Engelman, and Fairchild, 359

52 Governor to Dominions Secretary, n. 608, 23 September 1940, NPA s4 2-1 file: 'Naval and Air Bases for U.S.A.'; Notes of meetings 16 September 1940, 21 September 1940, NAP s4 2-1 file: 'United States Bases'; for more on American policy and the negotiations see Richard Straus, 'The Diplomatic Negotiations Leading to the Establishment of American Bases in Newfoundland, June 1940–April 1941.'

53 Conn, Engelman, and Fairchild, 365

54 CWC Minutes, 5 September 1940

55 Skelton to Campbell, 5 August 1940, DRCN doc. 125

56 Skelton to Governor, n. 7, 13 September 1940, PAC RG25 D-1 vol 781 file: 395

57 Governor to Secretary of State for External Affairs, 30 September 1940, DRCN doc. 398

58 Dominions Secretary to Governor, 17 October 1940, DRCN doc. 400

59 Governor to Secretary of State for External Affairs, 28 December 1940, ibid., doc. 407

60 CWC Minutes, 13 December 1940

61 Secretary of State for External Affairs to Governor, 20 January 1941, DRCN doc. 410

62 For a fuller discussion of the Knox draft see Straus, 55.

63 Ibid; for the concern of the Commission of Government, see Governor to Dominions Secretary, n. 717, 3 November 1940, NPA s4 2-1 file: 'Naval and Air Bases for U.S.A.'

64 Emerson memo, 28 November 1940, ibid
65 Straus, 66–7
66 King to Massey, 27 January 1941, DRCN doc. 267
67 CWC *Minutes*, 31 January 1941; see also DRCN doc. 269–72
68 High Commissioner in Great Britain to Secretary of State for External Affairs, 4 March 1941, DRCN doc. 279
69 Ibid; DRCN doc. 275
70 Lester B. Pearson, *Mike: The Memoirs of the Right Honourable Lester B. Pearson*, vol 1, 190
71 CSC memo, 4 March 1941, PAC RG25 B3 vol 2150 file: 133, file I
72 CWC *Minutes*, 5 March 1941
73 The clause read: 'When United States is engaged in war, or in time of other emergency, it shall have all such rights in the territories and the surrounding waters and air bases as may be necessary for conducting military operations.' DRCN doc. 285
74 Massey to King, 7 March 1941, ibid
75 King to Massey, n. 323, 8 March 1941, PAC RG 25 G2 vol 2397 file: 976-40c pt. II
76 Pearson, *Mike*, vol 1, 191
77 Massey to King, n. 412, 11 March 1941, PAC RG 25 G2 vol 2397 file: 976-40c pt. II
78 King to Massey, n. 354, 12 March 1941, ibid
79 Massey to King, n. 444, 14 March 1941, ibid
80 King to Massey, n. 382, 18 March 1941, ibid
81 Pearson, *Mike*, vol 1, 191
82 A.D.P. Heeney memo, 25 March 1941, PAC RG25 G2 vol 2397 file: 976-40c pt. II
83 Pearson, *Mike*, vol 1, 192
84 Pearson to Robertson, 26 May 1941, PAC RG25 G2 vol 2397 file: 976-40c pt. III.
85 Ibid; the original Hickerson letter to Moffat (6 May 1941) is in the same file.
86 Ibid
87 CWC *Minutes*, 9 April 1941
88 See DRCN Appendix E.
89 Woods memo, 11 April 1941, DRCN doc. 428
90 Keenleyside memo, 27 March 1941, PAC RG25 G2 vol 2397 file: 1793-40c; both Skelton and Ralston had earlier brought up the possibility of sending an agent to Newfoundland; see CWC *Minutes*, 27 March 1941, 1 October 1940, and DRCN doc. 187.

91 Robertson memo, 15 July 1941, PAC King Papers J4 vol 308, file: 3270
92 Ibid
93 CWC *Minutes*, 15 July 1941
94 King to Burchell, n. 56, 17 July 1941, PAC RG25 G2 vol 2397 file: 1793-40c
95 Malcolm MacDonald to Robertson, 9 September 1941, DRCN doc. 193; see also Kathern Hayman, 'Origins and Function of the Canadian High Commission in Newfoundland, 1941–49.'
96 Most of the correspondence on this issue is printed in DRCN doc. 197–203.
97 A.J. Pick interview, Ottawa, 27 May 1982
98 Pickersgill, *Mackenzie King Record*, vol 1, 202

CHAPTER FOUR Getting along with the Americans

1 'Intelligence Report–Newfoundland,' 1 August 1940, PAC RG24 A vol 2370 file: HQS-5199-Y. This did not stop the Germans from establishing an undetected weather station on the Labrador coast in 1943. See Alec Douglas, 'The Nazi Weather Station in Labrador,' 42–7.
2 G.N. Tucker, *The Naval Service of Canada*, vol II, chapter 2
3 Minutes of a Meeting Held at Government House, 20 August 1940, NPA S4 2-1 file: Commission of Government 1934–48, Justice and Defence
4 See DRCN doc. 141/143.
5 Donald Macintyre, *The Battle of the Atlantic*, 29–35
6 Ibid, 86–8; Joseph Schull, *The Far Distant Ships: An Official Account of Canadian Naval Operations in the Second World War*, 65
7 CWC *Minutes*, 27 May 1941. See Tucker, 189.
8 Macintyre, 86.
9 Dominions Secretary to Governor of Newfoundland, 3 June 1941, DRCN doc. 559
10 Governor to Dominions Secretary, 6 June 1941, DRCN doc. 561
11 CWC *Minutes*, 10 June 1941, 20 June 1941. See Tucker, 190.
12 Tucker, 190–1; see also CWC *Minutes* 15 July 1941; DRCN doc. 573.
13 Tucker, 191–3
14 Ibid, 197; C.P. Stacey, *Arms, Men and Governments*, 134
15 R.A. Divine, *The Reluctant Belligerent: American Entry into World War II*, 105–9; W.S. Churchill, *The Grand Alliance*, chapters 7–8
16 Dziuban, *Military Relations*, 123–4; Schull, 96
17 Macintyre, 135; Divine, 143
18 Woods to Gibson, 17 April 1941, PAC RG25 A-12 vol 2090 file: AR 26/3
19 CWC *Minutes*, 28 April 1941
20 M.H.M. MacKinnon, 'The RCAF in Newfoundland,' 217

21 DO to DEA, 15 December 1941, n. 222 PAC RG25 D-1 vol 778 file: 375 vol 1
22 Governor to DEA, 21 may 1941, n. 30, ibid. See also Douglas Anglin, *The St Pierre and Miquelon Affaire*, and William A. Christian, *Divided Island: Faction and Unity on Saint Pierre*, chapter 5
23 Robertson memo, 3 December 1941, ibid. The Canadians also feared that the islands would become a source of Vichy propaganda; see J.F. Hilliker, 'The Canadian Government and the Free French: Perceptions and Constraints 1940–44,' 87–108, and Paul Couture, 'The Vichy–Free French Propaganda War in Quebec, 1940 to 1942,' 200–15.
24 Robertson memo, ibid. The American position is examined in Hooker, ed., *The Moffat Papers*, 358–75.
25 Dominions Secretary to DEA, 15 December 1941, n. 222 PAC RG25 D-1 vol 778 file: 375 vol 1
26 A.J. Pick interview, Ottawa, 27 May 1982. See Hooker, 362–70; Pickersgill, *Mackenzie King Record*, vol 1, 318–24; and J.L. Granatstein, *The Ottawa Men: The Civil Service Mandarins, 1935–1957*, 97–106.
27 DEA to Massey, 24 December 1941, n. 2106, PAC RG25 D-1 vol 778 file: 375 vol 1
28 Macintyre, 133; Tucker, 197
29 CWC *Minutes*, 14 May 1942
30 Burchell to Robertson, 19 June 1942, DRCN doc. 602
31 Burchell to Woods, 18 August 1942, DRCN doc. 605. See Tucker, 198.
32 Tucker, 199; CWC *Minutes*, 16 April 1943
33 Schull, 100; Tucker, 197
34 Tucker, 138–9
35 Ibid, 202
36 Dziuban, 98; see also Richard Straus, 'The Americans Come to Newfoundland.'
37 MacDonald to King, 8 April 1941, DRCN doc. 153
38 Ralston to King, 11 April 1941, DRCN doc. 157
39 Dziuban, 168–9; 3,392 acres at Argentia, 198.35 acres at Quidi Vidi, 27.57 acres at White Hills, 2.5 acres at St John's harbour, and 867 acres at Stephenville. See also Cole to State Department, 27 March 1941, n 234, NAW RG59 811.34544 / 2079.
40 Tucker, 168, 175
41 Dziuban, 99; see also Frank Ryan, 'New Life in an Old Land'
42 C.P. Stacey, *Six Years of War: The Army in Canada, Britain and the Pacific*, 180.
43 See MacKinnon, 'The RCAF in Newfoundland,' 216.
44 Richard Gwyn, *Smallwood: The Unlikely Revolutionary*, 56

45 See W.G. Carr, *Checkmate in the North*, 238.
46 Memo by L.E. Emerson, 14 January 1942, DRCN doc. 913; Dziuban, 117
47 Dziuban, 87
48 Stetson Conn and Byron Fairchild, *The Framework of Hemisphere Defence*, 377. Dziuban discusses the major deficiencies of the plan, 87–90.
49 Conn and Fairchild, 379
50 Stacey, *Arms, Men and Governments*, 349
51 For a copy of ABC-22, see DCER vol 8 pt.II, doc. 160.
52 Stacey, *Arms, Men and Governments*, 349; Dziuban, 97
53 Pope, *Soldiers and Politicians: The Memoirs of Lt. Gen. Maurice A. Pope*, 164
54 Ibid, 162–7; Stacey, *Arms, Men and Governments*, 350–4; Conn and Fairchild, 382–4
55 DCER vol 8 pt.II, doc. 160
56 CWC *Minutes*, 15 October 1941
57 For example, see Robertson to Duff, 13 April 1942, PAC RG25 B-3 vol 2153 file: 1942–7 Defence: PJBD pt.I: 1942.
58 See DRCN doc. 926 / 928.
59 CWC *Minutes*, 5 October 1944; Stacey, *Arms, Men and Governments*, 367

CHAPTER FIVE Goose Bay: 'A fog of misunderstanding'

1 See Conn and Fairchild, *The Framework of Hemisphere Defense*, 377–84.
2 Ibid, 384
3 The average delivery time by sea was three months. See MacKay's introduction to DRCN, xliii.
4 Dziuban, *Military Relations between the United States and Canada: 1939–1945*, 181
5 See Milner, 'Establishing the Bolero Ferry Route,' 213–22
6 Ibid, 215; Conn and Fairchild, 399
7 Notes of Secret Meeting at RCAF Headquarters, 20 March 1941, Power Papers, vol 61, file: D1062
8 CWC *Minutes*, 21 March 1941
9 Roosevelt, *As He Saw It*, 15
10 Dziuban, 183
11 Kenneth Wright, 'How Goose Bay Was Discovered,' 43
12 Fry, Report on an Investigation for Landing Areas near Northwest River, Labrador, 10 July 1941, DRCN doc. 338
13 For a fuller description see ibid, and Carr, *Checkmate in the North*, 80–5. There is some question as to who first discovered the Goose Bay site. On

the one hand, Roosevelt notes that his party located the site but fails to mention Fry at all (Roosevelt, 19). On the other hand, Carr quotes Fry as saying that he had sent a preliminary survey to Ottawa before Roosevelt arrived at the site (Carr, 80). Dziuban strikes for middle ground and writes that after Fry's aerial survey the two groups met 'at a suitable landing site some distance away and proceeded on foot for a joint ground survey on 4 July 1941' (Dziuban, 183).

14 PJBD, Journal of Discussions and Decisions, 29 July 1941, DRCN doc. 343
15 Ibid
16 CWC *Minutes*, 5 June 1941
17 Ibid, 13 August 1941
18 Governor to DEA, n. 51, 4 August 1941, NPA GN 1/3/A file: 1/41
19 Ibid, n. 58, 29 August 1941
20 Milner, 215
21 Carr, 86–7; Chadwick to Tait, 10 August 1943, PRO DO35 / 1375. For life in the northern bases, see R. Bartlett, 'Servicing Arctic Airbases,' 602–8.
22 Dziuban, 188; Carr, 87
23 Carr, 248–51
24 Ibid, 253; Burchell to DEA, 8 November 1943, DRCN doc. 516
25 DRCN Appendix G; see also *Canada Year Book* 1945, 712
26 Chadwick to Tait, 10 August 1943, PRO DO35 / 1375
27 Herbert, *Independent Member*, 278
28 Massey, *What's Past Is Prologue: The Memoirs of the Right Honourable Vincent Massey, C.H.*, 395
29 Draft agreement printed in DRCN doc. 490
30 CWC *Minutes*, 16 September 1942; Draft agreement, ibid
31 Burchell to Robertson, 30 November 1942, DRCN doc. 492
32 The minutes of this meeting and a list of the participants are printed in DRCN doc. 493.
33 PAC RG25 A12 vol 2090, file: AR26/1
34 Robertson to Burchell, n. 44, 23 February 1943, ibid
35 Walwyn to Attlee, n. 47, 6 February 1943, PRO DO35 / 1375
36 Attlee to Walwyn, n. 225, 14 May 1943, ibid
37 Attlee to Walwyn, n. 226, 14 May 1943, ibid
38 Attlee to Walwyn, n. 225, 14 May 1943, ibid
39 Robertson to Massey, 26 June 1943, PAC RG25 A12 vol 2090, file: AR26/1
40 Quoted in Massey to Robertson, n. 1511, 6 July 1943, ibid
41 Walwyn to Attlee, n. 249, 11 July 1943, PRO DO35 / 1375
42 Massey to DEA, n. 1728, 26 July 1943, PAC RG25 A12 vol 2090, file: AR26/1
43 CWC *Minutes*, 20 August 1943

44 DEA to Massey, n. 1496, 23 August 1943, PAC RG25 A12 vol 2090, file: AR26/1

45 Massey to DEA, n. 2226, 15 September 1943, ibid

46 Robertson to Massey, 26 June 1943, ibid

47 Massey to DEA, n. 2321, 29 September 1943, ibid

48 CWC *Minutes*, 30 September 1943; see also MacKay memo, 30 September 1943, PAC RG25 G2 vol 2395, file: 72-NL-40c pt. 1.

49 DEA to Massey, n. 1733, 1 October 1943, PAC RG25 A12 vol 2090, file: AR26/1

50 Cranborne to Massey, n. 665/5, 7 October 1943, ibid

51 For Howe on these talks see Bothwell and Granatstein, 'Canada and the Wartime Negotiations over Civil Aviation: The Functional Principle in Operation,' 585–601.

52 Massey to DEA, n. 2614, 23 October 1943, PAC RG25 A12 vol 2090, file: AR26/1 and attachment. Article 5 would read: 'Newfoundland and U.K. military aircraft shall have the right to use the Air Base on terms not less favourable than those of the Government of Canada.'

53 There was some confusion here. Apparently Cranborne felt that Howe found these changes acceptable and would get 'concurrence' from Ottawa, but this was not the case. DRCN doc. 512

54 Clutterbuck memo, 25 October 1943, PRO DO35 / 1375

55 Clutterbuck memo, 27 January 1944, PRO DO35 / 1376

56 CWC *Minutes*, 3 November 1943

57 For example see Robertson to Clark, 2 November 1943, DRCN doc. 514.

58 Hopper to State Department, n. 525, 13 November 1943, NAW RG59, 842.7962 / 119

59 DEA to Massey, n. 86, 13 January 1944, PAC RG25 A12 vol 2090, file: AR26/1

60 DEA to Burchell, n. 161, 22 December 1943, ibid

61 Massey to DEA, n. 3086, 8 December 1943, ibid

62 Keenleyside to Massey, 8 January 1943 [*sic*], ibid

63 Massey, 389

64 Ibid

65 Ibid, 388

66 Keenleyside to DEA, n. 64, 28 February 1944, PAC RG25 A12 vol 2090, file: AR26/1

67 Burchell memo for Robertson, 2 March 1944, ibid

68 Burchell memo for Robertson, March 1944, DRCN doc. 526

69 Chadwick to Tait, 10 August 1943, PRO DO35 / 1375

70 Clutterbuck memo, 27 January 1944, PRO DO35 / 1376

71 Beaverbrook memo, 18 November 1943, PRO CAB 66 WP (43) 523

72 War Cabinet *Minutes*, 19 November 1943, PRO CAB 65 vol 36

73 Beaverbrook to Cranborne, 22 November 1943, PRO DO35 / 1375

74 See Cranborne's memo for the War Cabinet, 8 November 1943, PRO CAB 66 WP (43) 507.

75 Cranborne to Beaverbrook, 22 February 1944, PRO DO35 / 1376

76 MacKay memo, 11 March 1944, PAC King Papers, J4 vol 367, file: 3878

77 MacKay memo, 20 March 1944, PAC RG25 D-1 vol 823, file: 702

78 On this last point see MacKay's memo for the CWC, 19 June 1944, Power Papers, Box 61, file: D1060.

79 Memo for Malcolm MacDonald, 27 June 1944, PAC RG25 A12 vol 2090, file: AR26/1

80 MacDonald to Cranborne, 4 July 1944, PRO DO35 / 1376

81 Balfour to Air Ministry, n. 2163, 19 August 1944, PRO DO35 / 1376

82 Duff to Cranborne, 19 August 1944, ibid

83 Ibid

84 Ibid

85 Machtig memo, 29 August 1944, PRO DO35 / 1376

86 Cranborne memo, 18 August 1944; Machtig memo, 18 August 1944, ibid

87 Cranborne memo, 19 August 1944, ibid; Cranborne also noted: 'I take it that the Lord Privy Seal will also have to be consulted.'

88 Cranborne to Newfoundland Government, n. 471, 22 August 1944, ibid

89 Ibid

90 Cranborne memo, 30 August 1944, ibid

91 Newfoundland Government to DO, n. 360, 5 September 1944, PRO DO35 / 1375; MacDonald to Robertson, 8 September 1944, Power Papers, vol 61, file: D1060

92 24 October 1944

93 For example see Montreal Gazette, 23 and 25 October 1944.

94 22 October 1944

95 Hopper to State Department, n. 747, 26 October 1944, NAW RG59 842.7962 / 10–2644

96 Pearson to Robertson, 15 November 1944, PAC RG25 A12 vol 2090, file: AR26/1

97 Robertson to Pearson, 18 November 1944, ibid

98 Ibid

99 Macdonald to DEA, n. 500, 4 November 1944, Power Papers, vol 61, file: D1060. See also St John's Daily News, 18 and 31 October 1944.

100 Newfoundland Board of Trade memo, 4 November 1944, Power Papers, ibid

101 Outerbridge to Walwyn, 17 November 1944, NPA GN 1/3/A file: 1/44

102 Macdonald to DEA, n. 506, 7 November 1944, PAC RG25 A12 vol 2090, file: AR26/1

103 J.R. Baldwin interview, Kingston, 4 August 1982

CHAPTER SIX Civil aviation

1 M. Cohen, 'Canada and Newfoundland ... The Bonds Grow Tighter,' 56
2 Ibid, 130
3 *Fortune Magazine* (May 1943), 91
4 Ibid
5 See J.R.K. Main, *Voyageurs of the Air: A History of Civil Aviation in Canada, 1858–1967*, chapter 15.
6 Ibid, 125–6. See also J.T. Meaney, 'Aviation in Newfoundland,' 141–52; J.A. Wilson, 'The Expansion of Aviation into Arctic and Sub-Arctic Canada,' 130–41.
7 'Extract from a Report on Transatlantic Air Service,' 30 July 1936, DRCN doc. 1037
8 Main, 128
9 On Howe and TCA see R. Bothwell and W. Kilbourn, *C.D. Howe: A Biography*, chapter 8.
10 Robertson to Governor, 27 February 1941, n. 1 NPA GN 1/3/A file: 58/41
11 Tait to Woods, 26 March 1940, PRO AVIA 2/2310
12 Governor to Dominions Secretary, 13 September 1941, n. 455, NPA GN 1/3/A file: 58/41. The Newfoundlanders probably felt that because of the war neither company would be able to supply the necessary equipment.
13 Dominions Secretary to Governor, n. 866, 1 October 1941, ibid
14 For more on this see Burchell to DEA, n. 25, 23 October 1941, PAC RG25 G2 vol 2395, file: 72-RV-40c.
15 Burchell to DEA, 3 November 1941, DRCN doc. 1099. See also doc. 1098.
16 Burchell to Robertson, 23 October 1941, PAC RG25 G2 vol 2395 file: 72-RV-40c
17 DEA to Burchell, n. 29, 13 November 1941, ibid
18 Robertson to Burchell, 4 December 1941, DRCN doc. 1103
19 Burchell to DEA, n. 88, 9 February 1942, PAC RG25 G2 vol 2395, file: 72-RV-40c
20 Burchell to Emerson, 6 February 1942, DRCN doc. 1106
21 Burchell to Emerson, 9 February 1942, DRCN doc. 1108
22 Quoted in A.J. Pick to DEA, 8 May 1942, DRCN doc. 1112
23 For example, see Massey to DEA, 6 December 1941, DRCN doc. 1041. On the transatlantic service, see Main, 154–5.
24 PAC Escott Reid Papers, vol 10, file: 37
25 R. Bothwell and J.L. Granatstein, 'Canada and the Wartime Negotiations over Civil Aviation,' 592–3

26 Ibid, 595, and 'Canada and International Civil Aviation,' unsigned memo in PAC Howe Papers, vol 97
27 Baldwin to Howe and attached memo, 13 December 1944, PAC Howe Papers, vol 99
28 Governor to Dominions Secretary, 4 December 1944, DRCN doc. 1071
29 Churchill to Beaverbrook, 24 December 1944, PRO DO35 PREM 4 5/7
30 Cavanagh to State Department, n. 1108, 13 December 1945, NAW RG59 811.79600 / 12–1345
31 DEA to Burchell, n. 159, 10 July 1945, PAC RG25 G2 vol 2395, file: 72-NL-40c
32 DEA to Massey, 1 September 1945, DRCN doc. 1078; Massey to DEA n. 3046, 19 October 1945, PAC Howe Papers, vol 98, file: 61–6 (13)
33 See minutes of meeting, 10 August 1945, PAC RG25 G2 vol 2395, file: 72-NL-40c.
34 J.R. Baldwin memo, 23 July 1945, ibid
35 MacKay memo, 7 August 1945, ibid
36 Memo to Cabinet Committee on Reconstruction, 5 September 1945, ibid
37 See 'Bermuda Civil Aviation Conversations, Summary of Conclusions and Recommendations,' ibid
38 For this correspondence, see PAC RG25 G2 vol 2394, file: 72-AHF-40c.
39 Main, chapter 26; 'Exchange of Notes between Canada and the United States Relating to Civil Aviation at the Leased Bases in Newfoundland,' 4 June 1949, PAC RG25 A12 vol 2092 file: AR26/9
40 J.B. Brebner, 'A Changing North Atlantic Triangle,' 315
41 For examples of this see L.B. Pearson, 'Canada Looks "Down North,"' 638–47, and 'Canada's Northern Horizon,' 581–91.

CHAPTER SEVEN The problem of Newfoundland

1 Quarton to State Department, n. 912, 6 April 1940, NAW RG84 vol 5
2 Amery to Inskip, 19 June 1939, PRO DO35 723/N2/45
3 Inskip to Amery, 1 August 1939, ibid
4 W.E. Cole, 'Annual Economic and Financial Review, Newfoundland, 1942,' NAW RG84, vol 10
5 G.S. Watts in R.A. MacKay, ed., Newfoundland: Economic, Diplomatic, and Strategic Studies, 221
6 H. Quarton, 'Financial and Economic Conditions in Newfoundland during January 1941,' NAW RG84 vol 5, files: 310–628
7 Fred Waller, 'Monthly Economic and Financial Review,' for August 1941, ibid

8 Waller, 'Monthly Economic and Financial Review,' for December 1941, ibid

9 Cole, NAW RG84, vol 10

10 Ibid

11 Great Britain, DO, *Report on the Financial and Economic Position of Newfoundland*, 21–2

12 St John Chadwick, *Newfoundland: Island into Province*, 194

13 DO, *Financial and Economic Position of Newfoundland*, table 12

14 MacKay, *Newfoundland*, table 14, 523

15 DO, *Financial and Economic Position of Newfoundland*, 5; London *Times*, 14 January 1944

16 Ibid, table 7; Cole, 'Annual Economic and Financial Review, 1942'; MacKay, *Newfoundland*, table 15, 524

17 See DRCN doc. 1234 / 1278 / 1279 / 1282

18 DO, *Financial and Economic Position of Newfoundland*, 20

19 Cole, 'Annual Economic and Financial Review, 1942.' Burchell to DEA, 2 December 1941, DRCN doc. 1233

20 Cole, ibid; Burchell to DEA, ibid

21 Cole, ibid

22 Puddester to Clutterbuck, 5 July 1943, DRCN doc. 1246

23 DO, *Financial and Economic Position of Newfoundland*, 23

24 Governor of Newfoundland to Dominions Secretary, 5 April 1943, DRCN doc. 1178

25 Pearson to DEA, 12 May 1943, DRCN doc. 1181

26 DO, *Financial and Economic Position of Newfoundland*, 5; Peter Neary, 'Canada and the Newfoundland Labour Market 1939–49,' 490

27 MacKay, *Newfoundland*, 233–4

28 See David Alexander, *The Decay of Trade: An Economic History of the Newfoundland Saltfish Trade, 1935–1965*, for an in-depth look at Newfoundland's economic prospects at the end of the war.

29 Quarton to State Department, n. 2008, 31 March 1941, NAW RG84 vol 6

30 *St John's Daily News*, 16 and 17 September 1942

31 *St John's Evening Telegram*, 15 and 17 September 1942

32 *The Fishermen's Advocate*, 4 January 1946; Charles Granger interview, St John's, 9 June 1981

33 Joe Garner, *The Commonwealth Office, 1925–1968*, 25–6

34 Joe Garner memo, October 1941, PRO DO121 / 92

35 Shakespeare memo, no date, ibid

36 Emrys Evans memo, 10 May 1942, PRO DO35 723/N2/73

37 Machtig memo, 13 May 1942, ibid

38 Chadwick, *Newfoundland*, 182
39 Attlee to Governor of Newfoundland, n. 36, 25 November 1942, NPA GN 1/3/A file: 306/42. See Peter Neary, 'Clement Attlee's Visit to Newfoundland, September 1942.'
40 Newfoundland government to Dominions Secretary, n. 2, 7 January 1943, NPA GN 1/3/A file: 167/40
41 War Cabinet Paper, 9 March 1943, PRO CAB66, WP (43) 102
42 Governor of Newfoundland to Dominions Secretary, n. 93, 21 March 1943, NPA GN 1/3/A file: 167/40; War Cabinet *Minutes*, CAB65 vol 33, 15 March 1943
43 Great Britain, House of Commons *Debates*, 5 May 1943
44 A.P. Herbert, *Independent Member*, 257. For a good overview of the Goodwill Mission, see Chadwick, *Newfoundland*, chapter 15.
45 Hopper to State Department, 18 September 1943, NAW RG59 843.01/58
46 Herbert, *Independent Member*, 286
47 Ibid, 257
48 For the actual reports of the Goodwill Mission, see PRO DO35 1336.
49. War Cabinet Paper, 8 November 1943, PRO CAB66 vol 43, WP (43) 507
50 Ibid
51 Beaverbrook memo, 18 November 1943, ibid
52 War Cabinet Paper, 8 November 1943, ibid
53 War Cabinet *Minutes*, 19 November 1943
54 Great Britain, House of Commons *Debates*, 2 December 1943
55 Newfoundland Government to Dominions Secretary, n. 14, 12 February 1944, NPA GN 1/3/A n. 6-9, file: 8/44
56 *A Man of Influence*, 203
57 Pearson to Robertson, 1 February 1944, PAC Pearson Papers, N1 vol 3, file: 'Robertson, N.A. – Canada 1942–6'
58 Vol 1, 15
59 Granatstein, *A Man of Influence*, 117–18
60 Robertson memo, 22 December 1941, PAC King Papers, J4 vol 240 file: 2411; Granatstein, ibid
61 For example, see Maxwell Cohen, 'Canada and Newfoundland ... The Bonds Grow Tighter,' 56–7/130; C.J. Frother, 'Canada's 10th Province?' 84–6; A. Lacey, 'Canada's 10th Province?' 435–45
62 Lord Garner interview, London, 22 October 1981. See also Granatstein, *A Man of Influence*, 111.
63 Canada, House of Commons *Debates*, 12 July 1943
64 Robertson memo, 18 August 1943, PAC King Papers, J4 vol 308, file: 3270
65 Keenleyside, *Memoirs*, vol 2, 146–50

66 MacKay memo, 27 November 1943, PAC RG25 G2 vol 2406 file: 5665–40
67 Ibid
68 MacKay memo, 21 March 1944, PAC RG25 D-1 bol 823 file: 702
69 CWC *Minutes*, 12 April 1944
70 Keenleyside, *Memoirs*, vol 2, 202
71 Clutterbuck to Walwyn, 19 February 1944, PRO DO35 1154 / N628/1
72 Garner to Clutterbuck, 24 February 1944, ibid
73 Walwyn to Cranborne, n. 27, 25 September 1944, NPA GN 1/3/A box 6–9, 1944. This file also includes a copy of the report.
74 Ibid
75 Cobbold to Sir David Waley, 27 October 1944, PRO T220/60
76 Clutterbuck memo, 17 November 1944, ibid
77 Ibid
78 Keynes to Podmore, 18 December 1944, ibid
79 Cranborne to Anderson, 19 January 1945, ibid
80 Cranborne to Machtig, n. 707, 14 June 1945, PRO T220/60
81 Clutterbuck memo, no date, PRO DO35 1344
82. Addison to Dalton, 15 August 1945, PRO T220/60
83 Dalton to Addison, 30 August 1945, PRO DO35 1344
84 Addison to Attlee, 5 September 1945, PRO DO121 / 10B
85 Clutterbuck memo, October 1945 PRO DO35 / 1345. This memo was also attached to CP (45) 234 (Appendix B).
86 Ibid
87 Ibid
88 Robertson memo, 25 September 1945, DRCN vol II, doc. 112
89 Pickersgill and Forster, eds., *Mackenzie King Record*, vol 3, 35
90 Clutterbuck memo, October 1945, PRO DO35 / 1345
91 Pickersgill and Forster, *Mackenzie King Record*, vol 3, 67
92 Cabinet Paper, CP (45) 234, PRO CAB66
93 Great Britain, Cabinet *Minutes*, 1 November 1945, CAB128
94 Dominions Secretary to Newfoundland Governor, n. 519, 8 November 1945, ibid
95 Great Britain, Cabinet *Minutes*, 27 November 1945, PRO CAB66
96 MacDonald to DO, n. 2505, 10 December 1945, ibid
97 DO to MacDonald, n. 2193, 11 December 1945, ibid
98 Great Britain, House of Commons *Debates*, 11 December 1945
99 J.R. Smallwood, *I Chose Canada*, 226–8
100 See David Alexander, 'The Collapse of the Saltfish Trade and Newfoundland's Integration into the North American Economy,' 246–67.

CHAPTER EIGHT The national convention

1 For example, see the *Daily News*, 12 December 1945 and the *Evening Telegram*, 12 December 1945.
2 *Daily News*, 13 December 1945
3 See Working Committee on Post-Hostilities Problems, 'Post-war Defence of Newfoundland and Labrador – Canadian Position,' 28 December 1944, PAC RG2 18 vol 19 file: R22-8 vol 6.
4 PJBD, Journal of Discussions and Decisions, Report of Service Members, 14–15 June 1945, DRCN doc. 956. See also doc. 958–9.
5 Clutterbuck to Governor, 25 August 1945, DRCN doc. 967; Tucker, The *Naval Service of Canada*, 498–9
6 See DRCN, chapter 1, part 6, and doc. 957
7 H.A. Winter to J.E. Read, 2 May 1945, NPA GN 1/3/A file: 1/45
8 Read to Winter, 18 May 1945, ibid
9 R.A. MacKay memo, 2 January 1946, PAC RG25 G2 vol 2395 file: 72-NL-40c
10 DEA to DO, no. 13, 21 January 1946, PAC RG2 18 vol 73 file: D-19-1 (Nfld) 1945–47; Tucker, 499
11 The report of the Canadian delegation and the minutes of the meetings can be found in PAC ibid.
12 Ibid. For a copy of the agreement, see DRCN Appendix H.
13 St John Chadwick, *Newfoundland*, 193–4
14 'Newfoundland, An Act Relating to a National Convention 1946,' NPA GN 1/3 file: 449/46; S.J. Noel, *Politics in Newfoundland*, 247
15 Machtig to Syers, 7 June 1946, PRO DO35 1346
16 Macdonald to DEA, n. 154, 8 May 1946, PAC Claxton Papers, vol 114 file: Nfld Cables between Canada 1946–47
17 See minutes of meeting, 24 June 1946, PAC MacKay Papers, vol 2 file: ICCNR, Minutes of Meetings July 46–Feb. 47.
18 See Noel, 246–7, and Chadwick, 196.
19 Noel, 247–8
20 'Memorandum of Meeting on Financial Aspects of Union with Newfoundland,' 16 October 1946, PAC MacKay Papers, vol 2, file: ICCNR, General Correspondence, Mar–Nov 1946
21 J.S. Macdonald, 'Memorandum for the Undersecretary,' 17 October 1946, PAC MacKay Papers, vol 3, file: Nfld, Despatches and Memos, Oct 46–Sept 47
22 Cabinet *Conclusions*, 30 October 1946
23 Pearson to Robertson, 12 November 1946, included in 'Preliminary Material for Cabinet Committee on Canada-Newfoundland Relations' (21

November 1946), PAC MacKay Papers, vol 4 file: Cabinet Committee on Canada-Newfoundland Relations 1946–47

24 See the minutes for the first six meetings of the ICCNR in PAC MacKay Papers, vol 2 file: ICCNR, Minutes of Meetings July 46–Feb 47.

25 'Memo of Discussion,' 20 November 1946, PAC Claxton Papers, vol 114, file: Nfld Cables between Canada, 1946–47

26 Cabinet Committee, *Minutes*, 2 December 1946

27 ICCNR, *Minutes*, 16 December 1946

28 Macdonald memo for Pearson, 17 October 1946, PAC MacKay Papers, vol 3, file: Nfld; Despatches and Memos, Oct 46–Sept 47; J.W. Pickersgill interview, Ottawa, 19 May 1982. See also MacKay, 'Smallwood's Visit to Ottawa, 1946, 230–2.

29 ICCNR, *Minutes*, 17 December 1946

30 Ibid, 18 December 1946

31 Cabinet *Conclusions*, 24 December 1946. See also Pearson memo for the Cabinet, 24 December 1946, PAC RG2 18 vol 88, file: N-18-vol 1 (1946 Dec).

32 For example, see Macdonald to DEA, n. 20, 10 January 1947, PAC MacKay Papers, vol 2, file: ICCNR, General Correspondence and Memos, Pt. II, Dec 46–Feb 47.

33 For the whole story see Smallwood, *I Chose Canada*, 266–8.

34 Newfoundland, *Minutes of the Commission of Government*, 8 February 1947, PRO DO41 / 31. See Smallwood, 268; Noel, 253–3; and Chadwick, 197.

35 Bridle to MacKay, 20 February 1947, PAC MacKay Papers, vol 2 file: ICCNR, General Correspondence, Dec 46–Feb 47

36 Robertson to Pearson, n. 380, 4 March 1947, PAC Mackay Papers, vol 3 file: Nfld, Despatches and Memos, Oct 46–Sept 47

37 'Memorandum on Conversation with Sir Alexander Clutterbuck,' 5 March 1947, PAC MacKay Papers, vol 3 file: Nfld, Despatches and Memos, Oct 46–Sept 47

38 Robertson to Pearson, n. 430, 11 March 1947, PAC MacKay Papers, vol 2, file: ICCNR, General Correspondence and Memos, Pt. III, Mar–April 1947

39 Cabinet *Conclusions*, 26 March 1947

40 Ibid, 28 March 1947, Baldwin memo for Pearson, 29 March 1947, PAC RG2 18 vol 89

41 G.K. Donald in the American consulate noted that 'various sources' had told him that this was the case. Donald to State Department, n. 401, 2 May 1947, NAW RG59 843.00 / 5–247

42 Addison to Dalton, 21 April 1947, PRO T220/61

43 Dalton to Addison, 28 April 1947, ibid

44 'Memorandum on Visit of Newfoundland Delegation,' 8 May 1947, PRO
   T220/61. Verbatim accounts of the meetings can be found here as well.
   See also 'Summary of Questions Raised by a Delegation for the Newfoundland National Convention,' PAC MacKay Papers, vol 3, file: Nfld,
   Despatches and Memos Oct. 46–Sept 47. The London delegation consisted of Bradley, Peter Cashin, Chesley Crosbie, Pierce Fudge, Malcolm
   Hollett, Albert Butt, and William Keough.
45 Report of Meeting, 29 April 1947, PRO DO35 3448
46 Bradley and Keough did not sign this memo.
47 'Memorandum on Visit of Newfoundland Delegation,' 8 May 1947, PRO
   T220/61
48 Donald to State Department, n. 419, 21 May 1947, RG59 843.00 / 5-2147
49 For Cashin's reactions see the *Evening Telegram*, 10 May 1947, and for his
   denial, see the 12 May edition. For editorial opinion see the *Evening Telegram*, 15 May 1947, the *Daily News* 10 May 1947, and the *Sunday Herald*, 25 May 1947.
50 23 May 1947. See the May 17 edition for a very critical opinion.
51 *Daily News*, 7 May 1947; *Evening Telegram*, 8 May 1947
52 Macdonald to DEA, n. 245, 14 May 1947 and n. 251, 16 May 1947, PAC
   MacKay Papers, vol 3, file: Nfld, Despatches and memos, Oct 46–Sept 47
53 'Trade and Tariff Aspects of Union of Newfoundland and Canada,'
   (unsigned) May 1947, PAC MacKay Papers, vol 3, file: ICCNR; General
   Correspondence, May 1947
54 Ibid. This calculation was based on 1938–9 figures; based on later years
   the quantity would be significantly higher.
55 'Effect on Canadian Export Trade of Newfoundland Joining the United
   States,' ibid
56 Baldwin memo to the Cabinet, 16 June 1947, Annex II, PAC RG2 18 vol 89,
   file: N-18 (June 1947)
57 See ibid, 'Report of Legal Sub-Committee,' and 'Labrador,' both in PAC
   MacKay Papers, vol 3, file: ICCNR; Correspondence May 1947.
58 13 June 1947, PAC MacKay Papers, vol 4, file: Cabinet Committee on
   Canada-Newfoundland Relations 1946–47
59 Pickersgill, *Mackenzie King Record*, vol 4, 50
60 Cabinet *Conclusions*, 19 June 1947
61 Pickersgill, *Mackenzie King Record*, vol 4, 53
62 The minutes of these meetings can be found in PAC MacKay Papers, vol 4,
   file: Nfld-Canada Discussions, Minutes of Meetings 1947.
63 For a list of the subcommittees and those individuals involved, see 'Newfoundland Delegations and Committees,' PAC Claxton Papers, vol 19, file:
   Newfoundland – Reference Material.

64 Bridle memo for Pearson, 4 July 1947, PAC MacKay Papers, vol 3 file: ICCNR; General Correspondence June–July 1947

65 See Baldwin memo for St Laurent, 11 July 1947, PAC St Laurent Papers, vol 19, file: 100-8

66 Bridle note to Pearson, 12 July 1947, PAC MacKay Papers, vol 3, file: ICCNR; General Correspondence June–July 1947

67 Pickersgill, *Mackenzie King Record*, vol 4, 54

68 Cabinet Conclusions, 18 July 1947. For the whole story see Gwyn, *Smallwood*, 88, and Smallwood, *I Chose Canada*, 271.

69 Pickersgill, *Mackenzie King Record*, vol 4, 55

70 See MacKay memo for St Laurent, 27 August 1947, PAC MacKay Papers, vol 3, file: ICCNR; General Correspondence, Aug–Sept 1947.

71 Pickersgill, *Mackenzie King Record*, vol 4, 76

72 See ibid, 77–80. King told St Laurent: 'I believed New Brunswick was dead against Newfoundland coming in on practically any terms,' 80.

73. For copies of the telegrams and Bradley's replies, see the attachment to J.S. Macdonald to DEA, n. 429, 13 September 1947, PAC MacKay Papers, vol 3, file: Nfld, Despatches and Memos Oct 46–Sept 47. See also Smallwood, *I Chose Canada*, 272.

74 Baldwin memo, 27 August 1947, PAC MacKay Papers, vol 3, file: ICCNR; General Correspondence Aug–Sept 1947

75 Baldwin memo, 5 September 1947, PAC RG2 18 vol 128, file: N-18 1947 (Aug–Sept)

76 Minutes of Meetings with Newfoundland delegation, 29 September 1947, PAC MacKay Papers, vol 4, file: Nfld-Canada Discussions, Minutes of Meetings 1947

77 Pickersgill, *Mackenzie King Record*, vol 4, 80

78 Ibid, 81

79 Cabinet *Conclusions*, 28 October 1947

80 Pickersgill, *Mackenzie King Record*, vol 4, 81

81 For the colourful story of the debate, see Smallwood, *I Chose Canada*, 272–9; Gwyn, 91–5.

82 Smallwood, ibid, 284

83 Pearson memo, 4 February 1948, PAC MacKay Papers, vol 3 file: ICCNR; General Correspondence Jan–Aug 1948

84 This correspondence can be found in PRO DO35 / 3456.

85 Clutterbuck to CRO, n. 163, 17 February 1948, ibid. Cabinet Conclusions, 5 February 1948

86 Pearson to Robertson, 4 February 1948, PAC MacKay Papers, vol 3, file: ICCNR; General Correspondence, Jan–Aug 1948

87 Robertson to Pearson, n. 141, 5 February 1948, ibid

88 MacKay memo, 11 March 1948, PAC RG2 18 vol 129, file: N-18 1948 (Mar–May)
89 Quoted from Chadwick, *Newfoundland*, 203–4
90 Noel, *Politics in Newfoundland*, 255
91 D.B. Pitblado, 28 January 1948, PRO T220/93

CHAPTER NINE 'We are all Canadians now'

1 Quoted in Peter Cashin, et al., 'Newfoundland and Confederation, 1948–49,' 248.
2 Smallwood, *I Chose Canada*, 289. There is a considerable body of literature dealing with the campaign, including: S.J.R. Noel, *Politics in Newfoundland*, chapter 16; St John Chadwick, *Newfoundland*, chapter 17; Richard Gwyn, *Smallwood*, chapter 12; Frederick Rowe, *A History of Newfoundland and Labrador*, chapter 23; Donald Jamieson, 'I Saw the Fight for Confederation,' 70–104. There are several other memoirs of the campaign in volumes 3 and 4 of *The Book of Newfoundland*.
3 Horwood and Gwyn note that two Water Street businessmen purchased senatorships. Gwyn added that the price varied from $11,000 to $25,000. Cashin, 249; Gwyn, 99
4 J.S. Macdonald to DEA, 29 April 1948, n. 184, PAC RG2 18 vol 129 file: N-18 1948 (March–May)
5 Gregory Power interview, St John's, 28 May 1981
6 Cashin, 251. See also Gwyn, 100.
7 Gwyn, 99; Cashin, ibid
8 Gwyn, 100
9 Ibid
10 12 April 1948
11 *Daily New*, 26 May 1948
12 L.O. Sanderhoff, 'Memo, no. 1,' 23 March 1948, NAW RG59 611.4331/3-2548. On Smallwood's offer to Crosbie, see Gwyn, 104.
13 T.B. Sanders, 'Memo of conversation,' 31 March 1948, NAW RG84 Box 1745 file: 710
14 A. Foster memo, 24 May 1948, NAW RG59 FW 843.00/5-1948
15 A. Foster, 'Memo of conversation,' 21 April 1948, NAW RG59 FW 611.4331/4-2048; J.D. Hickerson interview, Washington D.C., 18 February 1982. See also David Alexander, *The Decay of Trade*, chapter 1.
16 A. Foster memo, 21 May 1948, NAW RG59 843.00/5-1948
17 Noel, 256. See also Gwyn, 104.
18 Taken from Canada, DEA, *Report and Documents Relating to the Negotiations for the Union of Newfoundland With Canada*, Appendix 5

19 Noel, 257; Smallwood, 306; Gwyn, 107–9
20 Gregory Power interview, St John's, 28 May 1981
21 On this question see Noel, 259–60; Chadwick, 206; George C. Perlin, 'The Constitutional Referendum of 1948 and the Revival of Sectarianism in Newfoundland Politics,' 155–60.
22 Power interview; J.R. Smallwood interview, St John's, 20 May 1981
23 Bridle to DEA, 19 June 1948, n. 100, PAC RG2 18 vol 129 file: N-18 (June–July)
24 See Smallwood and Bradley to Howe, 21 June 1948, PAC Howe Papers, vol 58, file: 26 (1), Noel, 258; Gwyn, 111.
25 Abbott to Foster, 20 July 1948, NAW RG59 843.00 / 7-2048
26 Smallwood and Bradley to Howe, 21 June 1948, PAC Howe Papers, vol 58, file: 26 (1). It is uncertain whether Howe replied to this letter.
27 DEA, *Report and Documents*, Appendix 5
28 R.A. MacKay memo and attached letter, 6 May 1948, PAC MacKay Papers, vol 3 file: ICCNR; General Correspondence Jan–Aug 1948
29 Cabinet Paper, CP (48) 187, 19 July 1948, PRO CAB129 vol 28
30 Robertson to DEA, 2 July 1948, n. 1006, PAC MacKay Papers, vol 5 file: Legal Procedure for Admission of Newfoundland, 1947–49
31 Ibid; Escott Reid memo, 7 July 1948, PAC RG2 18 vol 129 file: n-18 1948 (June–July)
32 British High Commissioner to CRO, 17 July 1948, n. 661, and 13 July 1948, n. 650, PRO DO35 / 3459
33 Pickersgill and Forster, eds. *Mackenzie King Record*, vol 4, 344
34 Ibid; J.W. Pickersgill, *My Years with Louis St Laurent*, 78–9
35 Canada, House of Commons *Debates*, 19 June 1948
36 Abbott to State Department, 9 June 1948, n. 92, NAW RG59 843.00 / 6-948. A copy of the telegram can be found here as well.
37 Clutterbuck to Machtig, 23 July 1948, n. 652, PRO DO35 / 3459
38 Pickersgill, *My Years*, 80
39 Pickersgill, *Mackenzie King Record*, vol 4, 345
40 Cabinet *Conclusions*, 27 July 1948
41 Pickersgill, *Mackenzie King Record*, vol 4, 345
42 See the memos of MacKay's visit in PAC MacKay Papers, vol 3 file: ICCNR; General Correspondence Jan–Aug 1948.
43 Press Release, 30 July 1948, PAC MacKay Papers, vol 6 file: Memos on Nfld, Personal (1947–49)
44 December 1948
45 Smallwood to King, 31 July 1948, PAC King Papers, J1 vol 442
46 ICCNR *Minutes*, 19 August 1948
47 Ibid, 23 September 1948
48 Cabinet Committee *Minutes*, 10 October 1948; MacKay 'Memo for the

Cabinet Committee on Newfoundland,' 30 September 1948, PAC MacKay Papers, vol 4 file: Cab Com on Nfld minutes

49 MacKay memo, ibid

50 Collins to King, 10 August 1948, PAC King Papers, j2 vol 456

51 Pickersgill, *Mackenzie King Record*, vol 4, 360

52 Elmer Driedger interview, Ottawa, 14 June 1982

53 See the minutes of the meeting between the Newfoundland delegation and the cabinet committee for 27 October 1948, in PAC MacKay Papers vol 4 file: Nfld–Canada discussions, Minutes of Meetings 1948.

54 See R.W. Mayhew, 'Memorandum to Cabinet,' 8 November 1948, PAC MacKay Papers, vol 3 file: ICCNR; General Correspondence Jan–Aug 48; Cabinet Committee *Minutes*, 2 November 1948; Newfoundland Delegation–Cabinet Committee meeting *Minutes*, 13 November 1948.

55 Mitchell Sharp memo, 29 October 1948, PAC RG19 vol 3605 file: N04

56 Skelton memo for Howe, 2 November 1948, PAC Howe Papers, vol 60 file: 26 (9); Cabinet Committee *Minutes*, 20 October 1948

57 MacKay memo for Sharp, 8 November 1948, PAC Howe Papers, ibid

58 J.R. Baldwin memo, 29 October 1948, PAC MacKay Papers, vol 3 file: ICCNR; General Correspondence, Jan–Aug 1948

59 Skelton memo, 2 November 1948

60 Baldwin memo, 29 October 1948

61 Cabinet *Conclusions*, 3 November 1948

62 Pickersgill, *My Years*, 81

63 Pearson to St Laurent, 5 November 1948, n. 341, PAC RG2 18 vol 130 file: n-18 1948 (July–Dec)

64 Claxton to Pearson, 27 March 1947, PAC Claxton Papers, vol 114

65 Cabinet *Conclusions*, 9 November 1948

66 Mitchell Sharp interview, Ottawa, 4 June 1982

67 St Laurent's and Walsh's statements can be found in DEA *Report and Documents*, Appendix 9.

68 On this last point see Peter Neary, 'Newfoundland's Union with Canada, 1949: Conspiracy or Choice?' 110–19.

69 Claxton to Clutterbuck, 8 December 1948, PRO DO127 / 80; Cabinet Conclusions, 1 December 1948

70 Admiralty memo, attached to Syers to Clutterbuck, 21 April 1949, PRO DO127 / 98

71 For the correspondence, see Heeney to Clutterbuck, 19 December 1949, Attlee to High Commissioner, 26 January 1950, ibid

72 'Note of Meeting Held at the Foreign Office,' 19 November 1948, PAC RG25 A12 vol 2092 file: AR26/7/2 vol 1

73 'Effect of Union upon Newfoundland Agreements,' unsigned, 29 November 1948, ibid

74 E. Hopkins to Wershof, 22 December 1948, ibid

75 Wershof to Legal Advisor, 22 February 1948, n. 412, ibid. Lists of the various treaties can be found in this file.

76 See Hopkins to Wershof, 15 January 1949, n. 102, ibid; Hopkins to Wershof, 16 February 1949, n. 308, ibid. Later another case surfaced: Article II of the Convention between the United Kingdom and France (1904) giving the French some fishing rights in Newfoundland; see Wershof to Legal Advisor, 22 February 1949, n. 412, ibid.

77 These countries included France, China, Sweden, Norway, Italy, Ireland, Belgium, Denmark, and Switzerland. See Hopkins to Wershof, 15 June 1949, n. 102, ibid.

78 'U.S. bases in Newfoundland; status upon union with Canada,' unsigned, 12 November 1948, PAC Claxton Papers, vol 116 file: Defence: Nfld. Bases. W.P. Snow memo, 10 August 1948, NAW RG84 Box 1745 file: 710

79 Cabinet *Conclusions*, 3 November 1948

80 Wrong to Claxton, 13 November 1948, WA-2927, PAC RG25 A12 vol 2092 file: AR 26/9

81 Claxton to Wrong, 17 November 1948, EX 2675, ibid

82 Wrong to Claxton, 18 November 1948, WA-2959, ibid

83 Acting Secretary for External Affairs to Wrong, 18 November 1948, EX 2679, PAC RG25 A12 vol 2092 file: AR26/9

84 Wrong to DEA, 3 December 1948, WA-3079, ibid; Cabinet *Conclusions*, 24 November 1948

85 DEA to Wrong, 29 January 1949, EX 225, PAC Claxton Papers, vol 116, file: Defence: Nfld. Bases

86 Oral message, 19 March 1949, ibid

87 Wrong to Heeney, 27 October 1949, WA-2990, ibid

88 See John Swettenham, *McNaughton*, vol III, 194.

89 'Memorandum for Mr MacKay,' unsigned, 30 June 1949, PAC MacKay Papers, vol 5 file: U.S. Bases in Newfoundland and Defence Documents 1943–49

90 PJBD 'Recommendations of March 28–30, 1950,' and Pearson and Claxton memo for the Cabinet, 15 March 1951, both in PAC RG25 A12 vol 2092 file: AR26/9, and Swettenham, vol III, 194–5

91 Wrong to DEA, 13 February 1952, WA-433 and 19 March 1952, WA-759, both in ibid

92 Smallwood, *I Chose Canada*, 319

93 See the memo of conversations, 4 October 1948, PRO DO35 / 3465.

94 House of Commons *Debates*, 7 February 1949

95 Ibid. See also R.A. Spencer, *Canada in World Affairs*, vol 5, 358; Herbert Mayo, 'Newfoundland's Entry into the Dominion,' 505–22.

96 House of Commons *Debates*, 7 February 1949

97 Ibid, 14 February 1949

98 Mayo, 517

99 House of Commons *Debates*, 16 February 1949; Pickersgill, *My Years*, 82

100 Great Britain, Cabinet *Minutes*, 3 February 1949, PRO CAB128 vol xv, and for Noel-Baker's memo, see CP (49) 17, 1 February 1949, PRO CAB129 vol xxxii Pt. 1.

101 217

102 Herbert, *Independent Member*, 405

103 Herbert gives a detailed account in ibid, 417–50. See also Chadwick, 211.

104 For an account of the bill's passage in the House of Lords, see Chadwick, 223–4.

105 Gwyn, 120; Elmer Driedger interview, Ottawa, 14 June 1982

106 Abbott to State Department, 9 February 1949, n. 14, NAW RG59 843.00 / 2-949. See also McEvoy to MacKay, 9 March 1949, PAC MacKay Papers, vol 6 file: McEvoy, J.B. Personal Correspondence.

107 On this episode see Pickersgill, *My Years*, 84; Smallwood, 322–3; Gwyn, 117–18. The idea reportedly was first discussed by Pickersgill, Smallwood, and MacKay at the University Club.

108 Pickersgill, ibid, 83

109 Walter Harris memo, 16–17 March 1949, J.W. Pickersgill Papers

110 In a draft letter St Laurent wrote: 'From everything I hear, the Lieutenant-Governor, whoever he is, will probably feel that Mr. Smallwood should be invited to form the provincial Executive Council pending the election.' 8 March 1949, PAC St Laurent Papers, vol 66. J.W. Pickersgill interview, Ottawa, 19 May 1982

111 Gwyn, 121

112 Quoted in ibid, and Chadwick, 225

CHAPTER TEN Conclusion

1 Read memo for R.A. MacKay, 18 December 1944, DRCN doc. 541

2 See Gwyn, 76, and Granatstein, *A Man of Influence*, 118.

Selected bibliography

PRIMARY SOURCES

A *Public Archives of Canada, Ottawa*
Brooke Claxton Papers MG32 B5
C.D. Howe Papers MG27 III B20
William Lyon Mackenzie King Papers MG26 J
R.A. MacKay Papers MG30 E 159
Ian Mackenzie Papers MG27 III B5
Lester B. Pearson Papers MG26 N
J.W. Pickersgill Papers MG32 B34
J.L. Ralston Papers MG27 III B11
Escott Reid Papers MG31 E46
Norman Robertson Papers MG30 E163
Louis St Laurent Papers MG26 L

Department of External Affairs Records RG25
Department of Finance Records RG19
Department of National Defence Records RG24
Department of Trade and Commerce Records RG20
Liberal Party of Canada Records MG28 IV 3
Privy Council Office Records RG2

B *Public Record Office, Kew*
Admirality and Naval Departments: War History Cases and Papers ADM 199
Air Ministry Civil Aviation Files AVIA 2
Cabinet
– Memoranda (from 1945) CAB129

– Minutes (from 1945) CAB128
Dominions Office
– High Commission and Consular Archives, Canada: Correspondence DO 127
– Newfoundland: Sessional Papers DO 41
– Original Correspondence DO 35
– Private Office Papers DO 121
Ferry and Transport Commands AIR 38
Foreign Office: Political Correspondence FO 371
Prime Minister's Office
– Confidential Papers PREM 4
– Correspondence and Papers 1935–50 PREM 8
Treasury
– Finance Files T 160
– Imperial and Foreign Division: Files T 220
War Cabinet
– Memoranda CAB66
– Minutes CAB65

C *Newfoundland Provincial Archives, St John's*
Records of the Commission of Government GN series

D *National Archives, Washington*
Central Files of the Department of State RG59
Records of the Foreign Service Posts of the Department of State, St John's
Consulate Files RG84

E *Queen's University Archives, Kingston*
C.G. Power Papers

F *Bodleian Library, Oxford*
Lord Addison Papers
Clement Attlee Papers

G *British Library of Economics and Political Science, London*
Hugh Dalton Papers

H *Government Sources*
Canada. Department of External Affairs. 'Concluding Plenary Session,' *External Affairs* I (January 1949) 9–14

- *Documents on Canadian External Relations*, vii–viii, 1939–41, edited by
  D.R. Murray (Ottawa 1976)
- *Documents on Relations between Canada and Newfoundland, 1935–1949*,
  edited by Paul Bridle (Ottawa 1974). Two volumes
- 'Newfoundland and Canada: Terms of Union Signed,' *External Affairs* i
  (January 1949) 3–8
- *Report and Documents Relating to the Negotiations for the Union of New-
  foundland with Canada* Ottawa 1949
- Canada. House of Commons. *Debates*
- Great Britain. Dominions Office. *Report on the Financial and Economic Posi-
  tion of Newfoundland* (London 1946)
- *Papers Relating to the Report of the Royal Commission. 1933* (London,
  1933)
- *Newfoundland Royal Commission 1933 Report* (London 1934)
- Great Britain. House of Commons. *Debates*
- Great Britain. House of Lords. *Debates*
- Newfoundland. *Census of Newfoundland and Labrador, 1935, Interim Report*
  (St John's 1936)
- *Report by the Commission of Government on the Economic Situation,
  December, 1934* (London 1935)
- *Report by the Commission of Government on the Unemployment Situa-
  tion, May, 1935* (London 1935)

i *Newspapers*
Newfoundland
The Confederate
The Daily News
The Evening Telegram
The Fishermen's Advocate
The Independent
The Monitor
Newfoundland Govenment Bulletin
The Sunday Herald

Others
London *Times*
Montreal Gazette
New York Times
Toronto *Globe & Mail*
Winnipeg Free Press

J *Memoirs, Diaries, and Letters*

Herbert, A.P. *Independent Member*. London: Methuen & Co. Ltd 1952

Hooker, Nancy H., ed. *The Moffat Papers: Selections from the Diplomatic Journals of Jay Pierrepont Moffat, 1919–1943*. Cambridge, Mass.: Harvard University Press 1956

Keenleyside, Hugh L. *Memoirs of Hugh L. Keenleyside*. Vol. 2: *On the Bridge of Time*. Toronto: McClelland & Stewart 1982

Loewenheim, Francis L., H. Langley, and M. Jonas, eds. *Roosevelt and Churchill: Their Secret Wartime Correspondence*. New York: E.P. Dutton & Co. Inc. 1975

Massey, Vincent. *What's Past Is Prologue: The Memoirs of the Right Honourable Vincent Massey, C.H.* Toronto: Macmillan Company of Canada 1963

Pearson, Lester B. *Mike: The Memoirs of the Right Honourable Lester B. Pearson*. Vol. I, 1897–1948. Toronto: University of Toronto Press 1972

Pickersgill, J.W. *My Years with Louis St Laurent: A Political Memoir*. Toronto: University of Toronto Press 1975

Pickersgill, J.W., ed. *The Mackenzie King Record*. Vol. I, 1939–1944. Toronto: University of Toronto Press 1960

Pickersgill, J.W., and D.F. Forster, eds. *The Mackenzie King Record*. Vols. II–IV, 1944–1948. Toronto: University of Toronto Press 1968–70

Pope, Maurice A. *Soldiers and Politicians: The Memoirs of Lt. Gen. Maurice A. Pope*. Toronto: University of Toronto Press 1962

Smallwood, Joseph. *I Chose Canada: The Memoirs of the Honourable Joseph R. 'Joey' Smallwood*. Toronto: Macmillan Company of Canada 1973

Ward, Norman, ed. *A Party Politician: The Memoirs of Chubby Power*. Toronto: Macmillan Company of Canada 1966

K *Interviews*

J.R. Baldwin

Paul Bridle

St John Chadwick

Elmer Driedger

Lord Garner

Charles Granger

J.D. Hickerson

Donald Jamieson

Lord Noel-Baker

Alfred Pick

J.W. Pickersgill

Gregory Power

Mitchell Sharp
J.R. Smallwood

SECONDARY SOURCES

A *Books*
Alexander, David. *The Decay of Trade: An Economic History of the Newfoundland Saltfish Trade, 1935–1965*. St John's: Institute for Social and Economic Research 1977
Ammon, Charles G. *Newfoundland: The Forgotten Island*. London: Fabian Pub. Ltd 1944
Anglin, Douglas G. *The St. Pierre and Miquelon Affaire of 1941*. Toronto: University of Toronto Press 1966
Bothwell, R., and William Kilbourn. *C.D. Howe: A Biography*. Toronto: McClelland and Stewart 1979
Boutilier, James, ed. *The RCN in Retrospect, 1910–1968*. Vancouver: University of British Columbia Press 1982
Carr, William. *Checkmate in the North*. Toronto: Macmillan Company of Canada 1944
Chadwick, St John. *Newfoundland: Island into Province*. Cambridge: Cambridge University Press 1967
Christian, William A. *Divided Island: Faction and Unity on Saint Pierre*. Cambridge, Mass.: Harvard University Press 1969
Churchill, Winston S. *Their Finest Hour*. New York: Houghton Mifflin 1949
– *The Grand Alliance*. New York: Houghton Mifflin 1950
Conn, Stetson, Rose C. Engleman, and Byron Fairchild. *Guarding the United States and Its Outposts*. Washington: Office of the Chief of Military History 1964
Conn, Stetson, and Byron Fairchild. *The Framework of Hemisphere Defense*. Washington: Office of the Chief of Military History 1960
Currie, A.W. *Canadian Economic Development*. Toronto: Thomas Nelson and Sons (Canada) Ltd 1960
Dawson, R.M. *Canada in World Affairs* Vol 2: *Two Years of War, 1939–41*. Toronto: Oxford University Press 1943
Divine, Robert, A. *The Reluctant Belligerent: American Entry into World War II*. New York: John Wiley and Sons, Inc. 1965
Dziuban, Colonel Stanley W. *Millitary Relations between the United States and Canada: 1939–1945*. Washington: Office of the Chief of Military History 1959
Garner, Joe. *The Commonwealth Office, 1925–1968*. London: Heinemann 1978

Granatstein, J.L. *Canada's War: The Politics of the Mackenzie King Government, 1939–1945.* Toronto: Oxford University Press 1975
– *A Man of Influence: Norman A. Robertson and Canadian Statecraft, 1929–68.* Ottawa: Deneau Publishers 1981
– *The Ottawa Men: The Civil Service Mandarins, 1935–1957.* Toronto: Oxford University Press 1982
Gwyn, Richard. *Smallwood: The Unlikely Revolutionary.* Toronto: McClelland and Stewart 1968
Harvey, Heather. *Consultation and Co-operation in the Commonwealth.* Westport, Conn.: Greenwood Press 1972. First printed by Oxford University Press 1952
Holmes, John W. *The Shaping of Peace: Canada and the Search for World Order 1943–1957,* vol. i. Toronto: University of Toronto Press 1979
Langer, William L. *The Challenge to Isolation, 1937–40.* New York: Harper and Brothers 1952
Lodge, Thomas. *Dictatorship in Newfoundland.* London: Cassell and Co. Ltd 1939
Macintyre, Donald. *The Battle of the Atlantic.* London: B.T. Bastford Ltd 1961
MacKay, R.A., ed. *Newfoundland: Economic, Diplomatic, and Strategic Studies.* Toronto: Oxford University Press 1946
Main, J.R.K. *Voyageurs of the Air: A History of Civil Aviation in Canada, 1858–1967.* Ottawa: Queen's Printer 1967
Molson, K.M. *Pioneering in Canadian Air Transport.* Winnipeg 1974
Neary, Peter, ed. *The Political Economy of Newfoundland, 1929–1972.* Toronto: Copp Clark 1973
Nicholson, Colonel G.W.L. *More Fighting Newfoundlanders: A History of Newfoundland's Fighting Forces in the Second World War.* St John's: Government of Newfoundland 1969
Noel, S.J.R. *Politics in Newfoundland.* Toronto: University of Toronto Press 1971
Roosevelt, Elliot. *As He Saw It.* New York: Duell, Sloan and Pearce 1946
Rowe, Frederick W. *A History of Newfoundland and Labrador.* Toronto: McGraw-Hill Ryerson Ltd 1980
Schull, Joseph. *The Far Distant Ships: An Official Account of Canadian Naval Operations in the Second World War.* Ottawa: Department of National Defence 1961
Smallwood, J.R., ed. *The Book of Newfoundland.* Six volumes. St John's: Newfoundland Book Publishers, Ltd 1937–79
Spencer, Robert A. *Canada in World Affairs* Vol 5 *From* UN to NATO, *1946–1949.* Toronto: Oxford University Press 1959

Stacey, C.P. *Arms, Men and Governments: The War Policies of Canada,*
1939–1945. Ottawa: Department of National Defence 1970
– *Canada and the Age of Conflict: A History of Canadian External Policies.*
Vol II. Toronto: University of Toronto Press 1981
– *The Military Problems of Canada: A Survey of Defence Policies and Strate-*
gic Conditions Past and Present. Toronto: Ryerson Press 1940
– *Six Years of War: The Army in Canada, Britain and the Pacific.* Ottawa:
Queen's Printer 1966
Swettenham, John. *MacNaughton.* Vols. I and III. Toronto: Ryerson Press 1968–9
Thomson, Dale, C. *Louis St. Laurent: Canadian.* Toronto: Macmillan Com-
pany of Canada 1967
Tucker, Gilbert Norman. *The Naval Service of Canada.* Vol 2: *Activities on*
Shore during the Second World War. Ottawa: King's Printer 1952

B *Unpublished Theses*
Christopher, Brother. 'The Influence of Economic Factors on Newfoundland's
Entrance into Confederation' MA thesis, University of Ottawa, 1957
Clark, Richard L. 'Newfoundland 1934–1949 – A Study of the Commission
Government and Confederation with Canada' PHD thesis, UCLA 1951
Cuff, H.A. 'The Commission of Government in Newfoundland: A Preliminary
Survey.' MA thesis, Acadia University 1959
Cunningham, W.B. 'Newfoundland Finance, with Particular Reference to the
Union with Canada, 1949.' MA thesis, Brown University 1950
Hayman, Kathern. 'Origins and Function of the Canadian High Commission in
Newfoundland, 1941–49' MA thesis, University of Western Ontario
1979
Mayo, Herbert. 'Newfoundland and Canada, the Case for Union Examined.'
PHD thesis, Oxford 1948
McCorquodale, Susan. 'Public Administration in Newfoundland during the
Period of the Commission of Government: A Question of Political Develop-
ment' PHD thesis, Queen's University 1973
Stewart, Ian M. 'The "Revolution of 1940" in Newfoundland.' MA thesis,
Memorial University of Newfoundland 1974
Straus, Richard. 'The Diplomatic Negotiations Leading to the Establishment
of American Bases in Newfoundland, June 1940–April 1941.' MA thesis,
Memorial University of Newfoundland 1972

C *Articles*
Alexander, David. 'The Collapse of the Saltfish Trade and Newfoundland's
Integration into the North American Economy,' in *Newfoundland in the*

Nineteenth and Twentieth Centuries, edited by J. Hiller and P. Neary, 246–67 Toronto: University of Toronto Press 1980

– 'Newfoundland's Traditional Economy and Development to 1934,' in *Newfoundland in the Nineteenth and Twentieth Centuries*, edited by J. Hiller and P. Neary, 17–39. Toronto: University of Toronto Press 1980

Bartlett, Robert. 'Servicing Arctic Airbases,' *National Geographic*, LXXXIX (May 1946), 602–8

Bothwell, R., and J.L. Granatstein. 'Canada and the Wartime Negotiations over Civil Aviation: The Functional Principle in Operation,' *International History Review* II (October 1980), 585–601

– '"A Self-Evident National Duty": Canadian Foreign Policy, 1935–1939,' *Journal of Imperial and Commonwealth History* III (January 1975), 212–33

Brebner, J.B. 'Relations of Canada and the United States,' *CHR* XXIV (June 1943), 117–26

– 'A Changing North Atlantic Triangle,' *International Journal* III (1948), 309–19

Browne, W.J. 'The Lasting Sitting of the House of Assembly,' *Newfoundland Quarterly* (Spring 1934), 29–30

Cashin, Peter, Harold Horwood, and Leslie Harris. 'Newfoundland and Confederation, 1948–49,' in *Regionalism in the Canadian Community 1867–1967*, edited by Mason Wade, 227–63. Toronto: University of Toronto Press 1969

Cohen, Maxwell. 'Canada and Newfoundland ... The Bonds Grow Tighter.' *Canadian Business* XV (September 1942), 56–7, 130

– 'Newfoundland: Atlantic Rampart,' *Yale Review* XXXII (1942–3), 555–70

Couture, Paul. 'The Vichy–Free French Propaganda War in Quebec, 1940 to 1942,' Canadian Historial Association, *Historical Papers* (1978) 200–15

Douglas, Alec. 'The Nazi Weather Station in Labrador,' *Canadian Geographic* CI (December 1981 / January 1982), 42–7

Fortune, 'Canada's Postwar Air Policy,' XXVII (May 1943), 90–2

– 'Thunder over the North Atlantic,' XXX (November 1944), 153–60, 197–206

Fraser, A.M. 'Newfoundland' *The Canadian Banker* LVI (Spring 1949), 35–47

– 'The Nineteenth-Century Negotiations for Confederation of Newfoundland with Canada,' Canadian Historical Association, *Historical Papers* (1949), 14–21

Frother, C.J. 'Canada's Tenth Province?' *Canadian Business* XIV (February 1941), 84–6

Haglund, David G. '"Plain Grand Imperialism on a Miniature Scale": Canadian-American Rivalry over Greenland in 1940,' *American Review of Canadian Studies* II (Spring 1981), 15–36

Hiller, James. 'Confederation Defeated: The Newfoundland Election of 1869,' in *Newfoundland in the Nineteenth and Twentieth Centuries*, edited by J. Hiller and P. Neary, 67–94. Toronto: University of Toronto Press 1980
- 'The Origins of the Pulp and Paper Industry in Newfoundland,' *Acadiensis* xi (Spring 1982), 42–68
Hilliker, J. F. 'The Canadian Government and the Free French: Perceptions and Constraints 1940–44,' *International History Review* (January 1980), 87–108
Hillmer, Norman, 'The Anglo-Canadian Neurosis: The Case of O.D. Skelton,' in *Britain and Canada: Survey of a Changing Relationship*, edited by Peter Lyon, 61–84. London: Frank Cass and Co. 1976
- 'The Pursuit of Peace: Mackenzie King and the 1937 Imperial Conference,' in *Mackenzie King: Widening the Debate*, edited by John English and J.O. Stubbs, 149–72. Toronto: Macmillan Company of Canada 1978
Jackman, L. J. 'Newfoundland's Case for a New Deal,' *Atlantic Guardian* v (April 1948), 12–16
Jamieson, Donald C. 'I Saw the Fight for Confederation,' in *The Book of Newfoundland*, iii, edited by J.R. Smallwood, 70–104. St John's: Newfoundland Book Publishers 1967
Jennings, G. 'Newfoundland Trusts in the Sea,' *National Geographic* cxlv (January 1974), 112–41
Keenleyside, H. L. 'The Canada–United States Permanent Joint Board on Defence, 1940–1945,' *International Journal* xvi (Winter 1960–1), 50–77
Lacey, A. 'Canada's Tenth Province?' *University of Toronto Quarterly* xii (July 1943), 435–5
Lodge, Thomas. 'The Present Position of Newfoundland,' speech given to the Royal Institute of International Affairs, 13 May 1941
McGrath, Sir P.T. 'Will Newfoundland Join Canada?' *Queen's Quarterly*, xxxvi (Spring 1929), 253–66
MacKay, R.A. 'Canada and the Balance of World Power,' *CJEPS* viii (1941), 229–43
- 'Smallwood's Visit to Ottawa, 1946,' *Dalhousie Review* l (1970–1), 230–2
MacKinnon, M.H.M. 'The rcaf in Newfoundland,' *University of Toronto Quarterly* (April 1946), 213–21
Maddox, W. 'Canadian-American Defense Planning,' Foreign Policy Association, *Reports* (15 November, 1941), 210–20
Mayo, H.B. 'Newfoundland and Confederaion in the Eighteen-Sixties,' *CHR* xxix (June 1948), 125–42
- 'Newfoundland's Entry into the Dominion,' *CJEPS* xv (1949), 505–22
Meaney, J.T. 'Aviation in Newfoundland,' in *The Book of Newfoundland*, v,

edited by J.R. Smallwood, 141–52. St John's: Newfoundland Book Publishers, Ltd 1979

Milner, S. 'Establishing the Bolero Ferry Route,' *Military Affairs* xi (Winter 1947), 213–22

Mitchell, Harvey, 'Canada's Negotiations with Newfoundland, 1887–1895,' in *Historical Essays on the Atlantic Provinces*, edited by G.A. Rawlyk, 242–59. Toronto: McClelland and Stewart 1967

Neary, Peter, 'Canada and the Newfoundland Labour Market, 1939–49,' CHR LXII (December 1981), 470–95

– 'Canadian Immigration Policy and the Newfoundlanders, 1912–1939,' *Acadiensis* xi (Spring 1982), 69–83

– 'Clement Attlee's Visit to Newfoundland, September 1942,' *Acadiensis* xiii (Spring 1984), 101–9

– 'The French and American Shore Questions as Factors in Newfoundland History,' in *Newfoundland in the Nineteenth and Twentieth Centuries*, edited by James Hiller and Peter Neary, 95–122. Toronto: University of Toronto Press 1980

– 'The Issue of Confederation in Newfoundland, 1864–1949,' unpublished paper (1976), in the Centre for Newfoundland Studies, Memorial University

– 'Newfoundland's Union with Canada, 1949: Conspiracy or Choice?' *Acadiensis* xii (Spring 1983), 110–19

Pearson, L.B. 'Canada and the North Atlantic Alliance,' *Foreign Affairs* xxvii (April 1949), 369–78

– 'Canada Looks "Down North",' *Foreign Affairs* xxiv (July 1946), 63–47

– 'Canada's Northern Horizon,' *Foreign Affairs* xxxi (July 1953), 581–91

Perlin, George C. 'The Constitutional Referendum of 1948 and the Revival of Sectarianism in Newfoundland Politics,' *Queen's Quarterly* lxxv (Spring 1968), 155–60

Rothney, Gordon O. 'The Denominational Basis of Representation in the Newfoundland Assembly, 1919–62,' CJEPS xxviii (1962), 557–70

Ryan, Frank, 'New Life in an Old Land,' *The Beaver* cclxxii (March 1942), 26–30

Saunders, Stanley, and E. Black. 'Newfoundland – Sentinel of the St. Lawrence,' *Behind the Headlines* iii (1943)

Stacey, C.P. 'The Canadian-American Joint Board on Defence,' *International Journal* ix (1954), 107–24

Stanley, G.F.G. 'Further Documents Relating to the Union of Newfoundland and Canada, 1886–1895,' CHR xxix (December 1948), 370–86

Straus, Richard, 'The Americans Come to Newfoundland,' in *The Book of Newfoundland*, vi, edited by J.R. Smallwood, 555–60. St John's: Newfoundland Book Publishers, Ltd 1975

Whiteley, G. 'Newfoundland, North Atlantic Rampart,' *National Geographic* LXXX (July 1941), 111–40

Wilson, J.A. 'The Expansion of Aviation into Arctic and Sub-Arctic Canada,' *Canadian Geographical Journal* XLI (September 1950), 130–41

Wright, K. 'How Goose Bay Was Discovered,' *The Beaver* (June 1946), 42–5

Index